AN INTIMATE LONELINESS

Supporting bereaved parents and siblings

GORDON RICHES
PAM DAWSON

OPEN UNIVERSITY PRESS
Buckingham · Philadelphia

Open University Press
Celtic Court
22 Ballmoor
Buckingham
MK18 1XW

e-mail: enquiries@openup.co.uk
world wide web: http://www.openup.co.uk

and
325 Chestnut Street
Philadelphia, PA 19106, USA

First Published 2000

A catalogue record of this book is available from the British Library

ISBN 0 335 19973 9 (hb)   0 335 19972 0 (pb)

Library of Congress Cataloging-in-Publication Data
Riches, Gordon, 1948–
    An intimate loneliness: supporting bereaved parents and siblings
/ Gordon Riches and Pam Dawson.
        p.   cm. — (Facing death)
    Includes bibliographical references and index.
    ISBN 0–335–19973–9 (hardcover). — ISBN 0–335–19972–0 (pbk.)
    1. Grief.   2. Bereavement—Psychological aspects.   3. Children—
Death—Psychological aspects.   4. Brothers and sisters—Death—
Psychological aspects.   5. Loss (Psychology)   I. Dawson, Pam.
1943– .   II. Title.   III. Series.
BF575.G7R535   2000
155.9′37—dc21
                                                    99–29752
                                                    CIP

Typeset by Graphicraft Limited, Hong Kong
Printed in Great Britain by St Edmundsbury Press, Bury St Edmunds, Suffolk

*To the sons, daughters, brothers and sisters
who left too soon*

Contents

Series editor's preface

It is a great pleasure to welcome Gordon Riches and Pam Dawson's first book, to the Facing Death Series. Our early volumes concentrated upon aspects of palliative care and cancer care. Then came Tony Walter's (1999) path-breaking book *On Bereavement*, which is now complemented superbly by *An Intimate Loneliness*, in which the authors address the question of support for bereaved parents and siblings.

This is a book full of practical relevance to those who work with the fathers, mothers, sisters and brothers of those who died prematurely. The authors begin from the assumption that such bereavements, whilst often tragically avoidable, nevertheless constitute 'normal' and 'taken for granted' aspects of modern culture. It is precisely because this culture individualizes these experiences, however, that making sense of them either personally or structurally causes us so many problems. This makes *An Intimate Loneliness* a very important book.

In recent years a 'new' model of bereavement has been developing, discussed at length in Tony Walter's volume in the Facing Death series. Now we have a book firmly rooted in this social and cultural approach to the analysis of bereavement which in looking at the specific issue of parental and sibling loss turns the new theoretical model to such palpable practical advantage. I suspect that many practitioners will feel deeply gratified that much of their professional experience in recognizing social and cultural factors in bereavement is now being given a new legitimacy. This is a perspective for too long silenced by the predominant psychological discourse of bereavement. Now it has a voice and as a result our attention can turn, properly, to the relationship between endogenous and exogenous factors in understanding bereavement and the delicate interplay between embodied identity, our theories of loss, and encounters with the social world.

Gordon Riches and Pam Dawson provide a clear framework for this approach by reminding us from the outset that the death of a child or sibling usually serves to rupture a pre-existing social and familial network. This network must be understood in its history and context before attention is narrowed onto the apparent 'sequelae' of bereavement. So we are invited to consider the effect of bereavement on partner relations, including the gendered differences in these, and taking into account the influence of others – friends, colleagues, neighbours – beyond the immediate family network. A similar approach to sibling loss leads us to understand what the authors style the 'double jeopardy' of losing a brother or sister and at the same time some aspects of one's own parents.

By means of this analysis the 'coping' strategies available to bereaved parents and siblings come to make more sense. From here four important principles which should underpin help-giving to bereaved parents and siblings are then identified. First, respect of cultural diversity; second, respect for ways of talking and ways of keeping silent; third, respect for individual coping strategies; and fourth, respect for the reality of local social worlds. It is precisely because Riches and Dawson have been able to ground their arguments in the actual experiences of particular bereaved people (their book is peppered with fascinating case illustrations) that they are able to distil such sound practical conclusions from these principles of respect.

Gordon Riches and Pam Dawson have taken a subject matter which few would deny is painful and distressing as well as at the same time intellectually taxing. Despite the deeply troubling material with which they work, the authors write with a remarkable clarity and elegance. Above all they bring to the subject of bereavement a sense of humanity, warmth and optimism that cannot fail to impress the reader. Their book deserves to be read by anyone who has had personal experiences of the losses described here, as well as practitioners and researchers in the bereavement field. *An Intimate Loneliness* shines out as a beacon of hope and inspiration, and what more can we ask of any piece of social or cultural analysis?

David Clark

Reference

Walter, T. (1999) *On Bereavement: The Culture of Grief*. Buckingham: Open University Press.

Acknowledgements

Our thanks go to the many friends, colleagues, bereaved parents, organizations and bereavement supporters who have helped in gathering material for this book and in commenting on its progress.

In particular, we would like to thank Jane, Audrey, Pat and so many other members of The Compassionate Friends; Irene and John and the members of Parents of Murdered Children; Jean, John and Jenny and the members of Survivors of Bereavement through Suicide; Jane and the members of Support After Murder and Manslaughter; Carol and Sarah at The National Association of Bereavement Services; parents and all the children at Childhood cancer Support for the Family, Farnborough Hospital; The Laura Centre (Leicester); The Eclipse Bereavement Centre (Cheshire) and The ABC Centre (Derby).

We would like to thank our respective employers – The University of Derby and Bromley Health Authority – for their support of this project. Our thanks also go to those people who have, in one way or another, contributed to the final shape of this book: Pam Abbott for getting us going in the first place; the reviewers who supported our original proposal; David Field for his editorial expertise in our earlier writing; David Clark, whose encouragement kept us going; Jan MacLaren who found time under difficult circumstances to read and comment on the final draft; all those friends we have made at some memorable conferences on death, dying and bereavement; and, of course, to our long-suffering families.

Finally, our special thanks go to Jane Keeling and staff at the University of Derby Library who continue to give so much support in searching and obtaining research literature, and to Sarah and Maureen who patiently transcribed hours of interviews.

Introduction: an intimate loneliness

> Losing a child is probably the most painful and devastating event that a parent can ever experience. One expects to lose one's parents, and to become a widow or widower is entirely possible, although painful. But, in our society, to lose one's child to death seems out of order, unthinkable, a stunning, devastating turning of the tables.
>
> (Milo 1997: 443)

This book grew out of a research project begun in 1993. The Compassionate Friends in England gave us our starting point and funding was provided by the University of Derby. The Compassionate Friends is an international self-help organization of bereaved parents who offer support to families following a child's death, providing group meetings, one-to-one befriending, telephone support and annual conferences. We began by exploring the marital difficulties that bereaved parents appeared to experience after their child's death. We set out to examine some of the misunderstandings and tensions noted by volunteer supporters working with recently bereaved parents.

Very soon after beginning this project, it became clear that loss is interpreted in different ways by different parents. In time, our research expanded to cover the family as a whole and we have collected numerous stories of the lives and deaths of children as seen by mothers, fathers, brothers and sisters. The marked differences between some of these stories, and the variety of ways in which parents told them, directed our attention to how family members each made personal sense of their loss. We became aware, in particular, that these stories showed that the death and its consequences were being interpreted differently. Moreover, we lost count of the surprise, hurt or exasperation that different family members felt towards their partners, surviving children or parents because they appeared not to be sharing the particular sort of pain that they themselves were feeling. The ease or difficulty with which they shared conversations about the deceased child and their feelings about whether the family was closer or further apart, appeared to be affected by how each saw the others coping.

Throughout our interviewing we were offered examples of how people had helped provide comfort and direction in coming to terms with the death. We were also given examples of the obstacles bereaved family members encountered in finding some way back to a sense of normality in their family relationships. A continuing theme in parents' and siblings' mourning was their search for meaning, for explanation and a sense of wider purpose behind the death and their own continuing living. Even though these explanations varied, parents and siblings universally appeared to have benefited from the support of others during this search.

Since we embarked on this research project Pam [Dawson] took up the new post of Bereavement Co-ordinator for the London Borough of Bromley. We had worked together for some years in the field of social science and, more recently in social aspects of death and bereavement. This book has grown from our joint experience of research, practice and teaching in bereavement and grief support.

Social and cultural contexts in coping with bereavement

In this book we explore links between the sense that individual family members make of their bereavement and the quality of their everyday social relationships. Family role, the nature of their work, their colleagues or school friends, their neighbours, the strength of their local community and the culture within which these relationships are experienced all contribute towards the variety of strategies bereaved parents and siblings adopt in trying to cope with their grief.

Published research recognizes a wide variation in grief responses among bereaved people. Rando (1991) warns against the tendency to 'overpathologize' parents' grief reactions, especially those that appear to fall outside of conventional models of grief offered by counselling handbooks. Bereaved parents and siblings experience a wide range of reactions and deal with them in many different ways. These ways change over time. Some appear to take longer than others to grieve. Some appear to begin to grieve much later than others. Some appear to grieve more deeply than others. Rather than evaluating whether or not these behaviours are appropriate we set out to explore some of the ways that social role, culture and differing position in relationships appear to affect individual responses.

We develop the argument that social and cultural factors affect how people interpret the meaning of their loss and, therefore, affect how they experience and express their grief. We also aim to show that differences in the ways people make sense of their bereavement can add to problems in couple and family relationships. People adjust to loss differently and this can lead to misunderstanding. Finally, through discussion of some key ideas and case examples, we offer bereavement support workers insights into how such a variety of grief responses can be accommodated within existing social relationships.

An intimate loneliness

Why call a book about bereaved parents and siblings *An Intimate Loneliness*? In our interviews, many parents expressed the view that: 'unless you have been through it, you have no idea what it is like . . . no one does . . .'. In different voices, but no less hurt by their feelings of isolation and invisibility, surviving brothers and sisters offered accounts of exclusion, guilt and resentment along with often unheard and unexplained feelings of grief. Throughout our research we discovered bereaved parents and siblings who felt uniquely alone with their grief even when surrounded by the rest of their family.

Many couples experienced difficulty in talking to each other after the death. Similarly, many surviving children felt that their sibling's death has irrevocably changed their family and made their own place within it less secure. They frequently expressed deep resentment at the lack of interest shown by anyone in how they felt. There were ambivalent feelings of protection and frustration with their parents for their emotional fragility and tendency to exclude them. This sense of unique aloneness presents a particular challenge to professionals and volunteers offering support to bereaved parents and siblings.

Intimacy and making sense of bereavement

There is growing evidence that for many people, the benefits of talking – about feelings of grief, about what has happened and about what it means for the future – are central to making sense of loss and grief, yet many bereaved people described how hard it was to find someone who was prepared to listen. Among those we interviewed who found an understanding ear, many described the enormous benefits they felt when someone demonstrated the intimacy and acceptance that allowed them to tell their story.

Being able to picture what it is like to lose a son, daughter, brother or sister is unimaginably hard. It is valuable to talk, but it is even more comforting to be heard by someone who appears to recognize that need to talk and appreciates it is hard to do so. Much of this book is concerned with examining the link between opportunities for intimate communication (and in the case of younger children this is not just verbal) and successful adjustment to loss. We chose this title to illustrate the paradox of child-death: bereavement can drive apart those who normally would be expected to give support, isolating individuals from their most intimate relationships. Those who cope most resiliently with such traumatic experiences often seem to be the ones who can most easily make sense of the meaning of their loss. The part played by relationships – with other family members, with friends and with professional or volunteer supporters – is central to discovering ways of picking up the pieces and carrying on with the rest of one's life.

Death, relationships and the challenge to reality

If sharing painful thoughts and feelings in a safe and intimate setting can be so valuable, why do family relationships sometimes deteriorate after a child's death? The chance to turn and confront our fears accompanied by someone we trust can reaffirm our confidence and sense of self. At the same time, exploring our feelings can threaten us, exposing our weaknesses and vulnerability. The reluctance of fathers, husbands, siblings and sometimes mothers to confront and expose this vulnerability can increase the sense of distance between family members.

The paradox of this 'intimate loneliness' lies in parents and siblings needing the support of other people but finding it hard to ask for it, and finding it hard to give. Following the death, parents may no longer be 'there' for surviving siblings. Wives and husbands may no longer be 'there' for their partners. By being caught up in their attempts to support their most distressed member, the balance of care in families may be disturbed and personal needs put on one side. Some of the children we have worked with commented that their teachers showed concern about their lost sibling and about their parents, but not directly about them.

Why is there a tendency for everyday, taken-for-granted relationships to deteriorate or lose their significance? Our self-esteem, our sense of family and our working model of the world rely largely on opportunities for intimate conversation with those who really 'know' us. We all use stories about our family life to create a sense of who we are – a sense of self-identity. These stories or 'narratives' – sometimes called 'internal working models' (Hart 1996) are formed through our reflections about ourselves and through the impressions other people have of us. Their evaluation of us affects how we see ourselves. Anthony Giddens (1991) argues that these 'reflexive self-narratives' are really important in helping us make sense of our place in modern societies.

In these days of nuclear families and geographical mobility, our offspring are very significant to us. They give us a role and a sense of purpose in our lives. Family stories help clarify and confirm what we mean to each other. Conversations based on family memories maintain and reinforce everyone's place in the family. Changes to these routines require the negotiation of new roles and the construction of new stories. When children are born, leave home or get married, or if couples separate, then family patterns change. New events require new stories, and each member has to adapt their 'internal working model' to fit the altered circumstances. Shared reminiscences in the context of stable relationships help anchor our sense of self and maintain our grip on reality in an uncertain and rapidly changing world. These autobiographical conversations help support our self-esteem and place our position both in the family and in the wider world.

The death of a child and of a brother or sister therefore fundamentally threatens this sense of who we are. It wipes out many assumptions about the future and shakes the permanence of our relationships. It calls into question the point of many of our family activities and roles. Parenthood offers a valued and often personally fulfilling social position. Modern society emphasizes its importance. To a greater or lesser extent, parental identity is destroyed by a child's death, and this, in turn, diminishes the self. Wheeler (1994) shows how this may be particularly intense with the loss of an only child.

Similarly, bereaved siblings may lose that part of their parents that was 'attached' to their deceased brother or sister, in addition to the more direct loss of a playmate, rival and collaborator. The grief of a bereaved twin may be every bit as intense as that of a parent. Siblings close in age to their lost brother or sister also lose someone who has been crucial in defining their own sense of self. Their anchorage to reality may also crumble following the death, and their uncertain sense of personal identity may be even less coherent. Opportunities for mentally processing these traumatic changes and unfamiliar feelings are therefore crucial. Sharing intimate feelings and receiving help in exploring confused and frightening perceptions can provide a touchstone for rebuilding identity.

Problems of communication following bereavement

But who is there to talk to? A child's death creates obstacles to intimate relations on a number of levels. Many of the family's routines are disrupted or destroyed. The 'internal working models' used to make sense of the family are no longer appropriate. They create pain when they are called on to make sense of what is happening. Wider social networks lose their point and benefit. Bereavement poses a fundamental threat to each family member's sense of self-identity. Taken-for-granted assumptions about the world and about one's place within it are challenged by this evidence of personal mortality. Life suddenly appears fragile, impermanent and arbitrary. Those apparently safe and comfortable relationships once relied on may be the very ones broken by the death.

Many children provide a willing and tolerant audience for their parents' rehearsal of private feelings and opinions. Many siblings share a mutual understanding of their parents' idiosyncrasies and use each other's experience of the outside world to gain personal insight into their own futures. The loss of this reassurance represents the disappearance of a primary social support. There is a hole in the domestic landscape where the child used to be and there is a flaw in the model of the family that each member relied on to shore up their own sense of self. At a deep level, trust in the world has been broken and mental energy is taken up with adjusting to this loss. This loss of certainty may make it harder for previously intimate relatives to 'be there' for each other.

Bereaved parents may be isolated by their preoccupation with the loss of the part of themselves that remains attached to the deceased. They search for a mental place to which the child has gone. They question how the death came to be, what it can mean and how they can possibly go on with their lives. At the same time, they are aware of the grief of others close to them. Typically, some will add guilt to their grief, knowing that they can only neglect their partners and surviving children. Some are socially and emotionally paralysed by their grief. On the other hand, others may bring down the shutters on their own distress, working hard to shelter and support the rest of the family, doing their best to hold it together. Parents and surviving children may swing, unpredictably, between these two states, not knowing why they feel they are coping one minute but in deep despair the next. Children may take their cue from their parents or elder siblings. Different family members may react very differently, adding to their sense of personal isolation and to the overall impression that nothing can ever be the same again.

Contradictory grieving: reconciling crises of meaning among family members

In thinking about support for bereaved parents and siblings, it is helpful to bear four principles in mind:

1 Bereaved parents and siblings are the surviving part of a *family network* that has been 'damaged' by the death. This overall perspective must therefore be constantly kept in mind in any assessment of need. The disappearance of normal routines and breakdown in family communications can present many 'secondary losses', which add to grief and individual isolation.

2 Each family member's reaction to bereavement will be affected by *differences in social position* both in the family and in other social networks. Perceived impact and consequences of the death may vary within families, contributing to misunderstanding and impaired communication.

3 *Different aspects of the culture* from which the family comes *and different aspects of the sub-cultures* to which individual family members belong will encourage particular attitudes, expectations and beliefs about death, and about 'appropriate' responses. Different age, gender, occupational and peer groupings can provide contrasting interpretations for each family member, adding to problems of misunderstanding about each other's feelings.

4 One of the major challenges bereavement poses to bereaved parents and siblings is its demand for their *adjustment to ways of acting and thinking* about themselves and their family. This presents a major 'task' of mourning for each member: to adjust their own internal working model of self and of the deceased to give meaning to the bereavement. At the same time, the family as a whole faces the challenge of reconciling these individual meanings into a shared picture of what has happened to them.

Grief, social support and resilience

Research into the death of a partner has revealed that adjustment can create longer term positive outcomes, including the learning of new skills and the discovery of new abilities (Middleton *et al.* 1998). Lauer *et al.* (1985) discovered a heightened sense of family cohesion among children involved in the home care of their terminally ill sibling. Although change can be painful, successful adjustment offers opportunities for self-development, self-knowledge and enhanced social relationships (Lindstrom 1995).

In the following chapters we examine processes of adjustment following the death of a child, noting that personal adjustment following bereavement involves changes in social position and, therefore, changes in identity. The reactions of others – their advice, support, embarrassment, criticism or avoidance – can play a key role, not only in how one feels during the early stages of bereavement, but also in how one interprets the new status of bereaved parent or sibling.

Emergency, health and funeral personnel, chaplains, social workers, teachers and counsellors, family members and friends may all be in a position to offer valuable touchstones by which fundamental life changes can be comprehended and acted on. Informed understanding of the variety of these adjustment processes, and of the obstacles that might hinder them, can help bereavement support. As Rando (1991) so forcefully argues, bereaved parents can and do survive their children's deaths. The aim of this book is to explore ways in which they can be supported in this survival while bearing in mind the family as a whole.

Aims of this book

By making change, adjustment and meaning a primary focus of this book, we aim to illustrate how relationships with self, with partners, with surviving children and with wider social networks affect parents' and siblings' ways of coping with bereavement.

In practice, much 'formal' bereavement support comes in the form of one-to-one counselling, regardless of the evidence that many difficulties resulting from a death manifest themselves as marital and other relationship problems. By recognizing that individual members are part of a larger network of family relationships, that this network follows a changing life-course and that the age at which the child dies will have implications for the stage the family is at, support workers can explore personal experiences of grief in the light of how others in the family are coping.

Underlying each of the following chapters, we argue that problems of meaning – how bereaved people perceive their loss and their own role within it – directly affect their ability to reconcile their own grieving with that of other close family members. In brief, misunderstanding, a sense of resentment and isolation all can arise from a number of social and cultural differences:

- how bereaved people see themselves: their age, life-stage, gender, family role, life goals;
- how bereaved people see their surviving family members: their sense of duty and responsibility towards them, their expectations of them regarding their own needs;
- the kind of relationship they had with the deceased: its importance to them and what it meant for their self-identity;
- the cause and manner of the death: its 'meaning' in the wider society, its suddenness, violence, the degree of publicity and stigma surrounding it;
- cultural beliefs and attitudes: assumption about death and mourning, about parenthood and family life, about men and women's place in grief and emotion 'work';
- the bereaved person's involvement in sub-cultural and social networks outside of the family.

We aim to explore how bereaved parents and siblings cope with what may be one of the most profound challenges to the meaning of life that anyone can face. Much evidence points to the sense of disorientation that often accompanies the death of a close family member. Perceptions of what the death 'means' for the survivors will have a direct influence on how they 'reorient' themselves to their changed circumstances. The strategies they use to cope may strongly influence whether or not they ask for support, who they ask for support and if they are perceived as being in or out of step with the rest of their family. Family members may have to share their interpretations of the death for their differences to be reconciled. They may need to understand why these are different if they are to accept them without hurt, resentment or a sense of loneliness.

Hence, this book also aims to draw out the implications for anyone offering bereavement support. Intimacy is not merely about trust and openness. More fundamentally it relates to the sharing of another's intensely held – but sometimes widely differing – perceptions of reality:

> the intimate person is wise enough to accept other people's points of view as quite literally connected to their very survival, (s)he accepts as a truth that being wrong or right and the fear of admitting that is important . . . Intimacy is impossible unless that 'rightness' door is first closed.
>
> (Stark 1978: 73)

At the same time, we aim to illustrate the role that culture plays in creating these differences. By this, we include professional cultures, clinical cultures, counselling cultures, cultures of particular bereavement support groups like The Compassionate Friends, as well as the differing experiences and expectations that result from experience of age, gender and ethnically based cultures.

Approaching bereavement from a socio-cultural perspective

In this book we bring together a number of useful concepts that we have encountered in our work with bereaved parents and siblings. We have considered what the published literature has to say about them. We have also included our experiences from setting up a bereavement service and from supporting families of children with life-threatening illnesses.

Primarily, this book stresses a social and cultural approach to understanding bereavement and support. We suggest that death, whether 'expected' or sudden, 'natural' or avoidable, is *normal*. We do not mean that many of the senseless causes of premature death are acceptable and should not be a cause of political pressure – for example, pressure exerted by groups such as 'Roadpeace'. Rather, we offer the sociological observation that road traffic accidents, murders, incurable illnesses, suicides and disasters still claim the lives of children on a regular, daily basis. 'Society' – or more specifically the *culture of modern society* – tends to push awareness of these personal tragedies to the back of our mind. Grief appears to be an individual event and an individual problem, and many books on bereavement, although acknowledging the social dimension, still perceive support in terms of 'counselling' on a one-to-one basis. It has not always been so. In the past, and currently in many more 'traditional' societies, death is central to the culture and is demonstrated in commonly held belief systems, ceremonies, public rituals and collective agreement about how the event can be explained and dealt with. So when a child dies, although this cultural framework may not lessen the anguish of the loss, it does provide a ready made set of *meanings* that help the bereaved person to place the death within a common set of assumptions (Anderson 1998).

Meanings are crucial because their presence or absence can affect how successfully bereaved people adapt to the changes that face them. The culture of modern society does not offer everyone a clear framework for interpreting the meaning of their own personal tragedy. The decline of strongly held religious faith, popularization of a variety of belief systems, increasing materialism, fundamental changes to local communities and family patterns have contributed to shifting and contradictory meaning structures. In the past, explanations for premature death were generally part of a collective belief system, rarely questioned by the mass of the population. In modern societies, individuals are often cut adrift from any meaning structure they might possess by the unexpectedness of their bereavement. They may have to make sense of their experiences and emotions in a personal way, drawing on the particular social networks in which they find themselves.

Hence, *social connectedness* – the experience of everyday support, patterns of family interaction, friends, relationships with people at work and in the neighbourhood, specialized agencies, self-help groups and so on – are all crucial in coming to terms with bereavement. It is in the context of these local networks that bereaved people are abandoned or guided in their personal discovery of frameworks that can help them make sense of their loss. It is also these networks that constrain or encourage individuals to explore confused and painful emotions. *Language, conversation and shared symbols* lie at the heart of these daily interactions. It is through conversation that feelings are expressed or avoided. Talk reflects the attitudes and reactions of other people, signalling either their willingness to receive distressing experiences or their discomfort at the prospect of someone 'letting go'. It is within these relationships that bereaved people can discover that their despair is recognized and cared about, or that it is socially threatening and should be kept firmly under control.

Therefore, the nature and value of *social support* is a central issue in this book. We were surprised by the percentage of parents and siblings we interviewed (some interviews lasting over three hours) who said 'that's the first time I have ever had the chance to talk it through'. Modern society is highly structured by time constraints and economic demands. Contemporary cultural attitudes are not geared to slow, thoughtful and often emotionally challenging conversations. If they do take place, it is usually within a fairly structured therapeutic setting and anyone seeking such support may open themselves up to the suspicion that they have some sort of mental illness.

Support need not be 'expert', and growing evidence points to the value of self-help groups in enabling some bereaved parents and siblings to explore a range of meanings (Klass *et al.* 1996). At the same time, there is also clear evidence that others find all the support they need in close friends and caring family members. There are others who attest to the value of their local community in sharing their grief and giving them a sense of purpose following the death. These communities have been both religious and secular. Finally, others praise the value of the support – both offered and sought – from 'professionals' in a variety of settings: chaplains, counsellors, nurses, psychotherapists, teachers and trained volunteers.

The final idea that we have included in planning this book is drawn from developments in sociology and the study of culture. *Identity* refers to the way in which individuals see themselves. This view of 'self' includes a sense of our own purpose, personal worth and assumptions about how others see us and evaluate our place within society. The strength or weakness of our social connectedness to others and the extent to which we rely on one, two or a range of relationships in the maintenance of our identity affects the resources we can draw on to repair a self damaged through bereavement (Forte *et al.* 1996). Our view of our self is a complex and continually changing picture, which is strongly influenced by our '*significant others*':

> In the course of group and family interactions, certain persons assume special importance. . . . They become internalised extensions of our sense of self. These are our significant others. Grief, from this perspective, can be understood as a response to the disintegration of the understandings we have created with others. . . . It is the loss of the part of our self they alone maintained . . .
>
> (Forte *et al.* 1996: 31)

It is also influenced, at a more stable and long-term level, by how we value those aspects of our self about which we can do little, such as our age, gender, class and race. It is within these constraints that we learn the extent of our choices and the boundaries of our aspirations. It is hard to recognize how strongly individual parents and siblings are affected in their views of themselves by general cultural messages about motherhood, fatherhood and 'normal' family living. Lastly, identity is affected by our perceptions of the esteem in which our everyday roles are held and how well we seem to be performing them.

Hence, the death of a child or of a partner, of a sibling or of a parent, especially prematurely, threatens the bereaved person's sense of identity. It may take away the core social connection on which a young child, parent or a close sibling – twin in particular – relied for their sense of self. Other marital and family relationships can also be seriously affected by the death, weakening even further the processes relied on previously to maintain identity. So, not only do the bereaved have to adapt their assumptions to cope with a changed external world, not only do they have to find some meaning behind the death to help with adjustment, they also face a potential internal collapse of those assumptions about who they thought they were. As one bereaved parent said:

> I had failed as a mother, I was useless as a wife ... What kind of mother lets her child get killed? Nothing made sense anymore. I couldn't stand my husband near me. I went through the motions with the other children. I just felt I wasn't there.

Normal grieving can be seen, therefore, as a difficult period of adjustment from a taken-for-granted socially familiar position to a painful and socially difficult one. A number of writers portray grief as the psychological cost of forced adaptation to a new and unwelcome role. We feel it is also useful to explore bereavement as the damage to identity caused by the loss of a relationship that is central to a personal sense of self and purpose. Grieving can then be considered as a process in which the relationship with the dead child has to be reconstructed. Recent thinking suggests that, rather than letting go, this involves bereaved parents and siblings finding ways to transform the relationship so that they can continue to 'hold on' to their deceased loved ones (Klass *et al.* 1996; Walter 1996). This involves bereaved people in an active 'stock-taking' of memories and assumptions about the deceased that, in time, can provide an internal picture with which they can continue to relate.

This process can be made easier through sharing these recollections. Many parents and surviving children noted in our interviews that it also helped them discover new aspects of their loved ones' characters. Sharing memories and exploring the significance of their lives helps confirm the impact they continue to exert on the living. In cases of sudden and violent death, or where the deceased lived only for a short while or died before birth, or where the deceased previously occupied an ambivalent or conflicting relationship with the bereaved person, this process of sharing memories of the life may be difficult or impossible. If the bereaved person is isolated – especially from others who also knew the deceased but whose memories are different – then construction of a comfortable set of memories may be very difficult. If the death was particularly traumatic, then preoccupation with its nature, with the last few moments and with subsequent problems over access to the body or to its disposal may also get in the way of bereaved people reaching back into the life for fonder memories of the deceased.

Outline of the book

This exploration of meaning and its implications for supporting bereaved parents and siblings is divided up into seven chapters, each with its own main concern. Each chapter carries forward the issue of meaning, and has additional features in common with the others: selected reference to ideas found in published studies of parental and sibling grief, examples from our own research or practice, and some key concepts or ideas that enable analysis of case studies.

In Chapter 1, we summarize the principle ideas on which the book is based, briefly reviewing central concepts within the literature such as loss, bereavement, grief and mourning, before going on to outline the value of ideas relating to self- and social adjustment. We look at the range of possible effects that bereavement might have on self-identity, and consider some recent theories of adjustment to loss. The struggle to make sense of self in a radically changed set of circumstances, often with little or no preparation, is examined using examples of parental and sibling bereavement.

Chapter 2 applies these ideas to the ways that a child's death can create a crisis of parental and partner identity, producing in some parents a sense of disorientation from everyday life, dislocating wider social networks and causing feelings of estrangement even from partners and surviving children. This chapter examines how the internal conversation with the self (the self-narrative) is disrupted, creating a further sense of unreality, loneliness and, at its most extreme, a sense of pointlessness in continuing to live. The part played by partners, friends, work colleagues, neighbours, other bereaved parents and cultural expectations in coping with these crises is explored.

In Chapter 3 this problem of meaning is applied to bereaved siblings, taking into account that often their grief takes second place to that of their parents. The dislocation to their own less mature and still developing sense of self is explored. We consider the 'double jeopardy' experienced by many bereaved siblings: they lose both their brother or sister, and are in danger of also losing important aspects of their parents. The distress of younger children may be wholly overlooked, and the distress of older children may be all too easily confused with crises of adolescence. The impact of parent's own orientation to grief on surviving siblings' ability to adjust is also examined.

Chapter 4 explores the variety and range of grief responses among parents and siblings, noting specific 'coping' strategies: being alone, keeping busy, sharing their experiences and personal 'internal' reflection. Drawing on data from our own and other published studies, we examine specific case examples that help the reader recognize the benefits and the disadvantages to each of these responses. We summarize these themes into four 'typical' perspectives through which bereavement is viewed, examining the links between culture, gender, age, role in family and likelihood of movement between and through these various grief positions. We also examine the social and cultural influences that may contribute towards parents or siblings becoming 'stuck' with the first and most lonely of these perspectives.

Chapter 5 looks in greater detail at examples of causes of death that may contribute towards parents or siblings finding difficulty in perceiving their bereavement from any other than the first of these perspectives. Sudden, violent, inexplicable or particularly stigmatized causes of death may prevent

parents or siblings from either moving backwards into warmer recollections of their children's lives, or from moving forwards into picking up the
threads of a purposeful life without their lost loved one.

Chapter 6 explores the implications of our approach for the kinds of
bereavement support family members feel is helpful. Based both on our
own experiences of working with parents and siblings, and on the implications for professional support found in much of the bereavement research,
we summarize the kinds of contact and relationships that have helped both
during the time of death and its early aftermath, and in the years that follow.

In our conclusion (Chapter 7), we reflect on the complexity of bereavement in a plural post-modern society and its implications for professional
and volunteer support, noting the range of help available and the variety of
ways in which professional services might help bereaved parents and siblings. We consider practical issues of what constitutes appropriate support,
together with problems of establishing an authentic 'intimate relationship'
with family members who have been bereaved.

1 Order out of chaos: personal, social and cultural resources for making sense of loss

Introduction

People experience bereavement differently. The nature and intensity of their grief varies. Many factors, in addition to genetic make-up, influence the range of responses bereavement researchers have identified. In this book, we examine social and cultural resources because they can affect the ease with which bereaved parents and siblings adjust to loss. These resources provide the tools for making sense of the intellectual and emotional chaos that bereavement can bring. Parents' ability to give meaning to their child's death is central to successful adjustment (Braun and Berg 1994). Even suffering can eventually be interpreted by some parents as the cost of positive changes in their own views of themselves and the world in which they live (Talbot 1997).

The ideas we use to think about death and bereavement come from the culture in which we live. Our access to these ideas and the contribution they can make to personal adjustment is often influenced by the kind of social relationships in which they are encountered. This key aspect of grieving is sometimes marginalized in texts written primarily from a counselling psychology perspective.

In this chapter we examine some of the personal, cultural and social resources parents and siblings use to help make sense of their bereavement. We include the kinds of meanings researchers and practitioners use, because these too are used by bereaved people to interpret their experiences. We look at three distinctive approaches that place different emphases on personal, cultural and social aspects of adjustment and examine how issues of meaning affect the type of support offered to parents and siblings.

Resources for grieving

We use the term 'resources' because we want to stress that bereaved people are active individuals, making choices as they deal with their experience of loss. Parents and siblings are not simply victims of circumstance. Nevertheless, their ways of coping need to be understood in the light of the different resources that are available to them. This approach helps us evaluate the range of support available to different family members in different cultural settings.

We are not just referring here to particular services or information, or to the help that a friend or counsellor might offer. The term resources also includes distinctive attitudes and beliefs found in different cultures that may help people make sense of bereavement. Familiar social relationships, particularly with partners and other family members, also affect the individual's assumptions about their capacity to deal with bereavement.

Individuals build up a sense of their own resilience and vulnerability over a lifetime (Burkitt 1991). This perception of 'self' is crucial in understanding differences in the ways bereaved parents and siblings adjust to loss. The stability of an individual's identity relies on early internalization of positive views of their 'self', reflected by others during everyday interactions. It also depends on them being able to interpret their experiences in ways that confirm the view they have of themselves (Guidano 1991). Even in adulthood, this identity still depends to an extent on the positive regard offered by others in fulfilling their roles both in the family and in wider society.

The death of someone as significant as a son or daughter, brother or sister, can mean the loss of an important source of self-esteem and social purpose. Capacity to cope with bereavement may partly be affected by the parent or sibling's belief in their own personal resilience. The ways that parents and siblings adjust are influenced by how they have come to think of themselves in the roles they most regularly occupy. These roles are affected by expectations within the particular culture in which bereaved people live.

Figure 1.1 illustrates the links between culture, social relationships, views of the self and differences in coping with bereavement. Social relationships always exist within a wider cultural context, and together these shape the individual's attitude to death, experience of grief, opportunities and forms for expressing it and assumptions about the kinds of support he or she can expect from others.

Cultural resources

Cultural resources include systems of familiar ideas and recognizable patterns of behaving, such as:

- distinctive, shared beliefs about death, mortality and the 'natural' order of things;

Figure 1.1 Contingency model of responses to grief

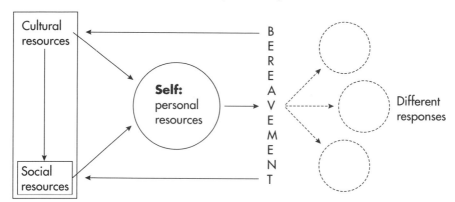

- general assumptions about the role of parents, the nature of families;
- descriptions of important social differences such as between mothers and fathers, adults and children, men and women, experts and lay people;
- shared attitudes about what is 'normal' and of social value;
- conventions relating to bereavement, grief and appropriate ways of behaving following a death in the family;
- assumptions underlying professional, religious or community-based support networks.

Conventions around dying, bereavement, expression of grief and appropriate forms of mourning exist in all societies (Craib 1995). As Parkes *et al.* (1997) describe, they differ enormously between and within different countries. Within most major western cities, cultural diversity will ensure these differences occur side by side. The beliefs that held older generations together, may be the very source of conflict that pulls the younger generation from the ways of its parents. Modern communication and entertainment contribute to cultural dilution, producing changing, confusing and often contradictory sets of conventions, each competing for the attention of individual family members.

Different cultures will make different arrangements for supporting their bereaved. Ender and Hermsen (1996) note that in so-called 'modern' societies many households have shrunk to a small and often changing nucleus of cohabiting partners and step siblings. Support services and specialized organizations may have taken over many of the roles that were performed previously by extended family members and neighbours.

Most modern societies are culturally 'plural'. That is, more and more nations are composed of a number of cultures with contrasting conventions, sometimes widely differing beliefs and varying priorities. Popular entertainment, the mass media in particular, draw on all of them to produce an ever growing variety of images that, in turn, feed back new ideas, particularly to the young of each culture. Hence a wide range of potential choices about lifestyle and personal identity exist in late modern societies. Some of these do provide 'resources' for making sense of bereavement, but many act in the reverse way, making the society as a whole unprepared for personal death and offering few clear guidelines about how to deal with the experience of grief (Handley 1991).

Social resources

Social resources include the types of roles an individual performs, the quality of personal relationships, and membership of groups that helps contribute to a sense of identity. These include:

- a marital or couple relationship in which grief can be shared and the meaning of bereavement discussed;
- open channels of communication and stable relationships between surviving family members;
- available groups and social networks outside the immediate family – friends, neighbours, work colleagues, for example;
- purposeful and fulfilling roles in addition to those within the family;
- opportunities to become involved in new relationships with other bereaved people or with experienced support 'professionals' familiar with grief.

Relationships and social support are a crucial factor in bereaved people's capacity to cope. Opportunities to share perceptions of a joint loss with a partner, to offer mutual support and remember the details of the deceased's life that no one else is likely to appreciate, can provide enormous comfort. Evidence indicates that bereaved mothers and fathers place their partner at the top of the list of people they turn to most for support (Thuen 1997).

In addition, relationships that provide a safe 'space' where bereaved people can open up their feelings without fear either of criticism or of hurting the feelings and sensitivities of the listener can provide a valuable resource. Confused thoughts, ambivalent feelings, strong emotions may all be better managed and understood when shared with someone in whom trust and confidence can be placed.

Families often are unable to provide this second resource because while they share the same bereavement, they do not necessarily share the same sense of loss (Gilbert 1996). Moreover, families and marital partners will already possess fairly clear perceptions of each other's strengths, weaknesses and idiosyncrasies. Patterns of family conflict and the issues around which they are acted out will be familiar, but not necessarily discussed. All families have characteristic strategies for coping with crises based on the assumptions that each member makes about the reactions of the others. Some family systems are more open in their discussions, more democratic in allowing each to contribute to eventual strategies. Others are more closed, with individual members imposing their definitions onto others and so repressing discussion and honest sharing of feelings. Evidence suggests that surviving siblings cope better with grief within a more open family system (Hogan and DeSantis 1994).

Bereaved people usually belong to other social networks in addition to their immediate family. Extended family members, friends, work colleagues and neighbours all represent a potential resource through which grief can be explored, expressed and made sense of. Alternatively, membership of other groups may distract attention – even if only briefly – from thoughts of personal grief. Work roles and responsibilities outside the immediate family can provide a sense of continuity and purpose in at least some areas of the bereaved person's life.

Finally, opportunities to build relationships with others who have themselves been bereaved, perhaps in similar circumstances, or with professionals or volunteers who can demonstrate their own understanding of the range and uniqueness of the reactions, offer another possible resource in adapting to loss.

Personal Resources

Personal resources help determine the individual's resilience or vulnerability in the face of bereavement. These include:

- a personal 'philosophy' that can make some sort of sense of the death;
- faith in established beliefs that provide frameworks of meaning that 'place the death in a recognizable context';
- opportunities to learn from previous critical life experiences;
- an 'inner-directed' autonomous identity that can distinguish personal boundaries;
- an ability to acknowledge and express personal feelings.

A number of researchers suggest that parents who already possess a personal 'philosophy' that helps them make sense of the death and gives them a purpose for continuing to live can adjust more quickly. Strongly held religious beliefs in a higher purpose or in the workings of 'destiny' appear to enable bereaved people to 'place' the death in a wider scheme of things (Braun and Berg 1994).

Past opportunities to learn and grow from difficult life experiences, including previous bereavements might also contribute to longer term coping with grief and the loss of security it brings (Storr 1997). In modern societies, a well-developed sense of autonomy and inner-directedness, resulting from internalization of a stable, positive view of self also appears to be a feature of personal resilience.

Following from this, opportunities to 'connect' with personal feelings and to express them verbally or through some other medium also contribute to a sense of personal strength, especially within the family (Hogan and DeSantis 1994). Evidence suggests that girls and women have less problems than boys and men in recognizing their feelings and sharing them with others (Duncombe and Marsden 1995).

Social meanings of death and bereavement

All change involves loss, and social arrangements exist that help guide people through the inevitable changes that occur during their lifecourse. While bereavement challenges the individual's sense of identity, death has to be managed socially in ways that create the least disturbance to society as a whole. Unexpected death challenges assumptions about the point of all our social roles – both inside and outside the family. The public and the private are closely connected. How we manage personal experiences of bereavement is influenced by how society as a whole copes with its bereaved people (Prior 1989).

In this section we consider how society manages changes resulting from death and how culture contributes to the meanings bereaved families use to understand their loss. We look particularly at the way informal, personal conversations help or hinder individual grieving while broader attitudes and beliefs surrounding bereavement inform these conversations.

Roles and identity

Family roles often provide the core constructs of our identity. We live through them rather than merely playing them. For certain parents and siblings, at particular times of their lives, the family role may be the principle source of their sense of who they are. The child is not only a highly significant person in the mind of the parent, he or she is also an active member of the parent's 'audience', continually involved in maintaining the parent's own identity. A child's death can therefore fundamentally threaten a parent's or sibling's sense of self.

The roles making up personal identity will differ according to our social position and who constitutes the individual's most significant others. These are not fixed, but shift and change over time. The role of parent or sibling may be more significant to some people than to others. With the death of a child each family member loses a different aspect of their identity. Hence, certain relationships will be more 'potent' in aiding adjustment than others. For example, support among work colleagues may be crucial for bereaved parents for whom an occupational role is a core construct of their identity. Peer support among teenage siblings may be more valuable than that offered by adult professionals or parents. Other bereaved mothers may offer insights and understanding unavailable from husbands.

Particular social roles are accompanied by wider cultural expectations, and categories such as motherhood and fatherhood exert powerful influences on how individuals feel they should behave. These may be supportive if they match personal perceptions following bereavement, but may be negative if these expectations cannot be met. Supporters need to be aware of the pressure for a bereaved parent or sibling to feel they have to 'play' out a particular role – such as being strong for others in the family. Similarly, family expectations in some traditional cultures may be a source of embarrassment and anger among adolescent members. Following bereavement, others may fail to see that bereaved parents and siblings who appear to be back to normal in their public roles are only playing the part – putting on a 'face' for the outside world.

Case example 1.1

Brenda's son died at the age of 21 from cancer. She worked as a nursery teacher. Her account showed the effort she put into presenting a 'normal' self while she was at work: '. . . the tiredness is unbelievable . . . this face drops so badly. I've actually walked out of the nursery and sat in the car and couldn't turn the engine on and just cried, because I've lasted the eight hours – and I've only got eight hours in me – in fact I've only got 7 hours and 59 minutes – and I'm not very good with myself. I find I have to be extra normal . . . extra, extra, extra specially . . . extra normal, yeah . . . and especially because I'm so loud and bubbly normally'.

The status of bereaved people

No change in status is easy. Bereaved people occupy neither the old social position nor the new. They exist in a limbo – 'betwixt and between' – where they are temporarily outside of the social structure and where their external appearance and internal feelings are confused and ambiguous (Turner 1974). It may take considerable time for personal feelings to catch up and begin to fit with the new status. Others in society play a crucial 'management' role in helping with these transitions (Strauss 1962). Doctors, clergy, funeral directors and counsellors, for example, are recognized as possessing responsibility for helping dying, deceased and bereaved people negotiate the movement from life into death.

The hardest status passages are those that are sudden, unpredictable, negative in their consequences and where it is difficult to find others who have gone through similar experiences. Here a sense of loneliness arises not just from personal feelings of loss, but more broadly from a wider sense of social exclusion. The sense of limbo that can be felt during the early months

– or even years – following bereavement can be accompanied by a loss of social purpose. Widowhood is a good example of being caught between expectations that come from being both a married and a single woman at the same time (Middleton *et al.* 1998).

Bereaved parents and siblings, similarly, have major difficulties in adjustment. In addition to their own grief they often feel excluded by others who feel unsure how to relate to their new status. Familiar family routines are broken. Personal relationships are severely tested as roles are no longer clear and core constructs of self lose their explanatory power. The mutual support each member relied on to make sense of their family role may disappear (Forte *et al.* 1996).

Bereavement in parenthood is a status passage few have been through and none wish to contemplate. Professionals given responsibility for directing these changes are often strangers. Formal arrangements for establishing cause of death and disposal of the body occupy bereaved people for a little while. Compassionate leave from work, time alone and initial concern from others help manage the potential problems that bereaved people might pose through behaving inappropriately in public.

Bereavement supporters thus play a social as well as a personal role. They help manage the challenge that arises from bereaved people's sense of liminality. Like the sick role, the bereavement role allows 'normal' society to make allowances for the emotion and disorientation that accompanies it. Meaning is central to adaptation. Professionals, other bereaved parents and siblings, friends and wider social discourses may each offer signposts that help or hinder bereaved people to discover where they are – both in relation to the deceased and in relation to other family members.

The social construction of death and grief

When we were young the picture of our self and the world we live in was largely given to us by our family. Other influences, especially teachers, friends and the mass media, also shape our knowledge of the world and our attitudes to it as we get older.

> In our world of everyday life, we each have access to our own personal reservoir of socially-derived knowledge. This knowledge consists of clear, consistent, and unquestionably valid 'knowledge about' people, places, and things, knowledge which has been tested and passed on to us by others, and which explains the what, how and why of social life . . .
>
> (Talbot 1997: 49)

We come to acquire a framework of meaning that helps us interpret everything we experience in the everyday world. It is variously called a 'socially constructed reality' (Berger and Luckman 1966), an 'assumptive world'

(Parkes 1993b), a 'prior meaning structure' (Braun and Berg 1994), and an 'internal working model (Moos 1995). These internal models allow us to make sense of our experiences in a consistent way. This 'world in our heads' is continually being updated as we encounter new experiences and new ways of interpreting them. Sharing these interpretations allows us to act predictably in concert with others. Conflict can easily arise where they are not shared.

A number of writers argue that the internal working models acquired by most individuals in modern cultures no longer prepare them for making sense of death (Giddens 1991; Handley 1991; Bauman 1992; Mellor and Shilling 1993). The models of the world represented by the media tend to associate death with old age or abnormal circumstances – neither of which are of general personal concern. Giddens argues that we no longer 'know' in any fundamental way that we will die. There is a natural order: parents die before their children; science and technology has made child-death an extraordinary event; even the elderly die of unnatural causes.

> In spite of evidence to the contrary, we live as if we shall live for ever and treat death as if it were an avoidable accident. Our belief that death happens only to others is neatly captured in Freud's anecdote about the couple discussing the topic, in which one says to the other: 'If one of us dies, I shall go and live in Paris.'
>
> (Handley 1991: 250)

The death of an offspring or sibling can shatter this assumptive world. A central problem in adjusting to child bereavement is our total lack of preparation for it. In modern societies we possess few mental frameworks that help us make sense of our child's death. It can feel close to madness. Reality literally breaks down for some bereaved people.

This threatens others who would prefer not to face the prospect of their own or their children's mortality. Death confronts our deepest assumptions about the nature of the world we live in:

> On the other side of what might appear to be quite trivial aspects of day to day action and discourse, chaos lurks. And this chaos is not just disorganisation, but the loss of a sense of the very reality of things and of other persons.
>
> (Giddens 1991: 36)

Hence it may be easier to reduce contact with bereaved people than to face the implications of their loss for our own life and family.

The notions of bereavement as 'limbo' and 'socially constructed reality' help explain why the death of a child or sibling can make bereaved people feel socially displaced. Child bereavement carries a stigma because surviving family members inhabit a different reality from 'normal'. One mother said to us 'Unless you have been through it, you cannot possibly know what it is like'. Few people want to know what it is like. This insight is terrifying. Our cocoon of security, our plans for the future, our assumptions about our families and ambitions for our careers are fragile, temporary and always closer to collapse than we care to imagine.

The model of the world held by bereaved people is crucial to their ability to adjust. Traditional or religious communities may offer the support of commonly held meaning structures that make immediate sense of the death. A predicted, well-prepared for and well-informed death, as opposed to a sudden or violent one in which information is scarce, may provide the support of a clearly understood process in which dying and bereaved people are able to keep some sense of control. These kinds of deaths are rare.

Modern, largely agnostic and highly mobile societies may offer few, if any, pre-existing meaning structures that can cope with bereavement. Making sense of the death may be a major problem for many parents, and respected professionals and close friends can help them acquire information and a sense of how to place the death in a broader perspective. Caution must be exercised by supporters in not imposing their own meaning structure on those they are trying to help.

Case example 1.2

Monica attended a support group for mothers whose infants had died through miscarriage and still-birth. Her account illustrated the problems that can arise for newly bereaved parents when others 'further down the line' impose their own meanings on the group: 'this one woman was so convinced she was right. Whenever anyone else tried to talk, she immediately turned it round to her own experiences. She said no one understood how she felt, the doctors wouldn't give her any information and . . . she had a very bad time. Well, I thought the hospital had been really helpful to me . . . and my own doctor was so kind and . . . caring. I didn't go [to the group] again.'

Talk and the bereaved family's construction of meaning

The family often lies at the heart of an individual's cherished view of the world (Gubrium 1988). The death of one of its members can trigger painful differences in how each makes sense of, and deals with it. At one level, grief is the emotional cost of reconstructing a view of the world that can account for the death of a loved one (Gilbert 1996). Conversation is crucial to the family's attempt to make sense of its bereavement (Middleton and Edwards 1990). Effective mourning appears to require someone to mourn *to* (Brice 1987; Talbot 1997). Discussion about how the loss affects each member takes place within the context of what are sometimes called 'social discourses'.

Feelings involve thoughts, they involve our immediate sense of who
we are, our interpretations of our current projects which might be
threatened, disrupted or furthered by the events to which we are
responding. Feelings are thus bound up with the stories, myths and conventions of a culture which guide people on how to react in different
circumstances. As a result, certain kinds of emotional expression and
certain ways of understanding emotion become habitual and characteristic in a cultural group.

(Wetherell and Maybin 1996: 235)

In other words, sets of beliefs and assumptions about death and grief already exist within every culture, providing possible models for making sense
of death and loss. Soaps, magazine articles, comic strips and popular novels
provide examples of how fictional characters cope with bereavement. Religions provide another kind of discourse through which some bereaved
parents and siblings may make sense of the death. Where a strong faith is
shared, conversation about the nature of the death can help produce agreement about its significance for the family. Where different meanings are put
on the death, or where little sense can be made of it, family members may
feel even more isolated in their own personal grief.

Counselling psychology and theories of grief provide other models from
which bereaved parents and siblings might derive meaning. Although different in many ways to religious models of the world, the 'psychology' of
grief offers bereaved people a similar system of ideas that can be used to
interpret personal experiences and feelings. These models provide a mental
map on which family members may plot their differing experiences.

On the other hand, some sets of assumptions can also limit the meanings
that individuals may use to explain their experience of bereavement. For
example, traditional discourses of motherhood impose a view that reproduction and child rearing are a woman's principal role in life. If an only
child dies in circumstances in which its mother feels blame, her sense of loss
and self-criticism may be overwhelming. Only if she can step out of her role
as mother and wife will she be able to recognize that her sense of guilt and
despair is a 'normal' and temporary reaction out of which she can build a
fuller sense of herself and the world in which she lives (Talbot 1997).

However, as we argued earlier, popular discourses about death stress
stoicism, the healing properties of time, the heroism of keeping feelings to
oneself and 'getting on' with life. These are common and contribute substantially to the assumption in modern society that death is rare and tends
to happen to other people. Brabant's analysis of 'domestic' comic strips in
modern America suggests death is trivialized rather than denied (Brabant
1997–8).

The media is full of images of death and models of how people react to
it. Many are harrowing, many are simply entertainment. Some are both.

Most are 'sensational' and portray death as extraordinary. They all contribute to the range and confusion of ideas that inform – or misinform – bereaved parents and siblings, and add to the sense of social uncertainty felt by those who come into contact with them. Bereavement supporters need to realize how such public discourses may add to family members' sense of powerlessness and loss of control.

Case example 1.3

George's adult daughter was murdered. Two years after her death, his account indicated that he and his wife were still suffering intense distress. Their grief was intensified by the insensitivity of the media: 'we can't even turn the television on. I have to be so careful. Every damn programme seems to be about murder. You can't watch for more than a few minutes before someone gets killed. The violence, and all the blood, the graphic detail of the bodies . . . even autopsies. And that is entertainment!'

Constructions of death and grief in professional models of bereavement

What meanings do therapists, bereavement counsellors and researchers use in making sense of the grief experiences of those with whom they work? In this section we look at some of the discourses around death and grief that provide meaning for the professionals who work in this area. The three perspectives we outline here reflect the three different emphases – personal, cultural and social – noted throughout this chapter.

Many models of grief found in the literature acknowledge the influence of family and culture on grief, but still focus primarily on the bereaved person's personal resources when discussing the 'tasks' that have to be accomplished during its resolution. Often, by focusing on personal resources, these approaches place meaning on the 'broken' relationship with the deceased, seeing adjustment in terms of the individual's need to understand and deal with the emotional distress that comes from facing the finality of this loss (Stroebe 1993).

Recent 'new directions' in grief theory, on the other hand, present a more culturally sensitive perspective that stresses the diversity of meaning attached to grief and mourning, criticizing conventional grief counselling as being limited to a 'modern' view of society – that is of a largely western, liberal democratic and secular population consisting of private individuals. Conversely, as well as emphasizing collective sharing of memories of the deceased, this perspective recognizes that a substantial relationship with the deceased may well continue after the death.

Systems approaches to bereavement focus on the role of existing family and other relationships in the individual's adjustment, stressing the nature of communication between family members as a key to understanding how individuals make sense of bereavement. Increasingly systems approaches also incorporate cultural awareness, recognizing the impact of broader influences on the individual's attitudes and ways of thinking such as gender, power, sexual orientation and other social differences (Bor *et al.* 1996).

In psychologically based models death is generally assumed to be final and the counsellor's attention is primarily given to the 'internal' world of the client. New directions approaches accept alternative realities in which death is not necessarily final for bereaved people, and attention is given more to how they manage the changed relationship with the deceased. In a systems approach attention is given to how patterns of family and social interaction adapt to the changed role of the deceased, and in doing so, how it affects the sense that the bereaved individual makes of his or her own feelings of loss and grief. We shall look at each one of these in turn.

Psychotherapeutic models of grief and mourning

Psychological understandings of loss have been strongly influenced by theories of attachment and separation (Elders 1995). Notions of 'bonding' and of broken bonds inform many current models of grief. Emotional distress is assumed to be an inevitable psychological reaction to the involuntary breaking of attachments. Until recently, conventional wisdom held that 'resolution' of grief involved facing and accepting the finality of death. Healthy living involved letting go of impossible attachments and forming new bonds. Tony Walter (1996) describes how aspects of Freud (1913), Lindemann (1944) and Bowlby (1979, 1980) have contributed to dominant assumptions that finality of death and detachment from the deceased are key tasks in the grieving process.

Attachment, separation and personal resources

What insights into differences in personal resources are offered by psychological models of bereavement and grief? A valuable perspective offered by the work of Bowlby is that relationships provide the basis for the growth of independence. He argues that the ability to be alone, to be secure with one's own sense of personhood rests in large part on the quality and security of early relationships.

Individuals learn, as infants, how to view the world. Parents who create insecure attachments in their children are those who either reject their need to be reassured or who portray the world as a threatening place in which they cannot survive without the parent. This leads either to emotional coldness and fear of strong emotions or to an overdependence on others – a 'clinging' that invites rejection because of its neediness (Parkes 1996).

Parents' capacity to cope with the prospect or the reality of bereavement might therefore be affected by their ability to cope more generally with separation. Anxiety and inability to achieve mature relationships with others may not only cause major problems in dealing with the lost relationship, it may also add to these by making the support of others harder to seek or accept. The way they have related to their child before his or her death, and the way they respond to it, is also likely to have a major impact on surviving children's own sense of security and consequent independence later in life.

Winnicott uses the term 'potential space' to describe the circumstances that foster autonomy in children (Winnicott 1969). He argues that emotional calm comes with permission to be 'alone in the presence of the parent'. Security arises from the child knowing he or she is accepted, that the parent will be there if needed, but will not interfere with the child's exploration of the world in his or her own way. Here the child can begin to distinguish his or her own feelings from those of others. Rather than experiencing emotions imposed by an anxious or overcritical parent, this space enables the growth of autonomy, an ability to get in touch with personal feelings, and fewer problems in attaching to and separating from others.

These ideas offer an insight into why some adults appear to be better able to appreciate and express their feelings than others. It may point to the kind of personal resources that help parents cope better with bereavement, and indicate some of the problems bereaved siblings have if the chances of insecure attachment increase as a result of parents' grief reactions.

As we noted earlier, resilience or vulnerability among siblings appears to depend on the capacity of the family to acknowledge personal feelings and to share them without the fear of criticism or misinterpretation. They also illustrate how some members may 'take on' emotions from others without recognizing they have done so. It also demonstrates a theme we return to in Chapter 2, in which one parent – often the father – fails to recognize personal feelings of grief because they have taken on the emotional demands society requires of their particular social role – such as protector and organizer.

Grief, resilience and personal growth

What insights into resilience are offered by psychological models? Parkes (1996) argues that insecure attachments can be overcome by support from a counsellor. The main principle behind this 'psychodynamic' approach is to provide a model of a secure attachment between the counsellor and the bereaved person. The provision of a relationship that allows bereaved people to explore and face their feelings attempts to recreate the circumstances that should have led in the past to the resilience and independence that comes with secure attachment.

Another insight, provided by the humanistic school of thought, is that bereavement is a particular example of the range of crises that we all might experience during our lives. These crises provide opportunities for personal learning and, given the nurture of empathic support – from others and from one's own self – can be positive rather than negative events.

The humanistic approach assumes that individuals have a life-long capacity for growth and development, and that this can happen if experiences are embraced, understood and learned from. The social context in which they occur is important for determining whether or not this learning takes place.

Like the psychodynamic approach, attention to feelings is crucial. Individuals are thought to have the capacity for carrying through learning from one crisis to another with support from others who can help them to become aware of their strengths and learn from challenging experiences (McLaren 1998). The ability to recognize new meaning structures through which to make sense of these events is crucial. Research into parental coping indicates that parents with previous bereavements recognize the benefits of these experiences in making sense of their more recent loss of a child (Braun and Berg 1994).

This approach has many similarities with the psychodynamic model, with the development of a close empathic relationship between counsellor and bereaved person at its heart. However, whereas the perspective offered by Bowlby (1969, 1973, 1980) explains inadequate personal resources as resulting from earlier bonding experiences, Rogers (1957) and Maslow (1968) stress the importance of attending to learning in the here and now.

In the former, attention is on creating a secure relationship in which bereaved people can get in touch with feelings that habits of their previous relationship might have hidden from them. In the latter, attention is more on validating the feelings of the bereaved, focusing upon the range of meanings that might, in time, help them to recognize a way through their present distress. Much of this latter approach seeks to help individuals develop a sense of self-worth based on their own person-hood rather than on perceptions acquired through the conditional approval of others.

In practice, the distinction between the two approaches is probably lost on anyone experiencing profound grief. For the supporter, however, the subtle difference in assumptions is important. The first model assumes a deficit in bereaved people. Problems with grief are the result of an inability to confront personal feelings. These are the consequence of earlier insecure attachments and therefore long-lasting or particularly complicated grief is seen as an abnormal reaction in someone lacking in healthy personal resources. The second model assumes a more positive view of bereaved people. Everyone has the capacity to grow from their experiences. All they need is support in discovering the resources they already possess within themselves.

These ideas are helpful in explaining huge variations in the intensity and duration of grief. The humanistic approach acknowledges differences in people's position on the learning curve of life experience. It suggests 'maturity' of the self comes over time with reflection. It acknowledges that people do it in their own way and in their own time.

Bereavement counselling principles

Opportunities to reflect, to find a space in which the full implications of the loss can be contemplated, are central to principles of grief counselling. These assumptions are reflected in much of the work of Worden and others, where confronting the reality of the loss, working through emotional reactions, acknowledging and exploring various feelings of anger, guilt, and so on, provide an explicit framework or map, along with an empathic relationship, that supports bereaved people in letting go of their relationship with the deceased so they can fully reinvest in their relationships with the living (Worden 1991; Parkes et al. 1997).

Grief is often portrayed as a series of stages on a journey or 'trajectory' towards grief resolution. Although these stages vary within different models and there is some debate concerning the speed, sequence and direction of progress through them, they represent a view of grief based on the individual's ultimate acceptance that the death is real and irrevocable. Support is based around working through the pain of detaching from the deceased. Much bereavement support assumes a progression through these stages, each one containing specific tasks that have to be accomplished if grief is to be resolved.

A number of writers argue that this framework reflects the 'meaning structures' found in modern counselling psychology. This professional culture provides many of the assumptions on which bereavement counselling is based (Wortman and Silver 1989; Walter 1996). Worden's text *Grief Counseling and Grief Therapy* (1991) is an influential example of this model. Figure 1.2 lists the assumptions that underlie this approach. This summary also illustrates how the model allows progress during mourning to be evaluated.

Limitations

Although valuable in helping to understand problems of adjustment, there are a number of limitations to the meaning structures underpinning bereavement counselling:

- in spite of acknowledging the family context, this approach is still essentially individualistic, accepting on the whole the 'modern' model of western, rational, largely privatized, implicitly middle-class society;
- independence, autonomy and ability to relate to others are taken as self-evidently central to mental health and well-being;
- this model assumes death is final, while at the same time embracing as normal the spiritual needs of those who (still) possess religious beliefs;

Figure 1.2   Principles, tasks and support procedures

Principle	Task
1 It is hard to comprehend that death has actually occurred	To face the reality of the death in order to deal with the emotional consequences

Procedures: *Support the bereaved in detailed remembering of the death and events surrounding it.*

2 It is hard to recognize strongly felt emotions, e.g. anger, guilt anxiety, helplessness, sadness	To explore painful feelings about the deceased and self and express them

Procedures: *Give permission to feel negative emotions and help bereaved verbalize them.*

3 It is necessary to learn to live without the support of the deceased	To recognize lost benefits and find other ways of meeting needs without the deceased

Procedures. *Explore practical and relationship problems and ways of solving them.*

4 It is necessary to find a new place for the deceased in the bereaved's emotional life	To learn that even though the deceased cannot be replaced, new relationships are valuable

Procedures: *Help the bereaved acknowledge the intensity of their lost relationship and give permission for them to move on, in time, to new ones.*

5 Grieving requires time and is a gradual process	To recognize that grief is complicated and giving up the deceased is not easy

Procedures: *Help all family members appreciate that specific events such as holidays, birthdays and less obvious anniversaries will affect the bereaved in unexpected ways.*

6 It is normal that bereaved people may feel they are losing a grip on reality	To be reassured that symptoms of mental ill-health are not uncommon

Procedures: *Help the bereaved appreciate the general effects of bereavement and recognize that their own symptoms are natural and only temporary.*

7 People grieve differently	To recognize that loved ones may be experiencing profound grief but expressing it in unrecognizable ways

Procedures: *Help family members to explore feelings of discomfort with the way others may be expressing or failing to express their grief.*

Figure 1.2 (cont'd)

Principle	Task
8 Bereaved people need continuing support over an extended period	To be able to share grief and explore the loss for at least the first year and preferably for longer

Procedures: *Provide contact over an extended period and help introductions to other support networks and groups.*

9 Grief exaggerates defences and coping styles	To appreciate ways that personal coping may be postponing grief or contributing to unhealthy adjustment

Procedures: *Observe bereaved's responses to grief and offer opportunities for them to reflect on these in a trusting and supportive relationship.*

10 Bereavement may result in mental ill-health for some bereaved people	To be referred to professionally qualified help if necessary

Procedures: *To recognize the limitations of 'normal' grief support and be able to refer to appropriate specialized services if necessary.*

- it fails to account for a range of belief systems that accept the continuing existence and influence of the dead, and social behaviours in which some relationships with the dead continue;
- it assumes people need support in withdrawing emotionally from the deceased – and that failure to undertake this withdrawal is a sign of pathology;
- it overlooks the constructionist notion that people who are significant continue to influence us when they are not there physically.

The challenge of empirical evidence

To what extent are these psychotherapeutic assumptions supported by research? There appears to be some mismatch between the explanatory framework we have just outlined and the empirical evidence. Many of the key assumptions in grief therapy are now being questioned, notably the belief that 'avoidance' of grief is unhealthy. Cook (1988), for example, demonstrated the value of strategies that enabled bereaved fathers to control and repress distressing feelings. Bonanno *et al.* (1995) reported no more long-term negative effects in those who avoided intense feelings of grief than in those who experienced deep emotional distress. They also suggested that such avoidance might, in the longer term, be linked to a reduction in other symptoms including somatization. Stroebe and Schut (1995) argued that 'taking time off' from grieving was probably necessary for healthy long-term adjustment.

The 'myths' of bereavement therapy

A major contribution to this debate was made by Wortman and Silver (1989) whose summary of empirical evidence challenged what they called the dominant 'myths' of bereavement therapy. In reviewing what they claimed was the 'best' research (methodologically speaking), they presented the following observations:

- intense distress and/or depression is far from inevitable following bereavement;
- no link has been demonstrated between intensity of grieving and subsequent resolution;
- on the contrary, those who seemed most distressed during early stages of loss were more likely to be distressed one to two years later and, apart from one study, there is little evidence that 'suppressed' grief causes problems later in life;
- there is no obvious relationship between the intensity of parental attachment and levels of distress following infant death through Sudden Infant Death Syndrome;
- preoccupation with the reality of the loss, as demonstrated by high levels of rumination, appears to place bereaved people at *greater* risk of poor mental and physical outcomes later in life;
- 'resolution' of grief, as measured either by return to normal functioning or in being able to 'come to terms' with the death is *never* achieved for significant numbers of bereaved people. Indeed, where death is sudden, unexpected or in traumatic circumstances, most people appear incapable of finding any satisfying explanation.

Wortman and Silver concluded that at least three different patterns of grieving could be identified:

1 people whose grief fitted the conventional model, 'moving through' grief from high levels of emotional distress to low ones;
2 people who failed to experience high levels of distress at any point following bereavement;
3 people who experienced high levels of distress for much longer than would be expected, over many years.

They argued that lack of distress was insufficient evidence of pathology, and argued that counselling aimed at evoking deep emotions (where maybe none existed) was unjustified and liable to provoke rather than unearth anxiety. A surprising number of people appeared to survive bereavement relatively unscathed. For some, however, long-term grief continued to produce distressing effects that were often overlooked by others for whom the bereavement was a distant memory. Wortman and Silver's conclusion suggests we should treat many of the beliefs underlying bereavement counselling with caution as they reflect:

> a complex mixture of biased input and interpretation of data by outsiders, their own personal needs, as well as limited opportunity for open communication between parties, has led to a perpetuation of unrealistic assumptions about the normal process of coping with loss.
>
> (Wortman and Silver 1989: 355)

It is important to mention that this article triggered a series of responses, notably from Stroebe *et al.* (1994), debating the status of their conclusions rather than the quality of the evidence they were discussing. Stroebe's central point was that most studies are inconclusive and can at best only indicate tendencies rather than establishing unequivocal principles.

This debate draws attention to the dangers of generalizing theory from limited evidence, and warns all practitioners against using over simplified models to make sense of a wide range of grief behaviour. Both sides of the debate stress the problems that might arise from encouraging bereaved people to conform to a culturally inappropriate model of grief.

'New' models of grief

The chief difference between assumptions generally found in bereavement counselling texts and 'new' understandings is in their views of the relationship with the deceased. Separation and letting go of the dead are central to the former. Grief is seen as the emotional cost of facing up to the finality of the loss and the end of the relationship. Accepting the reality of the loss is seen as a prerequisite for regaining an autonomous self that can go on to develop new relationships with the living.

The origin of these assumptions can be found in psychotherapeutic and humanistic schools of thought, with bonding theory providing explanation of loss and human development trajectories helping establish grief as progression through a series of stages towards 'resolution' and normality. It is fair to note that most writers on the subject also caution against seeing this model as linear and against accepting it too literally. However, in spite of these warnings, a simplified picture of the phase/stage model has seeped into popular culture and has taken on the status of common-sense truth for many who offer bereavement support and for bereaved people themselves.

As already noted, a number of writers argue that much empirical evidence does not fit this model (Hagman 1995; Hogan and DeSantis 1996; Klass 1996b). Klass argues that grief resolution among bereaved parents involved 'intense interaction' with their dead children. Citing Anderson, he notes that 'death ends a life but it does not end a relationship' (Klass 1996b: 17). Similarly Walter, citing Littlewood, notes the impact of the continuing husband's presence in the lives of widows, many years after their bereavement (Walter 1996).

Continuing bonds

The emphasis in these 'new directions' is therefore on change and adaptation of the relationship rather than on loss and detachment. Rather than learning to let go of the loved one, the key task is to carry on without the living child while at the same time maintaining them as a presence in their everyday lives. In Klass's sample, as with our own, parents regularly reported sensing their child's presence, hearing the child's voice and seeing his or her influence on their own thoughts and feelings.

Kaplan (1995) demonstrates how parents' values and behaviour continue to be influenced by a growing awareness of the aspirations and beliefs their child held while alive. He identifies internal dialogues held in an active and changing way with memories of the deceased, as well as conversations between parents as they attempt to discover what the child meant to each other.

This model argues that memory is itself a dynamic part of the process of identity building in bereaved people. Rosenblatt (1996) argues that the idea of a single severance from the deceased person makes little sense. Memories emerge over time, and new aspects of the deceased child's life, and details of the death, may be triggered many years later. Unknown facets of the child's character and events in which they took part may be communicated by friends only after considerable time has elapsed.

The main points can be summarized:

- grief results not from losing a relationship, but from having to transform it;
- this relationship may well continue throughout bereaved people's lives;
- the deceased continues to influence the identity of the bereaved person;
- grief is not a progression from preoccupation with the deceased to re-attachment to the living, rather it is an oscillation between the demands of the living and continuing perceptions of the deceased;
- 'resolution' of grief does not involve letting go of the deceased, but in finding a way of 'holding on' to them in the light of their physical absence;
- successful grief work results not in giving up the deceased but in being able to contemplate their lives with warmth and affection rather than with a sense of overwhelming distress (Rubin 1984).

Marwit and Klass (1995) argue that the dead fulfil four kinds of role for the living: (1) as continuing role models; (2) as someone with whom survivors can check out personal values and priorities; (3) as a guide and mentor in times of crisis – or as someone with whom to share new successes and achievements; and (4) as a 'significant other' whose views of the world and of the bereaved person continue to be an influence.

Rethinking the relationship with the deceased

This approach has a number of distinctive differences from the psychological one outlined in the previous section. In the former, assumptions about the value of autonomy and independence receive a high priority, hence continuing bonds with the deceased are seen as temporary. Conversations with them, a sense of their presence, and other attempts to hold onto the 'lost' relationship appear as psychological defences, fantasies or hallucinations, providing a necessary cushion before bereaved people face up to the reality of their loss. Failure to 'let go' may be diagnosed as 'complicated grief' and interpreted as a form of unhealthy dependency. The cause may be assumed to be insecure bonding experiences as children, unresolved crises in personal development, or stress reactions arising from the traumatic circumstances of the death.

As with the human growth and development model, talk and other ways of representing thoughts and feelings are central to the model of adjustment in the 'new understandings' of grief. However, in this model, conversation is seen as much as a vehicle for sharing and creating memories with which the survivors can live comfortably, as it is an outlet for personal feelings of distress. The cognitive, biographical purpose of this talk is important, and reminiscences of the deceased appear to be vital in establishing an accurate and full picture of exactly who they were and what they meant to everyone who knew them.

Walter (1996) uses the term 'biographical' model to stress the importance of talking with others who knew the deceased in order to establish a clear personal understanding of who they were and capture as many details of their life as possible. He argues that 'writing the last chapter' is a crucial activity in resolving grief, allowing the circumstances of the death to be placed in the context of the life as a whole. It may not be easy to find others prepared to do this, and some parents and siblings may be reluctant to talk to strangers who did not know them.

Shared conversations refresh memories. These inner representations of the deceased are dynamic and changing. Bonds formed while the child was alive continue to grow and influence the present. A clear image of the deceased, sometimes made more real through dreams, a sense of being watched or of their presence 'not far away', of talking aloud as though they were able to hear provide a supportive resource for individual and family development (Klass 1996b).

Implications for bereavement support

The implications of this approach to bereavement for support and adjustment are different from the conventional one in a number of ways:

- not 'letting go of the deceased' may be healthy rather than pathological;
- visions, dreams and conversations with the deceased may be long-term aspects of bereaved people's adjustment rather than short-term 'hallucinations' and may contribute substantially to transforming the relationship;
- making sense of the death and 'writing the last chapter' may be a necessary prerequisite for making sense of the life as a whole;
- continuing interactions with the deceased and awareness of their 'presence' may be hidden from others for fear of being perceived as mentally unstable;
- bereaved parents and siblings may need to talk about their absent sons and daughters, brothers and sisters in exactly the same way as the non-bereaved, yet fewer everyday conversations may accept this as normal;
- memorializing may be a crucial part of keeping in touch with the deceased;
- the dead are an active, positive resource to be drawn on by the living.

Systems models of grief

Families as well as individuals follow typical 'life-courses', as couples move from being childless to having their first baby, to parenting school-aged children and caring for ageing parents of their own, to their own children growing up, leaving home and forming couples themselves.

Like the individual, families also possess identities – what Roger (1991) calls a family 'paradigm' and Byng-Hall (1979, 1998) calls a family myth. Each member's unique relationship with the others, each member's character and most loved, most irritating traits, are endlessly featured in the family's conversations and everyday interactions that make up the group identity of the family. At different points in the family's life-cycle, some members – such as the parents during the baby phase – will be more influential in creating these family stories. Certainly, each member will feel differing levels of commitment and greater or lesser distance from the heart of the family. Individual relationships, for example between father and daughter, between twins, or even between husband and wife, are unique to the two members sharing them, but collectively they are known about by all members and contribute to how each sees the family as a whole and their place within it. Over time, these stories gain the status of 'legends', acting as a set of symbols through which the family knows its members and represents itself collectively to others. Nadeau (1998) places this process of family story making at the heart of successful adjustment following a child's death. Rosen (1996), similarly sees the family as a crucial healing resource if it can share individual responses and feelings in an open and uncritical way.

So, just as the individual parent or sibling has to adjust their status position from being a relative of a living child to that of a bereaved one, the family as a group also has to adjust from being the complete whole that it was to the family minus one (or more) it has become. Each of the individual relationships has to shuffle around (Walsh and McGoldrick 1991). Each member loses a unique part of themselves and of the former family. Each member deals with this loss differently. Reactions appear at different times and in different degrees of strength and duration (Gilbert 1996). Each member's behaviour changes, the things they talked about, their irritating and loveable attributes alter or maybe disappear entirely. The attributes of the deceased member no longer actively contribute in the ways that they did to the identity and character of the family. Like the individual, the family is in limbo. Following the death, it is suddenly not what it was, nor yet what it will become. It is enormously fragile but can also feel threatening – to its own members and to others in the wider society whose lives in turn connect with the family.

The previous section illustrated the importance of sharing conversation and collective remembering. Because the family is such a familiar social network, a child's death means the loss of a number of unique and 'special' relationships that have come to help characterize the family. Difficulties that family members experience in talking to one another can prevent them telling the stories they need to share if they are to produce a new 'myth' that accounts for the death and its consequences. The impact of the changing shape of the group as a whole and the contribution of their shared conversation must be taken into account when trying to understand differences in grief and plan bereavement support. In the light of the previous section it is possible to see how parental narratives that focus on the lost child can too easily exclude surviving siblings (Rubin 1996).

Case example 1.4

An important narrative for late adolescents is leaving their parents and learning to live independently at college or in a job that takes them away from home. Two surviving daughters in our sample, one in the army, the other at University, both of whom lost younger brothers through cancer, expressed resentment at their parents' lack of interest in their new 'careers' together with personal guilt at feeling these negative emotions. It was small, but significantly 'normal' things that triggered their feelings, like their mother's lack of time to visit them in their first independent home, and lack of attention to details of new decoration and furnishings.

Grief and communication within the family

Nancy Moos (1995) summed up the impact of a child's death on patterns of family interaction:

- changes in communication patterns, changes in the family's shape and structure and changes in external relationships;
- noticeable increases or decreases in communication generally and in talk about particular topics;

- changes in who talks to whom, inclusions of previously excluded members or exclusion of previously included family members;
- the censoring of information (to siblings especially) is an example of this process;
- the family hierarchy may become unbalanced, previously dominant characters may become less involved while subordinate members may take over important responsibilities;
- 'special' relationships – such as between siblings or between a parent and a particular child – alter, and roles and duties within the family become unclear. Some members may withdraw from external relationships while others spend more time with them and less within the family;
- there may be stronger attempts to control and protect certain family members such as the mother or surviving siblings.

Moos suggests that each member has to be open with the others if they are to share feelings about the death and come to terms with how the family has to change. If this cannot happen because one or more of them have problems expressing their thoughts, or are discouraged by others from showing their distress, then the family system as a whole becomes an uncomfortable setting for sharing intimate feelings about the death. How each handles their experience will be predicted by the others. Existing family stories will have prepared each member to anticipate how the others are likely to react.

Where grief reactions are ignored, discouraged or evoke unbearable distress in others, opportunities for reminiscence about the deceased are reduced. Moos suggests that one family member can affect the capacity of the whole system to provide an emotionally secure place for exploring personal loss.

Family roles are changed and so functions fulfilled by the deceased child have to be reallocated in some way. He or she may have met important needs for parents and for other siblings. Adjusting to this loss may involve trying to find alternative ways of meeting them. Each member's needs may be different, and confusion and disagreement can result as they each seek their own solution.

Case example 1.5

Hilary nursed her 8-year-old son through a terminal brain tumour. She reported that he had always been special to her and, following his death, fearing she 'could never go through that again' said that she knew she held back from her two surviving children. Within three months, she had enrolled on a college course and reinvested some of her time and energy in achieving academic qualifications. In turn, this meant her husband and children had to adjust to her increased absence from the home and her new involvement in relationships outside the family. This pattern, in one form or another, does not seem uncommon.

Figure 1.3 Family systems model of grief (adapted from Moos 1995)

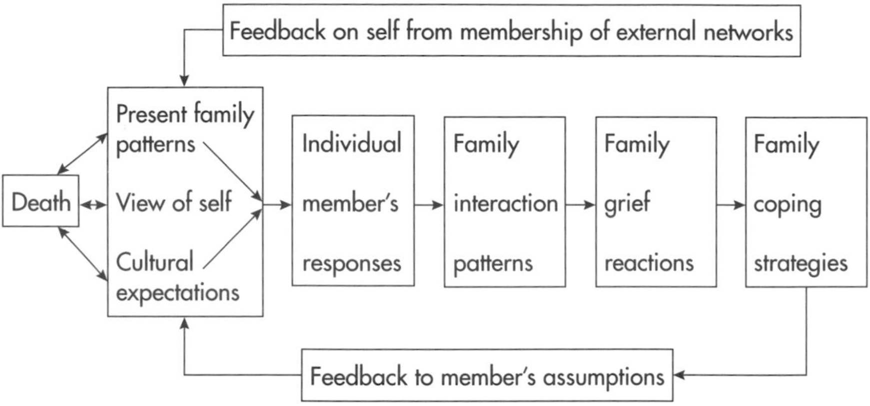

The family's role in socially constructing grief

Each family member therefore makes sense of the death in the context of the assumptions they hold about their family. These include perceptions of how each will react to the crisis and what the deceased meant to them. These assumptions act as a filter through which they anticipate the affect of the death on their family.

Each member's attitude contributes towards the family's overall adjustment, adding to the changes already caused by the deceased's disappearance from familiar routines. An anticipated death may allow more time for family members to adapt to these new patterns than a sudden death, though there is absolutely no guarantee that the nature of these adjustments will be positive or helpful to the others.

The changed interaction patterns produce new stories that reflect the family's particular bundle of grief reactions. These, in turn, produce individual coping strategies through which each member deals with the atmosphere in the home (Gilbert 1996). It may mean that some members avoid being there whenever possible, while others find it difficult to leave at all.

As noted earlier, external social networks also contribute to assumptions held by various members as they encounter their own and other family member's grief reactions. Personal interpretations of what the death means, though largely provided for young children by their parents, are also informed by important secondary relationships that can be particularly influential on views of self at different life stages. Adolescents, particularly, are often influenced by peers or by particular styles of thinking that help them create their own distinctive identity.

Figure 1.3 illustrates the importance of 'meaning structures' for parents' and siblings' adjustment. Braun and Berg (1994) argue that a child's death presents an irrevocable 'turning point', particularly in a mother's life, representing the most traumatic loss imaginable. Drawing on a wide range of evidence, they suggest that most bereaved parents can never return to the set of assumptions they held about the world prior to the death: 'Human beings struggle to reorder their reality to accommodate something that did not previously fit with their understanding of the world' (Braun and Berg 1994).

Parents who had never before experienced close family bereavement, who had never before contemplated life without their child and who possessed no 'philosophical' explanation for his or her death, experienced a shattering of existing beliefs, assumptions and values. Wheeler (1994) also found that many parents underwent a crisis of meaning after their child's death. She found that a reduced sense of purpose in life was linked to less time since the death, loss of an only child, loss of more than one child, or loss by suicide. Intense long-term distress in one family member may cause the others to fall back into supportive roles. This reinforces their task of 'protector' or 'carer' while marginalizing the implications of their own loss.

Disorientation is a likely consequence for many parents and siblings. This explains descriptions given by bereaved mothers of a loss of reality (Cornwell et al. 1977). The breakdown of one's internal working model presents a sense of 'anomic terror' (Giddens 1991). Much that was previously taken for granted about life, self and certainty in the future may now appear pointless. The family 'project' may have lost much of its meaning and the home may seem a bleak and desolate place for each member.

Braun and Berg (1994) found that parents whose children were fundamental to their meaning in life, who believed in the basic 'goodness' of the world and in its natural fairness, were particularly vulnerable to anomic terror following their bereavement. The collapse of a parent's internal working model threatens a major breakdown in the family's system of communication and relationships. Partners and surviving children may in turn be further disorientated by the loss of the parental identity of the mother or father.

Problems of representing the bereaved family to the outside world

The often overlooked value of the systems model of grief is its focus on the *family's* social adjustment, emphasizing that important aspects of the family's collective identity are lost along with the disappearance of the child (Braun and Berg 1994). For some of the families researched, holding on psychologically to the presence of the child, while at the same time coming to terms with their physical absence, appeared to be central to successful adjustment (Brabant et al. 1994).

Death of a child creates problems of how the family should represent itself to the outside world. Should the deceased child be included or omitted from public descriptions of the family? Brabant et al. (1994) identified two strategies: one in which the deceased child was 'front-stage' and referred to publicly, and one in which he or she was kept 'back-stage' and only included in the family's private conversations.

These authors draw attention to the problems created where there are conflicts over which of these strategies should be adopted by the family. There may be competing models that include or exclude the child's psychological presence within the family's coping strategies. Children can be particularly embarrassed by the inclusion of a deceased sibling in public conversation, and resentful of parents' preoccupation with memories of their life. Partners may disagree about the degree to which the deceased child should be a continuing feature of both family and external relationships. A simple detail like whether or not the child's photographs should be on display may cause communication problems between parents, and between parents and surviving siblings.

Conclusion: bereavement support and issues of meaning

Each of these approaches to understanding the meaning of bereavement has implications for its support. Parkes outlines a 'spectrum of helping strategies' ranging from direct action, through advice, information giving, reassurance, teaching and learning, listening, counselling and befriending (Parkes 1996: 54). He suggests that the earlier strategies are more likely to be encountered within health and other 'professional' services when bereaved people are most dependent, while the later ones reflect situations where the 'client' is more in control and actively seeking support.

This is a useful distinction to make in terms of the disorientation bereaved people feel and their strong needs to make sense of what is happening to them and to be able to adjust their view of the world to include their child's or sibling's death. Information may be crucial in piecing together the last moments of a child killed through accident, disaster or murder. It may be central to parents' ability to overcome guilt feelings associated with certain medical conditions such as Sudden Infant Death Syndrome. Longer term knowledge of the causes and predisposition of certain adolescents – especially young men – towards suicide might also begin to help depersonalize parent's sense of self- or other blame.

Advice on funeral and memorial arrangements, on taking photographs and keeping treasure boxes of infants, on predictable problems couples might encounter with each other and with surviving siblings may all help in making sense of present confusions and of longer term grieving when, looking back, arrangements helped 'write the last chapter' in a good rather than in an inadequate way.

The value of befriending, of having someone 'there' who shares the empty time and mourns the loss alongside the family, but who is not centrally involved in that structure, also contributes to re-establishing a sense of personal control and direction. If these befrienders have themselves gone through similar experiences, their empathy and the model of survival they can provide may be invaluable. It may also be, in itself, an important part of the meaning they are making of their own bereavement (Videker-Sherman and Lieberman 1985; Brabant 1997–8).

A number of writers recognize the importance of creating new stories that can accommodate these radically changed circumstances, and the powerlessness that grief appears to put in the way of this activity (Bright 1996). Hence the importance of conversations about the deceased and the manner of their death, of reminiscences about their life, and the sharing of feelings and thoughts about how life can be lived without them (Gersie 1991; Viney 1993). Where these conversations are shared with 'professionals' whether medical workers or counsellors, theoretical structures of grief processes such as we have outlined in this chapter are likely to underpin the kinds of support offered. These mental maps may be very helpful in offering reassurance. However, the clear philosophical differences between these models reflects the variability and range of possible meanings, and care must be taken not to impose structures that, in the longer term, are not helpful to the individual, or are at odds with their cultural background.

There is no single explanation of how people grieve and adjust to bereavement. Grief resolution may involve facing the reality of the loss and accepting that the relationship is over and moving on. It may, on the other hand, involve finding ways of changing the relationship so that the deceased can continue to be thought of and interacted with symbolically. Needs in bereaved parents and siblings will vary enormously. They may need help to move on and leave their loved ones behind. They may need help to keep a memory of them and to get in touch with others who can help them do this. They may need support in believing they possess the resources to cope with bereavement and that going back to work and getting on with their lives is a good way to do it. They may, on the other hand, need support to pause and get in touch with how they feel themselves, rather than focusing on how others in the family feel, or how they think 'society' expects them to behave in their family role. At the very least, models that help each member recognize that their own needs may be different from others in the family and that each may cope in their own way may reduce distress arising from misunderstanding.

Conventional models stress one-to-one 'counselling' with the emphasis on the emotional distress of the individual. Here, the key task is helping them face the reality of the death and detach themselves from the lost relationship. 'New' models of grief question the value of focusing exclusively on the bereaved person's feelings, suggesting that reducing emotional distress through maintaining a continuing, if changed, relationship with the deceased might also be an effective and 'natural' way of coping with bereavement.

Figure 1.4 Comparison of conventional, new and systems models of grief

	Conventional models	New understandings models	Systems models
Nature of grief	Consequence of severed bonds	Adjustment to change and continuing bonds	Filtered by position in family and culture
Relationship	Lost	Continuing but changed	Lost or continuing dependent on family communication patterns
Deceased	Internalized – 'frozen' as a precursor to 'letting go'	Inner representation who continues to change and develop over time	Absence exerting both direct and indirect effect on remaining family relationships
Grieving	Emotional reaction to pain of enforced detachment: personal, individual	Emotional response *and* cognitive activity of building a memory which is comfortable to live with: collective, shared, negotiated	Response filtered by family rules, external relationships and models available in wider culture
'Presence' of the deceased	Temporary, hallucinatory, pathological if sustained	'Absent' presence: role model, guide, part of bereaved's biography	'Social ghost': recognition and influence dependent on family communication patterns
Model of the world	Modernist: scientific, fact-based, individualist, rational	Post-modern: socially constructed. Identity based on internal conversations	Behaviour and systems functionally related: view of world filtered by position in family
Complicated grief	Failure to let go: avoidance of distress, traumatic circumstances, time limited	Inability to find appropriate meaning for changed relationship/preoccupation with manner of death/no one to share memories with, no time limit – can take forever	Dysfunctional families, communication patterns dominated by 'needy individuals', grief patterns socially learned, failure to address needs of the system as a whole
Research model	Positivist, empirical, psychological, quantitative research methods: large samples, objective measures, observer neutral	Constructionist, anthropological, socio-cultural, qualitative methods: case study, in-depth interviews/participant observation. Observer attempts to 'empathize' with subject's position	Action/intervention based, family systems approach: ecograms, family communication observations, case histories

Systems models stress the influence of family and other relationships on how the death is perceived, whether grief can be openly expressed, whether roles other than that of bereaved parent or sibling are called forth, and whether opportunities for conversational remembering of the deceased can begin to take place. Figure 1.4 offers a comparison of the principal differences and similarities between the three perspectives covered in this chapter.

Summary

Social, cultural and personal resources for making sense of bereavement

- Death is not simply an ending, but is also a changed social position, both for the deceased and for bereaved families. Society as well as individuals have to adjust to these changes.
- Personal identity has to be continually maintained. It relies on feedback from important roles for a sense of purpose, meaning and self-worth. The death of a child or sibling removes an important significant other and disturbs a set of role relationships within which identity is formed and maintained.
- Talk and conversation lie at the heart of meaning making processes. Family members already possess models for making sense of new experiences. Some models may be better at helping to give meaning to the death than others.
- All major social roles have attached expectations and obligations arising from the wider culture. Some of these may help with the expression of grief and adjustment to the death, some may hinder them.
- All societies have wider social discourses, expectations and conventions associated with the meaning of death, bereavement and the nature of grief. Individual family members draw on various impressions and interpretations gained in different subcultural settings and bring them back to the family dynamic.

Individual models of grief

- Bonding and the emotional pain of breaking bonds lie at the heart of conventional approaches to grief.
- It is natural and inevitable that loss will produce emotional distress. Avoiding it only prolongs grief's resolution.
- Grief reactions may vary, but acceptance of the finality of death is essential for bereaved people to 'move on'.
- Acceptance of death's finality is a gradual and often difficult process, characterized by a number of reactions: disbelief, anger at the deceased's disappearance, guilt, sadness, searching, intrusive thoughts about the deceased, disposal of belongings, adjusting behaviour and coming to terms with their permanent absence.

- Mourning is social. Family and other relationships can help or hinder the bereaved person's facing up to their feelings and adjusting to the loss. Where extended family and community networks have disappeared, health professionals and voluntary agencies have taken over this role.
- Professional models of grief are characterized by their rationality, generally being represented as a series of stages, each having goals and tasks to guide the bereaved person and their supporters.

New models of grief

- All theoretical models are based on cultural beliefs. Conventional models of grief reflect the culture of 'rationality and professional practice (individuality, privacy, rationality)'.
- Cultural meanings are central to the impact of death on close relatives. Support should only be offered from a position of deep knowledge of cultural beliefs and conventions of mourning.
- Social position within the family and roles played outside the family may affect perceptions of death and the meaning that is given to personal bereavement. Support should take account of how expectations vary according to membership of differing social networks.
- Evidence from studies of widows, bereaved parents and siblings contradicts the assumption that death irrevocably severs the relationship between the living and the dead.
- Evidence that failure to let go is unhelpful is not borne out in qualitative studies. Therapies that encourage detachment from the deceased may not always be helpful.
- Evidence suggests that avoidance or suppression of grief may not always be unhealthy. Moreover, individuals who fail to experience distress after bereavement may not be postponing or suppressing it. Therapies that encourage bereaved people to face painful feelings may not always be appropriate.
- Bereavement support may need to find ways of helping bereaved people 'hold on' to their lost loved ones, rather than encouraging them to let go.

Systems models of grief

- All experiences are filtered by assumptions grounded in one's social position within a family, community and culture.
- Bereavement affects not only each individual member of a family, but will also directly affect the ways in which the surviving members relate to one another.
- In addition to changes in the family's routines forced by the loss of one of its members, further changes in routines, communication patterns and roles will occur as a result of each member's perceptions of the grief of

the others, and of their own feelings of inclusion or exclusion from the death.

- Openness or censure over the expression of feelings, permission or restriction of conversations about the deceased arising from the grief responses of any one family member may set the 'tone' for all communication relating to the bereavement, impacting on the degree to which the family can operate as a resource for or as an obstacle to individual grief resolution.
- Each family member will be additionally influenced by relationships external to the family. These too may affect their assumptions regarding responsibility for other members and the degree to which they need or desire to explore their own feelings within the family.

2 A bleak and lonely landscape:
problems of adjustment
for bereaved parents

Introduction

This chapter explores how social relationships affect the way bereaved parents make sense of their child's death. We look at how friends, family and workmates help or hinder adjustment to bereavement. We outlined in Chapter 1 how the social and cultural contexts surrounding bereavement can lead to different interpretations of the death and to differing grief reactions. Here we explore the part that intimate relationships play in coping with bereavement, and how their breakdown can make grief such a lonely experience.

Some of the problems bereaved parents' face arise from the mismatch between what we are calling the culture of 'mainstream' society and the 'culture of bereavement'. Lack of sensitivity, empathy, avoidance, stigmatization and impatience with bereaved people's preoccupation with the death of their child are all consequences of the differences between these two cultures.

In addition, a more intimate set of problems arise from the mismatch between the grief reactions and coping strategies of each partner in the bereaved couple. The division of domestic labour between 'fathering' and 'mothering', and widely different expectations of the roles of fathers and mothers can lead to contradictory responses to the loss, and sometimes to conflicting ways of trying to make sense of it. Lone parents may be exposed to very ambivalent expectations arising from their attempts to fulfil both roles in the family. Planning effective support for individual parents is made additionally difficult when contrasting reactions in other family members – and the consequent changing shape of the family as a whole – is taken into account.

In the first section of this chapter we explore some of the particular obstacles that living in a typically 'modern' – that is, urbanized, technological, consumer oriented, largely agnostic and rapidly changing – society presents to bereaved parents trying to make sense of their child's death. Pressure to return to 'normal' as soon as possible and the stigma of parental bereavement can each create problems of adjustment, postponing or suppressing the need to explore how life has changed and what the death means.

Following from this, in the second section, we look at the value of support from wider social networks, and at the positive benefits that can come from professionals, friends, extended family and work colleagues.

In the third section we explore how a child's death affects marital and couple relationships. We examine the idea that men and women inhabit largely different emotional cultures, noting how gender affects both the kind of challenges faced by bereaved fathers and mothers, and the ways they attempt to overcome them.

Problems of 'modern' social attitudes towards death

Cultural beliefs and social conventions affect how we react to any momentous event. They offer guidelines about how we should express or control our feelings. The significance of children's deaths and their impact on bereaved parents and the communities they live in vary from culture to culture.

Many western societies are marked by their cultural diversity, racial mixes, minority ethnic groupings and plural belief systems. Shifting boundaries of class, gender, age, nationality, community and neighbourhood result in the observation that there is no uniform pattern to the way that the death of an offspring is experienced, grieved or supported (Parkes *et al.* 1997).

The death of a child is far from rare, but in modern societies attitudes towards death may make it *feel* unique for bereaved parents and siblings. Even in so-called 'developed' societies of the west, a surprisingly high proportion of parents outlive their children. In England and Wales, in 1995, nearly four thousand children died before they reached their first birthday. Although fewer died between the ages of 1 and 14, nearly another two thousand were added to the total figure before reaching their fifteenth birthday. By age 24, the figure had risen to 9089, and by 34, which was the upper limit of our own research sample, over 15,000 offspring had died in England and Wales. During two World Wars, and in Korea, Vietnam, Israel, the Gulf, Northern Ireland, Afghanistan, and in other conflicts around the globe, many sons from 'modern societies' died – and continue to die – before their parents. As our elderly populations live longer, more parents will inevitably survive their offspring. In terms of numbers, the loss of a child is far from unique yet many researchers confirm that the death of a child is still 'one of life's greatest tragedies' (DeVries *et al.* 1994).

Ambivalence towards death

Attitudes towards death in modern societies are often ambivalent and con-tradictory. On the one hand, murder, disaster and mass deaths feature as entertainment in block-buster films, and personal bereavement features regu-larly in popular magazines and television series (Brabant 1997–8). Images of violent death appear on news broadcasts virtually every night. On the other hand, popular magazines, newspapers and professional journals regu-larly include informed articles on bereavement, suicide and terminal illness (Walter *et al.* 1995). The vocabulary of counselling and ideas drawn from psychotherapy permeate everyday conversation. Top television and radio dramas deal with death and bereavement in often sensitive ways. At one level, death is far from a taboo subject. Nevertheless serious discussion about our own death, or about how we would cope if someone we loved died, are still generally seen as 'morbid'. We do not want to 'tempt fate' (Walter 1991a).

We may feel uncomfortable with someone whose child has died because the situation, although familiar in the media, is relatively unfamiliar in our own social network. In medieval societies, premature and often violent death was expected and commonplace. Poverty, wide-spread disease, disaster and political conflict guaranteed that childhood death was a familiar occur-rence in many cultures. Even in the 'developed' west up until the end of the 1940s many families would have shared the experience of losing a son or daughter to illness or war. Premature death, bereavement and ways of adjusting to it were a shared social experience. But over the past 50 years or so, diet, sanitation, medical science and relative peace have made childhood death a far less common occurrence in modern societies. Increased invest-ment in our children (both economically as well as emotionally), smaller families and the explosion of expert knowledge about child health and parenting have appeared to remove the need to anticipate how we would cope with our own children's deaths.

This is reinforced by the increasing longevity of other family members. Most people in the west have, statistically, high expectations of living a long, healthy and relatively affluent life. Since the end of the First World War, funerals have lost much of their ritual significance. Individual privacy and personal reserve have increased, and public expression of grief and sympathy have become less 'fashionable' (Walter 1991a). Modern societies appear to have 'tamed' the fear of death by shifting it to anxiety about the *causes* of death and admiration for those who face them heroically (Seale 1995b). Bauman argues that we share an assumption that, because every death has a specific cause, our own is in some way avoidable. People no longer die of old age. Death certificates record specific medical conditions as the cause of death. The time and nature of our own death, or of the deaths of those we love, is therefore removed from the list of things we regularly think about (Bauman 1992).

This argument is borne out through empirical study. Snyder (1997) found that students on a graduate programme still consistently overestimated their own age of death in spite of being shown actuarial tables about average ages of dying and of having the fallacy of personal invulnerability explained to them. Loo and Shea (1996), also working with college graduates, identified female students as being more sensitive to the death of others than male students. DeM'Uzan (1996) discovered a substantial percentage of patients with brain cancer who continued to live their lives without any real grasp of their own mortality.

Hospitals, hospices and undertakers provide a further barrier protecting us from the dying and the dead, postponing the insight that life is relatively short and all of us will die sooner or later. Placing elderly people in residential homes, or nursing them in the privacy of their own homes, hides evidence of our common mortality (Mulkay 1993). More affluent lifestyles, cosmetics, modern fashions and better diets enable people of all ages to display some characteristics of youth and physical attractiveness. The pace of modern living, with its emphasis on success, materialism and self-fulfilment, further discourages too much reflection on personal mortality (Mellor and Shilling 1993). Death may be a bridge that we will have to cross one day. However, that day can, perhaps, be indefinitely postponed (Bauman 1992).

In contrast to this 'hiding' from the fact of our own death, and to the tendency to grieve and mourn far more privately than in earlier and more traditional societies, there is ample evidence of 'huge upsurges' of public emotion following events such as the deaths of John F Kennedy and Princess Diana, and the aftermaths of Oklahoma, Dunblane and Hillsborough (Walter 1991b). At the same time, with the growth in professional knowledge and the ability to disseminate it, contemporary popular culture contains many 'expert' models of death and dying. Experiences of being terminally ill, the progress of bereaved people over the years following the death of a loved one, faith in the essential care and commitment of health professionals – specifically in those employed in caring for the dying but also more generally in friends, neighbours and community workers – have all been identified as themes that help individuals maintain a sense of order and security in the face of unexpected death or terminal illness in their own families (Seale 1995a, 1995b; Strauss 1993).

For most people therefore, death can be managed quite satisfactorily while it remains at a distance. As part of the plot of a good mystery novel, film or popular song (Plopper and Ness 1993), as the source of media and public emotion following the death of a well-known celebrity (Merrin 1999), and as a set of professional opinions that can be used to make sense of a colleague's or acquaintance's life-threatening illness (Seale 1995a, 1995b), death can be reconciled with the continuing order of our own, generally unaffected lives. In contrast, to actually imagine the death of our own child or sibling can be threatening at a very personal and fundamental level. This is not part of our plans. This is not how life *should* be or how we have been prepared to live it. Such a death threatens the mind-set that protects modern consciousness from the fragility, relative shortness and inevitable ending of all life (Giddens 1991).

The pressure to be 'normal'

'If you have not experienced the death of one of your own children,' a bereaved parent told us, 'you can never understand how I feel.' Another described The Compassionate Friends as: 'a very exclusive club. I hope to God you never have to join it.' Another said that, for many months after her daughter died, she felt that 'everything was unreal'; she was 'on a totally different plane'. This sense of unique difference from 'normal' people and dislocation from everyday life can create a major obstacle in understanding and offering support to bereaved parents. No matter how well-intentioned, support that does not take this difference into account may be ineffective.

Empathizing with someone who is dying, or with a parent or child who has been bereaved, is difficult. What should we say? How can we offer support? There are few cultural blueprints to follow in modern society. The bereaved parents we interviewed commonly resented well worn clichés like 'time is a great healer' or 'it must be a comfort to have your family around you . . .'. Such is the shock for many parents, that for a little while at least, even the closest of surviving relationships seem incapable of buffering their sense of aloneness and complete despair:

> one would expect that high emotional bonding between partners (cohesion), flexible adjustment to stresses (adaptability), good communication, high satisfaction, and good partner support would be associated with low degrees of bereavement. However, the mothers and fathers in this study were apparently so bereaved that their parental resources could not compensate for their grief beyond a certain level.
>
> (Thomas *et al.* 1997: 181)

Linda Layne (1996) in her study of pregnancy loss, identified why a child's death is so uniquely difficult to deal with in technologically sophisticated societies. Bereaved mothers in her sample had developed an unquestioned faith in the power of medical science, believing in its ability to deal with any problems that might arise in pregnancy. The deaths of their babies before they were born shattered this naïve belief. They were exposed to an unexplored 'truth': babies can and still do die (in substantial numbers) both before and soon after birth. Layne found their grief characterized a loss of innocence. Their dreams of birth and parenthood had been destroyed and their assumptions about the stability and certainty of the normal world in which they lived were broken. They felt bereaved not only of their babies, but also of their trust in the world and its technology. This tragic insight was amplified by the response of professionals, other mothers of surviving babies, partners, friends and relatives, many of whom sought to define their loss as 'abnormal'.

Our own research has found that mothers who lose babies during pregnancy feel an enormous sense of isolation. With a few notable exceptions, their general experience has been of nurses, midwives, doctors and even partners who advise them to forget it and 'get on with having another'. Bereaved parents of older children expressed the same sentiments in our study. They simply did not expect to outlive their children. They often experienced difficulty in getting other people to listen to accounts of their loss. They felt a reluctance in many people to recognize the significance of their bereavement. Many bereaved people felt pressure from acquaintances and even close friends to behave as normally as possible and not to lose control of powerful emotions (Barbarin and Chesler 1986; Littlewood *et al.* 1991; Fickling 1993).

Bereaved parents and siblings often feel that their own sense of loss is unique. Failure ever to have contemplated the death of one of their children, cultural messages of the psychological devastation caused by child-death, minimal personal experience of the death of other family members, unclear expectations about how to grieve, and a lack of wider social support all can combine to leave some parents substantially alone when faced with the death of their child. Because family dynamics are largely built around children, their loss can further isolate individual members even from each other (Dyregrov and Matthiesen 1987). Private images of the family's character, particularly myths about certain relationships within it, such as perceived favouritism or harboured resentments, may be exposed and confronted when a child dies. Research indicates that where parents had contradictory perceptions of the nature of their family following the child's death, they experienced greater problems of grief resolution than those who were able to share a common definition (Brabant *et al.* 1994).

Case example 2.1

Wendy had been remarried for over five years when her eldest son, Rick, from her previous marriage fell off the roof of their house and died after a short period in intensive care. She noted how supportive her present husband had been, how caring, compassionate and thoughtful to her as well as grieving the son he had come to think of as his own. At the same time, she acknowledged that for a short while, she shared with Rick's natural father a common sense of intense loss, especially around the time of his death and during the funeral. This family was remarkable in the way its boundaries opened up at this time to accept what normally could have been contradictory and conflicting needs.

When modern society offers so little preparation for a child's death and even less collective guidance following it, and when each family member is likely to be relatively committed to other social networks apart from the family, it is not surprising if each develops a different interpretation of their loss. The sense of isolation can therefore be doubly unique. A lack of interest or support from outside the family may be amplified by an increased inability within the family to talk about feelings and the meaning of the loss. Where such talk does take place, it may only confirm the perception that each family member is alone with their unique grief. Braun and Berg (1994) found that parents who could talk to an understanding person about the death were far more likely to adjust to their loss than those who had to deal with it alone.

The stigma of bereavement

The approach to identity we have adopted in this book stresses the active way in which individuals draw on wider cultural messages and images they encounter to construct a sense of self that fits their current social circumstances. Many writers, especially those exploring the impact of gender and ethnicity on personal identity, note how perceived difference from others affects their view of self and their sense of self-esteem (Gilroy 1997; Segal 1997; Woodward 1997). Sociological research also emphasizes the impact that stigmatized or 'spoiled' identities can have on social relationships and the way 'self' is presented – and accepted – in everyday life (Goffman 1963; Iphofen 1990).

In the same way, recent bereavement marks someone out as 'different'. As we noted in Chapter 1, like for someone in the sick role, allowances are made for unusual or socially unpredictable behaviour among grieving people. Wider social discourses, from soap operas to expert texts on grief counselling, inform bereaved people and non-bereaved alike of the differences from 'normal' that can be anticipated during this time. As with many stigmas, if grief is publicly visible, it can become a central feature affecting how others perceive and relate to bereaved people.

At certain times, bereavement can be physically identified as a socially significant 'difference'. Symptoms of physical and emotional stress (tiredness, short-temper, weepiness) mourning clothes, an inability to behave 'normally' (especially trivially in sharing jokes and banter) are all observable to others. At most other times, however, the social status of 'bereaved parent' will only become apparent through deeper interaction. Often, others will 'forget' that a friend or colleague occupies this status and conversations and jokes, previously accepted as normal, may be belatedly discovered to be insensitive or hurtful. With strangers, bereaved people can choose whether or not to 'pass' (Goffman 1963). That is, they can reveal their bereaved status, and risk the altered and uncomfortable response of others, or they can keep their bereavement and feelings of grief secret.

A fascinating study of 'petit mal epilepsy' – a largely invisible illness of a highly stigmatized nature – discovered how a sufferer only revealed her condition to very close and trusted friends. She used these friends and her family, to help hide the symptoms of this illness in everyday situations, where she felt discovery would add to her problems of relating (Iphofen 1990).

Case example 2.2

The 'strategy' of passing as a way of managing the effects of being stigmatized – whether it is embarrassment, sympathy, discomfort or avoidance – has been used by a number of parents in our own research. Brenda pointed out that in 'normal' conversation when people asked how many children she had and what they were doing, she would choose the answer she felt matched the social situation: 'If it is only a passing conversation, and there is little likelihood of us getting closer, I will simply say: 'I've got two daughters', and leave it at that. They don't want to know about Rob, or his cancer, and I don't want to go into it. The setting isn't right for a long and maybe embarrassing conversation. If I'm at a day conference though, and, say I'm working with a group all day, if I think it's helpful then I will talk a bit about him and how it still is affecting me . . .'

The importance of social relationships

We have argued that modern societies are characterized by rapid social change, by increasing complexity and by a decline in traditional family and community support networks. Most individuals now relate to more people, in briefer, more superficial ways, than they did in the past. More households are likely to be headed by a lone parent or to consist of stepfamilies. More people live alone (Grinwald 1995). Those intimate relations that we manage to retain appear to be invested with much higher expectations than they used to, and it is not surprising that they are collapsing under the weight of the demands we place on them (Rubin 1983; Beeghley 1997).

Availability of bereavement support

Against this background, it is easy to see how a child's death can present such a challenge, not only to the marital/couple relationship, but also to the family as a whole. The decline of community support throws individuals increasingly onto their own private resources for making sense of bereavement.

Hence, the amount of support each bereaved parent receives may depend on the lottery of whether or not available social networks provide opportunities for sharing the experience of bereavement and grief. It also can depend on the stage parents are at in the family life-cycle when the bereavement occurred. The deaths of young children and adolescents may attract more sympathy than still-born babies and infants who were unknown to anyone outside the family. Older parents, particularly of adult children who have left home, may have fewer people to turn to who knew their child.

Many bereaved parents feel that the support they do receive is inadequate and offered only over a limited period of time (DeVries *et al.* 1994). Many of our interviewees feel that people 'soon forget', or assume that after a few months (or even weeks in some cases) the bereaved person should be back to normal. Brabant *et al.* (1995) found that support from family members, friends, bosses, co-workers and clergy was often unforthcoming and, where is was offered, lasted for only a very short period of time. Difficulty in knowing what to say, feelings of awkwardness and inability to help, fear of triggering strong emotional reactions, and perceptions that fathers in particular did not need or want help were among the reasons given for this lack of support.

At the same time, bereaved parents may avoid potentially helpful relationships either through fear of losing emotional control or through a sense of exasperation with what now seem 'trivial' conversations. Men in particular may be unable to seek the help they need or to express their feelings in ways that show others they need it (Brabant *et al.* 1995). Perceptions of stigma associated with the nature of the death, such as suicide, AIDS or drug related deaths, may prevent parents seeking support even from other bereaved parents (Donaghy 1997). These more difficult problems of resolution, and their impact on the identities of surviving family members are examined in more detail in Chapter 4.

The link between 'healthy' grieving and good social support are well established – though the nature of this link is not always clear. Parents' sense of purpose and self-worth, badly damaged by their child's death, can be repaired by others whose opinions and esteem they value (Forte *et al.* 1996). Continuing caring relationships can help shore up the symbolic part of the self that was lost (Riches and Dawson 1996c; Umberson and Terling 1997). Relationships that help parents to make sense of the death and which continue to support this particular interpretation through long-term social networks are particularly helpful. Religious faith, supported by membership of a close-knit community of believers, can help in forming consistent images of where the dead child has gone, and the meanings behind his or her death (Klass 1991). Self-help groups such as The Compassionate Friends, can also offer opportunities to share interpretations other bereaved parents have used to make sense of their child's death and to give, as well as receive, social support (Videka-Sherman 1982; Klass *et al.* 1996).

Because marital relationships are limited in their ability to buffer the effects of parental bereavement (Thomas *et al.* 1997), and the emotional energy expended during the period following the death can put a strain on surviving family relationships, normal internal patterns of mutual support, where they previously existed (and this cannot be taken for granted) may collapse, with each family member feeling alone and emotionally vulnerable (De Montigny *et al.* 1996; Lang *et al.* 1996). Opportunities for supportive social contact outside the immediate family may therefore be a key element in helping bereaved parents overcome problems of adjustment.

Where such outside help is available it appears to come from a variety of sources. For example, ability to cope with the sudden death of an infant has been linked to availability of support from friends and caring neighbours. Lang *et al.* (1996) found that bereaved parents who were able to maintain common social networks outside of the family early on following the death of their child were further along in resolving their grief than couples who remained isolated. Thuen (1997) found that if external social support was available for one partner, it was often also available for the other, suggesting that strong links between the bereaved family and external social networks offered benefits to all family members. Bereaved parents reported that emotional support was not the only useful contribution made by friends and neighbours to their adjustment. Specific information about the condition from which the child died and practical help with domestic arrangements were said to be at least as valuable as opportunities to share feelings.

Relationship networks provided by certain occupations also may affect potential for coping. Mothers who are able to return to paid work after their child's death appear to experience less depression than women working exclusively in their own homes. Working bereaved mothers also reported experiencing significantly less intrusive thoughts. Greater discrepancies in grief reaction were found in couples where the mother did not work, producing an increased risk of marital difficulties (Dyregrov and Matthiesen 1991). Employment appears to provide a source for informal support from fellow workers as well as offering continuing opportunities for self-esteem. At a time when personal relationships and parental identity are uncertain, work can provide some stable sense of continuity in an area largely disconnected from the private world of the family. As we explore further in Chapter 4, work may force bereaved parents to take 'time out' from grieving while they cope with demanding tasks or dependent colleagues at work (Stroebe and Schut 1995).

The value of social support in adjustment to bereavement

Membership of supportive social networks is associated with positive mental health and a capacity to cope with critical life crises. Such relationships appear to offer both 'little ladders' that enable us to find ways of escaping, if only temporarily, from overwhelmingly stressful experiences, and larger 'levers' through which we can fundamentally reconstruct our views of the world and our place within it (Wellman *et al.* 1988). Research into depression indicates that absence of an intimate relationship with a partner in whom one can confide is an important factor in vulnerability following a major life event or difficulty. Previous low self-esteem, feelings of hopelessness and an inability to control events, all appear to contribute to mental ill-health in the face of crisis (Brown 1995). In contrast to this,

> social support has been defined as information from others that one is loved and cared for, esteemed and valued, and part of a network of communication and mutual obligation (. . .). Such information can come from a spouse, a lover, children, friends, or social and community contacts such as churches or clubs.
>
> (Stroebe and Stroebe 1995: 215)

Social support offers more than self-esteem, practical help or a shoulder to cry on. We have already stressed the importance of talk and other forms of representing feelings and thoughts in creating a narrative of what has, and is presently, happening. The demand for adjustment comes partly from personal assumptions and frameworks of meaning becoming manifestly inadequate to make sense of reality as it is presently being experienced. This sense of unreality, disorientation and loss of control can, to an extent, be mitigated through developing new narratives that begin to rationalize the feelings and thoughts that accompany bereavement and so regain some sense of control over events (O'Hara *et al.* 1994; Tehrani and Westlake 1994; Riches and Dawson 1996a).

Social support is not always emotional in content, and as implied in the review of the 'new models' in Chapter 1, information and opportunities for clarifying factual details are highly valued by bereaved parents. Social support that offers tools to aid in their adjustment empowers parents rather than making them dependent (Bright 1996; Talbot 1997). The biographical model of grief suggests that friends, teachers and other relatives might all provide insights into the life of the deceased child, and furnish parents with 'second-hand' accounts of aspects of the child's life that they had not known about. In a similar way, doctors, nurses or members of the emergency services who attended the death or who treated the child while alive can help parents build a fuller picture of the causes leading up to the death, and of the events surrounding it. Many professionals already recognize the import-ance of the need that parents have for the minutest of details that might help fill in a missing fragment of time or an unresolved link in the chain of events. This is particularly so in unexpected or inexplicable deaths such as road accident, suicide, or Sudden Infant Death Syndrome (Cornwell *et al.*

1977), and the contribution this information makes to parents' ability to give meaning to the death and to the life that preceded it is enormous.

Hence, the social support reported by parents to have been of value in adjusting to bereavement takes many different forms and fulfils a number of different needs. As a member of their social network, supporters may be in a position to offer one or many of the following:

- acceptance that they may never – and do not ever need to – return to 'normal';
- acknowledgement of the tiredness, disorientation and feelings of sadness that may hang around for many years, and, in some cases, for ever;
- willingness to express personal grief at their child's death, to be prepared to share one's own memories of them and to include them in one's conversations;
- preparedness to listen, over and over again, to the details leading up to and following the death;
- practical help with keeping the household running while parents are tied up with the many bureaucratic and administrative arrangements that have to be made after a death – and before, in the case of terminal illness;
- remembering, years after, important anniversaries of the child's birthday, the date of his or her death, and other dates whose significance can only become known after considerable time spent talking with the bereaved parent(s);
- willingness to make the first move, especially to fathers, particularly when they appear not to want or need support, but to phrase it in ways that do not imply they have a need to express deep emotional feelings – they genuinely may not have any at this particular point;
- tentative offering of signposts that help them locate strong feelings and odd thoughts that may make them feel they are losing their mental balance, but, at the same time, not imposing an interpretative framework as though it were the truth;
- gentle reflections on how the rest of the family appear to be coping – and willingness to help where misunderstanding and resentment are building up between family members (see case example 2.3);
- just being there, maybe not even saying or doing anything in particular, but being dependable, trustworthy, offering no judgements, listening, showing one cares;
- demonstrating, even if one did not know their child, that one wants to know her or him, and that you want to see the photographs and the school reports, and hear the story of their life;
- a thorough working knowledge of local contacts, support groups, bereavement literature, professionals in health and counselling, so that one can recommend, refer and generally extend their range of options in choosing the support they might need.

Case example 2.3

Brenda confirmed the value of the support mothers of children with cancer gave to each other both during treatment and after the death. Brenda felt able to communicate to Sarah – a very close friend she had met in the treatment unit – 'in no uncertain terms' how awful she (Sarah) was being to her surviving daughters. Acutely aware of the problems her own surviving children experienced ('they would sometimes go out of the house crying and there was nothing I could do to help'), Brenda was prompted to tell Sarah that she seemed to be taking out her irritability almost entirely on her daughters – and that their understandably rebellious response should be seen as part of their own grief and not as an extra burden for her mother to bear. Brenda correctly recognized that her friend would have been unlikely to take such criticism from anyone else. . . .

Parental grief, marital tension and gender

Mothers and fathers often seem to grieve differently. Many parents report that the experience either brought them closer together as a couple or made existing problems so bad as to result in breakdown (DeFrain 1991; Smart 1992). Research into parents coping with SIDS indicated that both parents were more likely to look to their partners for support than to outsiders, but that fathers were less able to express their feelings of emotional distress than mothers (Carroll and Shaefer 1994; Lang et al. 1996).

Many studies show that couple relationships deteriorate following an offspring's death, but evidence that parental bereavement is a cause of marital breakdown is far less strong and a source of lively debate (Rando 1991; Schwab 1998). Early studies have been influential in creating assumptions that a child's death is a factor in marital breakdown. Cornwell et al.'s research (1977) into Sudden Infant Death Syndrome found an increase in marital conflict. Two of the 19 couples they interviewed separated and over a third experienced 'severe' marital problems. Lauer et al. (1983) citing Kaplan et al.'s study (1976) noted that 50 per cent of marriages experienced conflict following a child's death from cancer. Kalnins et al. (1980) found 70 per cent of their sample of parents experienced marital problems. However, they concluded that the strain of nursing a dying child with leukaemia may have opened up existing difficulties in the marriage rather than being the direct cause of the breakdown. All of these figures have been challenged (Schwab 1998).

Rando (1991) was far more reluctant to link an offspring's death with marriage and couple breakdown. She noted the high incidence of divorce in contemporary society and argued that marital breakdown statistics following a child's death were often in line with national trends. She also cautioned about drawing conclusions from the low response rate in many of these studies. Often researchers acknowledge the difficulty in re-establishing contact with possible informants following a child's death (Najman *et al.* 1993). Rando's comments confirmed earlier findings of Kerner (1979) who investigated parent's coping with the death of a child through cystic fibrosis. Only one of their sample of 16 couples divorced apparently as a direct consequence of the child's death. Other couples also experienced difficulties, but at the same time a substantial number claimed that nursing the child through his or her illness had brought them closer together. A number of studies have found positive as well as negative outcomes to couples' experience of grief following the death of their child (DeFrain and Ernst 1978; Gottlieb *et al.* 1994; Martinson *et al.* 1994). Gilbert and Smart (1992) found that the least marital conflict occurred between bereaved couples who reported a pre-existing high level of satisfaction with their partner and with the relationship they shared.

Najman *et al.* (1993), in a large longitudinal survey of bereaved parents, found that the overwhelming proportion of marriages survive the death of an infant. In a recent comprehensive review of studies reporting the effects of child death on marital relationships, Schwab (1998) concluded that, although 'there was no convincing evidence that a child's death increased a couple's likelihood of divorcing, the literature nevertheless has tended to perpetuate just such a myth. He argued that many factors affected whether or not the marriage survived, including the quality of the relationship prior to the death, its cause, and the varying circumstances each parent experienced in the time during and after the death. He argued strongly that marital distress and communication problems should not be equated with marital breakdown, and, as with DeFrain's findings, noted that bereaved parents might feel considerable distance and irritation with one another for some time before regaining the same or an even greater level of intimacy than they shared before the death (Schwab 1998).

Different grief responses in mothers and fathers

Our own research suggests that tension can arise from differences in the way each partner expresses and manages their feelings. In his study of 110 bereaved couples Schwab (1998) found that inability of one partner to deal with the child's death or illness effectively appeared to be a key factor in the three divorces that his sample produced. These differences in grieving behaviour can get in the way of normal channels of communication, and can sharpen resentments that might have existed before the death.

At this point it is important to note that generalizations can be dangerous, and in our own research we have found many exceptions to the reported trends. However, overall, the majority of published findings indicate that fathers, at least in the early stages of bereavement, are more likely to put their energies into managing practical issues, to supporting their partners, to controlling their own emotions, to 'rationalizing' the loss in terms of its wider implications for the family and to finding ways of diverting their grief into practical activities (Hazzard *et al.* 1992; Gilbert 1996; Moriarty *et al.* 1996; McGreal *et al.* 1997). Mothers, on the other hand, are more likely to connect directly to their raw feelings, responding to the death through the experience and expression of strong emotion (Schwab 1992, 1996; Gilbert 1996).

In our own study, mothers were more likely to describe the death as losing a central part of themselves. All else became unimportant. These findings are consistent with the conclusions of numerous researchers: mothers appear to grieve more intensely, to be more immersed in their grief and to grieve for longer than fathers. Emotionally, fathers are more likely to feel anger and a need to blame someone. Mothers experience feelings of being cheated, of despair, of irritability, guilt, numbness and an inability to control their emotions. Mothers are more preoccupied with thoughts of the dead child (Littlewood *et al.* 1991; Rando 1991; Schwab 1992, 1996; Carroll and Shaefer 1994; Wheeler 1993; Moriarty *et al.* 1996; Murphy 1996; Mahan and Calica 1997; Puddifoot and Johnson 1997).

Littlewood *et al.* suggest that this pattern may not be helpful to fathers, concluding that in the longer term active strategies lose their ability to manage grief. Mothers, on the other hand, may move on from passive responses to more active strategies at a later time. Cordell and Thomas (1990) and Bryant (1989) both conclude that fathers may need more support in expressing their grief than has so far been recognized, arguing that men lack acceptable outlets for expressing emotional distress. Fitzpatrick (1998) notes that elderly bereaved men, including those who lost adult children, are likely to suffer higher rates of psychological and physical disorders than elderly women.

> Men are not taught how to grieve in healthy ways, and, in fact, maintaining the masculine role interferes with grieving. The roles that men assume lead them to maintain certain images that may be quite opposed to their true feelings. The man who is 'macho' cannot express his emotions. The 'competitor' cannot compete with death, and the 'protector' experiences failure when his child dies. The 'provider' focuses on work and avoids the emotions of grief. The death of a child is a problem that cannot be solved by the 'problem solver'. The 'controller' experiences feelings of helplessness, and the man who is 'self-sufficient' shuns emotional support from others. These dilemmas that grieving men face compound their suffering.
>
> (Cordell and Thomas 1990: 75–80)

A number of writers argue that, in modern western societies, men and women still inhabit largely different cultures, and that these different experiences go a long way to explaining the apparently unequal division of emotion work within families (Apter 1985; Altschuler 1993; Duncombe and Marsden 1995). Differences in gender socialization, differences in the role models presented to boys and girls in their formative years, the struggle adolescent boys have in distancing themselves from identification with their mother and with all things feminine, and the implicit responsibility men accept for helping maintain social order, have all been offered as factors that contribute to men's unwillingness to express emotion and inability to seek emotional support from others (Chodorow 1978; Hearn 1987; Hart 1996). Cook (1988) sees men increasingly confronted by a double bind, caught between traditional expectations for them to be strong, decisive and financially responsible for their families, and feminist/liberal expectations for them to be caring, sensitive and emotionally open.

Without doubt, different leadership roles exist within the family, in the same way that they exist in any relatively stable social group. Parsons and Bales (1956) identified both instrumental and expressive functions, arguing that mothers tended to fulfil the needs for emotional maintenance and repair of family relationships while fathers tended to act as the intermediary between the family and the outside world. Certainly these roles have changed substantially with the return of large numbers of women to the labour market, yet many of the couples we interviewed still tended to reflect this emotional division of labour in relation to expression of grief and perceptions of the needs of the surviving family. It is almost as though there is a need for one partner to keep a sense of control over the family's survival as a whole, while the other is released to become immersed in exploring the damage that the death has caused to the internal family relationships. These differences were clearly discernable in earlier research into parents' grief response to neonatal death (Benfield et al. 1978).

Differences in cultural expectations certainly help account for the pressure bereaved fathers' feel to be strong for their wives and surviving family, and their apparent stoicism in the face of poorer social support and fewer offers of intimacy or emotional release (Cook 1988; Bryant 1989; Cordell and Thomas 1990). Men frequently appear to lack a language through which to express their feelings and also seem culturally constrained to keep their sense of loneliness and feelings of inadequacy to themselves. The strategies they employ to deal with these pressures, and the difficulties they experience as a result of them, will be dealt with in further detail in Chapter 4.

Parental role and differences in grieving

A number of researchers link variation in grieving patterns between marital partners to differences in parental role. 'Motherhood' is central to assumptions about 'normal' happy, childrearing, and the identity of bereaved mothers is particularly vulnerable to damage (Hartrick 1996). 'Fatherhood', on the other hand, is associated more with images of protective masculinity, and bereaved father's may experience different pressures to 'limit' the impact of the death on their wives and surviving children.

Rando (1991) suggests that each parent had a different relationship with the child before he or she died, so will be mourning a different loss. Schwab (1996) assumes a direct link between the depth and centrality of the severed relationship and the intensity of grief felt by bereaved people. Because the mother's role is generally far closer to the child both in practical as well as emotional terms, there are bound to be clear gender differences in strength and duration of grief. In families where fathers are largely uninvolved in childrearing, and in cases of perinatal death, these differences may be more clearly marked. A number of writers argue that these differences are declining rapidly with men's increasing involvement in 'emotional' labour both before and after the birth. There are now many opportunities – through ultrasound and shared antenatal courses – for fathers to 'bond' with the infants during their wives' pregnancies (Bryant 1989; Wallerstedt and Higgins 1996; Mahan and Calica 1997; Puddifoot and Johnson 1997; Worth 1997).

Other differences result from 'special' relationships, which develop between each parent and each particular child within the family. As Nadeau (1998) describes so vividly, a particular parent and a particular child are connected by unique threads of emotion and shared experience. The death of a child therefore removes a number of unique relationships from the family system (Forte et al. 1996). Birth order, personality and other demands on parental time all contribute to the specialness of each relationship. Collectively they give the family its special character.

The hopes and ambitions that each parent invested in their deceased child were unlikely to have been identical or to have carried the same significance. Regrets, guilt, unfinished business, special memories and specific problems associated with the lost relationship are not necessarily shared or understood by both parents. It is possible that this lack of understanding may be increased in cases where one parent is a step-father or mother. Peppers and Knapp (1980) describe this process of developing unique relationships as 'incongruent bonding'. They argue that it can help explain similar incongruities – uneasy mismatches – in the type and intensity of each partner's grieving. If the child dies following a long illness, different involvement of each parent in the nursing care may also affect anticipatory and subsequent grief (Benfield et al. 1978; Lauer et al. 1983; Barbarin and Chesler 1986; Schwab 1996; Wallerstedt and Higgins 1996).

Rando (1991) notes that gender socialization will affect strategies for 'coping' with the death. Helmrath and Steinitz (1978) found that fathers involved themselves more actively in handling funeral arrangements, supporting their wives, involving themselves in work and generally expanding role identities, which helped fill the gap left by the parental-identity loss. Mothers, on the other hand, felt they had more permission to 'let go', to express their grief emotionally, and were more likely to preoccupy themselves with the lost parent identity, ignoring other aspects of their lives. We consider the obstacles to shared grieving arising from gender differences on page 69.

In addition, Corwin (1995) notes the increasing number of couples in long-term relationships who do not share the same cultural and ethnic backgrounds. She argues that misunderstandings arising from previously untested assumptions about the nature of death and appropriate responses to the loss of a child can produce resentment with a partner's approach to grief and mourning. Among Mexican and Puerto Rican people, for example, it is believed that the soul remains on earth until difficulties with the living are resolved. Ritual forms of expressing anger and deep emotional distress during the funeral and for a considerable time afterwards are expected. Similarly, in Greek and Italian cultures it is fully expected that parents will never overcome the loss of a child, and will demonstrate their grief in their clothing and their public restraint until they themselves die. These contrast with the restraint shown in public grieving in Anglo-American cultures and the comparatively briefer time they allow for mourning before it becomes seen as 'pathological'. These differences can lead to conflict between couple's extended families in addition to immediate communication problems they might have with each other.

Death of a child and problems of intimacy

Rando (1991) and Helmrath and Steinitz (1978) stress the effect that a child's death will have on the family as a system of interconnected relationships. Grief may be experienced as an 'individual journey' (Martinson 1991), but the loss of any family member will inevitably involve a readjustment of roles and relationships. It will also require a renegotiated view of the family's collective identity. As noted in Chapter 1, personal pain may obscure the changing nature of these relationships, and differences in how each member grieves can lead to misunderstandings and deep resentments (Gilbert 1996; Nadeau 1998). Alternatively, attempts to 'manage' these relationships may provide an escape from having to face personal pain.

These differences in the depth, pace and nature of grieving lead to problems in marital communication. Each partner is limited in the support they can offer the other because each is mourning a different loss – the contradiction between needing to release personal pain while at the same time trying to protect the other may lead to misunderstanding and a reluctance to share feelings. In a number of studies, men showed irritation with their wives for their continuing depression and their apparent lack of concern for the husbands' feelings. These fathers also felt pressure to put their own grief to one side while they supported their partners and the rest of the family. Conversely, wives felt an intense sense of loneliness, emphasized by their husbands' apparent lack of grief and emotional distance (Lang and Gottlieb 1991, 1993; Schwab 1996). Lang *et al.* (1996) found differences in husbands' and wives' needs for emotional and intellectual intimacy during the early months following an infant's death. Women who were able to share their thoughts and feelings with their husbands appeared to experience less intense grief reactions two to four years after the death than those who found such intimacy difficult. Men on the other hand, experienced less isolation and morbid fear if they maintained sexual intimacy with their wives than husbands whose physical relationship deteriorated.

Loss of sexual activity following a child's death is a difficult issue to research, yet the data that exist suggest wide variation in bereaved couple's sexual feelings (Johnson 1984; Schwab 1992). Rando (1991) notes that sexual difficulties are not unusual for several years following the death. Hagemeister and Rosenblatt (1997) illustrate the very different meanings that sexual intimacy can hold for husbands and wives. Some couples found sexual relations provided a source of comfort and reaffirmation of life in the face of the challenge to their family. For others, sex seemed totally irrelevant and inappropriate, and loss of intimacy more generally made such relations unlikely. Men were more prone to perceive sex as a source of comfort and psychic repair. Both men and women reported the need to be held and touched more following the death, though in a way that confirmed their connectedness with each other. This did not necessarily mean in a sexual way, though some couples reported an increase in such contact. The most difficult problems were reported among couples where these perceptions failed to coincide, and where one partner's sexual needs were interpreted by the other as an indication of weaker grief, while the other saw resistance to intimacy as a lack of concern for their own feelings of loneliness. The vulnerability of couple relationships to extra-marital affairs where this mismatch occurs has not been researched, but our own data, along with that of Hagemeister and Rosenblatt, contain examples of both husbands and wives who reported that sex outside of their marriage fulfilled needs for healing and comfort in ways their partners were unwilling or incapable of doing.

Other secondary losses may compound the original grief, and difficulty in discussing them can lead to further stress. Failure to share or explain emotionally poignant events, such as anniversaries in the deceased child's life that have significance for only one parent, exclusion from important milestones that have meaning only for the father or the mother, can each be deeply distressing yet appear petty and unreasonable if put into words as criticism of a partner's insensitivity. Lang *et al.* (1996) noted that bereaved mothers consistently retained the smallest details relating to their dead children's lives and deaths, investing dates and events with meanings that were totally lost on their husbands. In our own study, one mother, bereaved for a number of years, said of her husband:

It still feels like I am alone on this huge football pitch, running myself ragged trying to remember our son, to hold on to him, to still care. . . . And he (the husband) is standing on the touchline, like some coach, shouting instructions and encouragement. I wish . . . I wish, just for once . . . he would get on that damned field and help me out a bit!

These painful reminders may resurface throughout the parent's life, triggered by incidents that may have resonance only for one of them. Such secondary losses may be felt very differently by each partner, and may lead to conflicts that neither recognize as being linked to their child's death (Rando 1991). The couple's capacity to share these, to appreciate the variability of each partner's grief patterns, and to offset the intensity of their dependency on each other through keeping up joint friendships appear crucial to successful adjustment.

Misunderstanding and breakdown in couple relationships

Helmrath and Steinitz (1978) described the features of a typical marital relationship breakdown. They found that fathers, in being more likely to return to work sooner than their wives, were often presented with active distractions. They suggested that this apparent ability to shift attention from their bereavement back to work was due to weaker biological or emotional bonding arising from the uneven division of reproductive and domestic labour in most households. Cook (1988) argued that this ability to 'compartmentalize' was a skill possessed more by men than women. Duncombe and Marsden (1993) argue that there is still a clear division of emotional labour between men and women, with women carrying most of the responsibility for 'maintaining' intimate relationships. Whatever its cause, because men appeared to return to 'normality' more quickly, it led to a sense of increased isolation among their wives. Correspondingly, husbands felt a growing frustration over the women's apparent 'refusal' to let go of their grief.

At this stage, the husband believes that his wife is becoming obsessed with the death to the exclusion of other family members, and worries about her mental stability. His wife feels that he is callous and could not possibly have loved their child as much as she thought he did. Both share a short temper, tiredness and a sense of being unsupported, but each provides the other with a target and a cause for their deeper hurt. Exasperation at not being able to help his wife to get 'over it' is compounded by the husband's awareness that his wife is not supporting him or meeting his needs.

At work, there may be others with whom he finds it easier to talk, or who recognize his need to explore his loss. The gap that may have opened up between them may be compounded by the disappearance of normal routines and the contact with friends and acquaintances they brought. The husband returns from work to a distressed wife who needs to express her continuing grief. Resentful or withdrawn surviving children in the family may add to the complexity of this pattern. Where one partner is a step-parent, opportunities for misperception may be even greater.

Helmrath and Steinitz argue that the couple relationship can degenerate to a critical point where each partner becomes aware of their strongly felt differences and may, without the ability to deal with them, begin to accept their inevitability. Failure to communicate, repeated patterns of criticism or hurt silences are translated into a failure of the relationship. This 'crisis' may force some couples to discuss their misperceptions or seek help from elsewhere. They may be able to re-evaluate each other's perspectives and begin to appreciate the other's loneliness. Helmrath and Steinitz note that, for a significant percentage of their sample, the child's death led eventually to positive changes in lifestyles and outlook, but not before the parents had overcome considerable marital problems.

Our own research confirms features of this model but indicates that differences in grief reactions may be linked more to social role and involvement in social networks outside the immediate family than it is to gender. In a number of the couples we interviewed, the roles described by Helmrath and Steinitz were reversed. One father had not returned to work, 18 months after his son's death, while his wife returned to her part-time job within a few weeks, giving every appearance of coping better with her grief than her husband. Even more significantly, another bereaved mother who was not employed at all when her eldest son died, signed on for a college course within a few months of his death. Four years later, with a good honours degree behind her and a full-time career, she had filled her life with a new set of relationships, which helped place her intense grief within a wider framework. Her role in the family as wife and mother of their two surviving children, though still important, had become only one part of a busy professional lifestyle. Her husband, on the other hand, was a farmer, working largely on his own. With few distractions and plenty of time to think about his son's death he still exhibited many symptoms of intense complicated grief – regret, depression and continuing inability to share his feelings. Their continuing communication problems fit Helmrath and Steinitz's analysis, but arise from differences in their access to other activities and significant social connections rather than to gender. As employment patterns change, gender may decline in importance as a factor affecting emotional responses to bereavement.

Each partner is changed by the death. It is likely that neither will fully appreciate the extent to which the other is hurting. Opportunities to share feelings with a third party can offer important insights into these mutual misunderstandings:

A father stated that after having completed the inventory, he had looked at his wife's responses and realised how much more difficulty she was having and what she was experiencing. Even though he had known she was having troubles, he had not been able to appreciate the depth of her grief until her saw her Grief Experience Inventory responses.

(Schwab 1996: 110)

Grief and 'motherhood'

By focusing on identity it is possible to explain why some parents feel a greater sense of disorientation after child bereavement than others. Identity is created and maintained through the experience of living out our cherished and socially valued roles. Parenthood may be our one and only overriding source of self-hood (Rando 1991), or it may be but one among many roles in which we receive a sense of a successful and valued self (Forte *et al.* 1996). The death of a child may therefore pose a greater or lesser threat depending on how central that parental role is within bereaved people's overall identity. Another way of putting this is to ask the questions, to what extent was the bereaved adult's life seen from the point of view of a parent, and to what degree has this viewpoint been damaged by the death of a particular child?

A number of writers have argued that reproduction and childcare are so biologically and culturally associated with femininity that motherhood is a key characteristic of being a woman (Woodward 1997). The significance of 'family' and the possession of emotional skills may, in general, be far less crucial to men's self-esteem than to women's (Campbell and Silverman 1996). Fatherhood, on the other hand, is less central to images of masculinity, and has only recently been associated with emotional and domestic involvement with children, particularly small infants (Oakley 1980; Woodward 1997). Even here, the image of the 'new man' appears to be restricted to middle-class professional groups in modern societies who adopt this identity as a way of demonstrating their distinctiveness from more traditional working-class males. Fatherhood still appears to carry strong masculine overtones of provider and protector for all men (Lupton and Barclay 1997). Hence, the death of a child, while challenging the father's role as protector, re-confirms it in relation to holding the family together and supporting their bereaved wives.

At first sight, it appears that mothers are more likely than fathers to experience a fundamental identity loss through a child's death. The experience of physically sharing one's body with that of the growing foetus, of breastfeeding, of intimately caring for a dependent infant and of learning from a young age the vital importance of 'good mothering' each reinforce for women the importance of the mother role. The death of a child appears to represent a failure to fulfil this apparently natural and central role resulting in high levels of guilt among many mothers (Wallerstedt and Higgins 1996). However, if one accepts the argument of many feminist writers, these links are not so much biologically as socially constructed. Either way, it appears that 'mothering' activities, whether undertaken by women or by men, are more likely to fundamentally alter the way those who undertake them see the world.

Lupton and Barclay (1997) argue that these activities constitute a 'learned' set of skills and sensitivities based on the experience of having to care for first an infant, then a growing child, from a position of ultimate emotional responsibility. These involve feeding, changing, carrying, bathing, clothing, organizing, playing with, and generally emotionally managing the life of a dependent child. The time involved, and the physical and emotional investment these activities require, help characterize the 'bond' identified by Bowlby as being so important to adult development between mother and child (Bowlby 1973). It is a combination of the intensity of these demands, increasing economic pressures for mothers to return to full-time employment as soon as possible, and the benefits to the mother and child of father's increased involvement in these 'mothering' activities that have helped rewrite cultural expectations of fathers. Men now feel increased pressure to be present during antenatal classes, labour and birth, as well as taking a larger part in caring for the infant (Lupton and Barclay 1997). Fathers consequently are likely to be far more vulnerable to the pain of miscarriage or perinatal bereavement than in the past, but are still as likely to be overlooked in terms of emotional support (Pedicord 1990).

Lupton and Barclay suggest that the experience of mothering produces a particular attitude towards life that they term 'maternal sensitivity'. In the same way that the term 'nurse', once unquestionably a feminine noun, is now assumed to be either male or female, so too might 'mothering' be seen as an activity undertaken by men or women. 'Maternal sensitivity' is defined as a consciousness of emotional and physical needs and the ability to manage resources and relationships in order to meet them. This does not simply involve being able to perceive emotions in others and express them oneself, but also involves a broader awareness of the emotional consequences of actions and behaviours for relationships generally. The needs of others are more apparent and a sense of obligation for meeting them more strongly felt.

The skills and sensitivities of emotional labour are learned. Many men learn them from their wives following the birth of their first baby. Frequently, however, they forget them when they no longer have to take such a large part in childrearing, and many can only learn them partially owing to their greater involvement in wage-earning. In a minority of Lupton and Barclay's sample where roles were reversed and women were the principal wage-earners, their husbands had effectively learned and were carrying out key mothering activities within the family.

This distinction between mothering and fathering helps explain differences in adjustment to bereavement, not only between mothers and fathers in traditional families, but also between working mothers and home-based mothers, maternally 'sensitive' and maternally 'insensitive' fathers, and between different lone parents and parents in step-families. Single mothers or fathers may have to fulfil both mothering and fathering aspects of parenting, but engage with one rather than the other. Step-parents of bereaved children may not have shared crucial experiences in the child's development that made him or her so significant a part of the natural parent's identity. It is interesting to note that Dyregrov (1991), while identifying bereaved mothers as being generally more depressed than fathers, mothers who stayed within the home appeared to be more distressed at one, six and twelve months after the death than mothers who returned to full-time employment.

This approach also gets us away from stereotypical assumptions that all men are emotionally inexpressive and all women are naturally more caring. If mothering (as opposed to being a mother) is a learned set of skills and attitudes based on the experience of caring for others, then whoever does it, men or women, may learn more or less from it, may be more totally committed to it or see it as more peripheral to their wider identity. Hence, a child's death might devastate the cherished components of both parent's identity where each shared an intense involvement in their child's upbringing. If, on the other hand, many of these mothering activities were undertaken by only one parent or by child-care agencies, a lesser involvement in the child's upbringing might result in less maternal sensitivity and hence pose a lesser threat to overall identity.

Conclusion: supporting bereaved parents in adjusting to loss

Anyone offering support needs to appreciate the enormity of the obstacles facing many bereaved parents. Those of us who work with bereaved families have to be able to contemplate our own death and, probably even harder, the deaths of our children. We need to be aware of the ways that we have dealt with our own personal losses.

Modern society has equipped us poorly to do this. We can call on many intellectual models to help order and predict how others will respond, just as we can look at a map of a country we have never visited before, but it cannot prepare us for how it *feels* to be in such a strange and unfamiliar country, or prepare us for the things that can go wrong, or for the failure of the map-maker to include the bits of the landscape where we are lost (Gilroy 1997).

Dying is often compared to a journey. Terms like 'passing away', 'passing over' and 'lost' are common euphemisms, which help transform threatening events into descriptions that can be managed in everyday conversation (Anderson 1998). By placing the dead elsewhere – away from the 'normal' world – the living can continue with their lives. The anger and isolation felt by many bereaved parents reflect their forced migration from the old 'normal' life where their children went to school, celebrated birthdays and had friends round for tea. In the bleak landscape of the newly bereaved, other people's ordinary routines reinforce the extent of their exile from normality. Darcy Sims argues this means facing the fact that, though parents continue to love them, their children are dead, not lost (Sims 1997). Parents cannot return to the normal life they once lived. To survive, they have to find 'a new kind of normal' (Attig 1991). This means exploring the country they are now forced to inhabit, facing the assumptions and values of those who already populate it, rather than those they have left behind. Good support means empowering them with information, company and encouragement in this activity.

To a greater or lesser extent, a child's death forces parents to re-think their lives and their world (Talbot 1997), to reconstruct a new identity (Riches and Dawson 1997) and to reorganize the assumptions they used to hold about their family and the relationships within it (Gilbert 1996). They experience responses similar to migrants suddenly banished from their familiar landscape into a strange and frightening country – what Furnham and Bochner (1986) refer to as 'culture shock'. The routines that, only a day or so before the death were taken for granted, can now seem a million miles away. One mother expressed this clearly:

> I just couldn't believe how the world could go on. People went about their everyday lives and my baby had died. No one else knew or cared. What they were doing . . . their conversations . . . they seemed so *irrelevant*! I just wanted to scream at them, 'My baby's dead!'.

Comparing bereavement with 'culture shock' helps emphasize the value of social support, while at the same time reminding us that members of bereaved families themselves may find very different pathways through to some resolution of their new place in the world. Wooster College produces a handbook for foreign exchange students which begins:

> Culture shock is the loss of emotional balance, disorientation, or con-fusion that a person feels when moving from a familiar environment to an unfamiliar one. While it is a common experience, the degree to which it occurs will vary from one person to another. . . . The basic cause of culture shock is the abrupt loss of all that is familiar, leading to a sense of isolation.
>
> (Duker 1966)

When a loved one dies, many familiar features of bereaved people's social landscape change as well. Surviving family members are lost in this unfamiliar country. Disagreements about where they are and in which direction they ought to head increase the strain they feel individually. The various path-ways each follows to overcome their sense of disorientation can drive them even further apart. Many daily routines cease, or merely emphasize the absence of the dead child. Friends may avoid calling or find conversation embarrassing, and the point of work and enjoyment in leisure activities may be lost.

Potential supporters can be divided up into those who already inhabit this strange country (other bereaved parents), those who attempt to act as guides (professionals and trained volunteers), those who have come along to help carry the bags (close continuing friends, willing to adapt in the face of the changed demands on their relationship) and those who encourage membership of the expatriot community ('pretend you are still in the old country'). This metaphor helps point out the fragility of the support each bereaved parent and each surviving child can offer the other.

Talbot's research into the impact of the death of an 'only' child illustrates how social relationships can help or hinder 'healing'. In line with the title of this book, she argues that loneliness is one of the biggest problems faced by bereaved parents, and that literally being 'left alone' and 'unheard' is a major obstacle in adjusting to loss. They are unlikely to possess the energy needed to seek out caring and understanding friends, yet it is the company of non-judgemental, empathic listeners who can prevent bereaved parents from feeling alone and unheard (Talbot 1997).

Support from other bereaved parents can therefore be of enormous value. Brabant *et al.* sums up the crucial relationship between newly bereaved parents and those who have had, through their own bereavements, more time to adjust to living in this new culture:

> The event that destroyed the world in which they lived now becomes the event that defines their roles in the new one. The role of helper to the newly bereaved is a way of adjusting to a new world without forgetting the old . . . the opportunity to do so may also be critical to the grieving process itself.
>
> (Brabant *et al.* 1997: 264)

Summary

Problems

- Parents can feel high levels of disorientation following a child's death that are increased by apparent pressures to carry on as 'normal', by the avoidance or embarrassment of others to talk about the death and by their own fear of losing control of their emotions.
- Some parents – fathers in particular – may feel strong internal pressure to keep control of their emotions and support other family members. This active role may feel more appropriate, and may be beneficial in the short term, but over time can lead to feelings of mutual resentment and misunderstanding within the couple.

- Modern societies tend to deal openly with death as an abstract 'problem', but offer more patchy support in terms of social sensitivity to individuals who have to live over time with their own children's deaths. The growth of specialist services and the medicalization of death both contribute to removing personal death from the arena of everyday life. Individual views of the world, and family's shared models of themselves as a unit, are rarely capable of dealing with a child's death without considerable and often painful and lengthy reconstruction.
- Bereaved parents can experience a real sense of intimate loneliness resulting from differences in the way they and their partners experience and express their grief, and from differences in the cultural expectations each feel they have to meet. This may be further increased by differences in each parent's involvement in paid employment or other key life roles unconnected with the family.
- Therapists, counsellors and other grief supporters need to appreciate that men and women often see the world from very different cultural perspectives and find ways of developing empathy in each for the other's position (Philpot et al. 1997).
- Many couples rely on each other for access to outside social networks. Reduction or disappearance of routines that involve contact with friends, neighbours and wider family can add to a sense of individual isolation for each parent.
- Loss of sexual intimacy, failure to appreciate ways in which partners are dealing with grief, different cherished memories of the deceased and further resentments arising from partner's apparent withdrawal from family involvement can increase each parent's sense of isolation and abandonment resulting from the original loss.
- Oversensitivity to one parent's or surviving children's feelings, avoidance of sharing memories of the deceased child, management of information and other attempts to control the family's 'spontaneous' responses might reduce individual member's opportunities to explore and resolve their own feelings and their own adaptation to other family member's reactions.

Support principles

- A child's death disrupts relationships, systems and identities. Attention should not simply be directed at the psychological responses of individuals, but also at the relationship contexts: marriages, families, sibling relationships, surviving children/individual parent relationships. Failure to identify their direct effects on individual adaptation may reduce the effectiveness of individual counselling support.
- A child's death disrupts deep assumptions about the safety and security of the world. Talk is a key resource for reconstructing models of reality that can make sense of the death of a loved one.

- Following from this, death education should be part of school, college and management training curricula. The consequences of our shared mortality should be used to review personal values, priorities and the value of social relationships on a more regular basis.
- Differences in the depth, longevity and variability of grief should be more generally appreciated and built into institutional procedures for supporting the health and welfare of citizens, students, employees and patients. Long-term depression and idiosyncratic behaviours might stem back to earlier unrecognized *unheard* losses.
- Those who offer support need to appreciate the vast differences that exist between and within couples whose child dies. Fathers and surviving children often tend to be overlooked. Neither may be able to ask for help, and their existing social networks should be explored for opportunities in which their feelings can be explored and shared.
- Supporters need to recognize that differences in grief responses may well produce resentments that add substantially to family member's experience of stress, and that marriages/family relations might well have been experiencing problems before the death.
- Opportunities should be encouraged for sharing experiences in relationships outside the immediate family.
- The normality and 'OK'ness of taking time off from grieving through diversion into another activity should be confirmed, while its impact on other family members whose responses involve deep rumination over the loss should be borne in mind by the supporter. Respect for, and insight into, differences in dealing with loss should be encouraged.
- Variations in people's need to talk, and in the periods of time in which this need becomes apparent, should be acknowledged and built into support strategies.
- The *regularity* of death (including violent, unexpected and accidental deaths), the tenacity of families, couples and siblings in the face of bereavement, and the positive outcomes many couples recognize from sharing the challenge that the death has presented, should never be forgotten by supporters – though these insights might only become apparent to bereaved parents in time.

3 What about me? Problems of adjustment for bereaved siblings

Introduction

In recent years there has been a growth of literature describing the impact of bereavement on children and adolescents. This often describes typical reactions to the death, problems of comprehending its irreversibility and difficulties arising from children's inability to deal with grief as explicitly as adults. Some excellent guidance on how sensitive support can be appropriately offered to the bereaved child is now available (Dyregrov 1991; Pettle and Britten 1995; Smith and Pennells 1995; Corr and Corr 1996). However, this research has mainly concentrated on children and adolescents who have experienced the death of a parent, creating an approach that sees problems of bereaved children primarily in terms of their developmental stage, rather than in terms of the particular relationship they held with the deceased family member.

Although certain responses are linked to particular developmental stages, and without doubt children's capacity to grieve is closely related to their capacity to conceptualize and articulate feelings, there are important social and cultural aspects of lost relationships – especially lost sibling relationships – that contribute directly to problems of adjustment. These can all too easily be overlooked, and this chapter attempts to focus on the social position of surviving siblings within bereaved families.

The consequences for siblings of the death of a brother or sister are as varied as those already identified for parents. So, for some siblings, bereavement may have major long-lasting negative consequences for psychological and social well-being (Rubin 1996), while for others it can contribute to immense emotional growth and appreciation of the value of life (Hogan and DeSantis 1994; Stahlman 1996).

In common with the social process experienced by bereaved parents, the capacity of surviving children to adapt successfully to sibling bereavement appears to be closely linked with the quality of their intimate relationships, both within the family and with outside support networks (Birenbaum *et al.* 1989). Opportunities for exploring what has happened, for making sense of the death and being supported in discovering how life can be lived without their brother or sister appear to be crucial in providing siblings with the potential for resilience and healthy adjustment to their loss.

Nadeau (1998) argues that 'story-making' lies at the heart of effective grief resolution, and that intimate social relationships provide a crucial setting in which such stories might be constructed. This chapter focuses on the obstacles that often lie in the way of siblings finding a vocabulary or an audience for the creation of their own stories about their loss.

The uniqueness of sibling bereavement

Awareness of the problems of sibling loss is growing. Researchers into sibling bereavement argue 'it can only be expected that in the future, the numbers of children and young people who will experience sibling death through such things as violent crime, drugs, HIV, and suicide will increase' (Hogan and DeSantis 1996). We argue in Chapter 5 that a violent, 'senseless' death, and societal reactions to it, can spoil the memories family members might otherwise have created. A growing number of siblings might find themselves caught in sensational stories written about such deaths by others – by the media and the criminal justice system in particular. We believe that far more attention needs to be given to bereaved siblings of all ages (including adults), and to the siblings of children with life-threatening illnesses. This is not simply because their numbers are likely to grow, but also because the extent of the problems they face in adapting to loss is only now becoming fully recognized.

The problems that children and young people have to overcome in effectively constructing a story of the death of their brother or sister are interrelated in complex and varied ways. Social and cultural factors overlay individual psychological and developmental ones. The key message we hear over and over is that bereaved siblings feel they are overlooked. Our own work with sibling support groups is characterized by their sense of being excluded or left to their own devices while the most 'seriously' affected family members (first the dying child, second the memory of the deceased child, third the bereaved mother or father) seem to receive the greatest amount of attention. These oversights may be easily compounded, as it is for many fathers, by siblings' appearance of not needing or welcoming support. In many cases partially developed conceptual and emotional skills prevent them from understanding or articulating how they feel, and typically adolescent identity problems further camouflage the distress of surviving older children and young adults (Walker 1993). Cultural messages picked up from peers, from the popular media and from family membership can present contradictory expectations about how they should publicly react to the death of their brother or sister.

Research into bereavement following death from cancer has demonstrated some important principles about making sure siblings are involved during and after terminal illness (Lauer et al. 1985) but there is still a need for deeper understanding of the complex stresses they have to deal with following other causes of death, particularly socially stigmatizing, sudden or violent deaths such as from AIDS, suicide, murder and road traffic accident. Information, involvement, inclusion and understanding are all needed before the surviving siblings can even begin to explore their own feelings, and the chances of any recently bereaved parents possessing the emotional reserves to do this are arguably quite small.

Nevertheless, making sense of the cause has been shown to be crucial in other examples of 'senseless' death. Access to every minute detail, to all the possible explanations, to all the facts of the dying and the death, and to the disposal of the body, have been shown to be of immense value where personal responsibility, anger, guilt and blame feature in the reactions of bereaved people (Cornwell et al. 1977). These facts provide the basic material from which the sibling's own story of the death will be constructed. Without this information or anyone to share it with, the child or young person is thrown back onto their own imaginations. Our research indicates that in many cases these imaginary visualizations can be far worse than the truth.

The sibling relationship is unique. It is usually the longest and, in some ways, the most taken for granted social connection an individual will ever experience (Rando 1991). Its loss has consequences for self-identity, for personal development, for relationships with parents and other surviving siblings, and for long-term relationships throughout adult life (Lewis and Schonfeld 1994; Robinson and Mahon 1997). This simple observation is regularly overlooked, not only by those who support bereaved families, but by the siblings themselves.

The invisibility of sibling bereavement

Research into bereaved siblings has been relatively neglected in comparison with studies into the impact of parental death on children and studies of child-death on parents (Segal et al. 1995). Hogan and DeSantis (1992, 1994) argue that adolescent sibling bereavement is a complex phenomenon, often overlooked and still in need of more detailed understanding, in terms both of the immediate impact of the loss, and of the longer term, possibly life-long, effects.

Within the everyday world of children and adolescents, death and bereavement is largely overlooked – death education and pastoral care having a very low priority in most schools. Increasingly centralized curricula, standardized attainment targets and assessment driven teacher–pupil relationships, together with larger class sizes and an overworked teaching force do not provide the ideal circumstances either for picking up on emotionally distressed children, or for taking the necessary time to explore the source of their problems. Bereavement among the under 20s is an unexpected event and rarely planned for by educational or health services. At the same time, a child's death is rarely anticipated by parents and when it occurs they may be unprepared to support each other, never mind finding the reserves to appreciate what their surviving children may be going through.

Hindmarch (1995) describes bereaved siblings as 'the forgotten mourners'. Taking their cue from parents, they often attempt to be brave and avoid talking about the death in case they upset others. Balk (1990) argues that siblings often go out of their way to appear to be coping and so may not be given the chance to talk about their feelings. Black (1996) suggests that many parents will deny children the information on which they can begin to piece together what has happened in the misguided belief that they are too young to be able to understand, or that they should be protected from the full force of the death. Time and again, evidence illustrates that lack of attention, lack of parents' own emotional resources and just plain pre-occupation with the dying or deceased child, relegate surviving siblings to the sidelines, encouraging them to be, at best, passive spectators (Rando 1991; Rubin 1996).

It is not difficult to appreciate why this is so. A combination of factors – a feeling that children should be protected, the appearance that they grieve less intensely, that they seem less capable of conceptualizing the irrevocable nature of death, that they continue to be involved with their own friends or activities, and that they seem often to behave badly just at the time when parents feel they should not be asked to cope with any more distress – keep the spotlight of support away from the complicated and long-term needs of bereaved siblings (DeMinco 1995). Nevertheless, research evidence attests to the benefits of appropriately including these siblings at every stage when a child is dying, has died unexpectedly, is being buried or cremated, and is being grieved over, mourned for and memorialized in the life and attention of the parent or parents (Lauer et al. 1985; Hogan and DeSantis 1994; Stahlman 1996).

Many of the children and young people we have worked with express this sense of invisibility. Their feelings are borne out in the findings of research into sibling bereavement. Studies indicate that sibling grief can in many cases be profound and long-lasting, exerting a significant influence on adult mental health (Hindmarch 1995; Segal et al. 1995; Black 1996).

Case example 3.1

Following diagnosis of leukaemia, Harry received a successful bone marrow transplant from his younger brother, Jim. Jim is completely overshadowed by Harry. Even after the operation Jim saw himself as a hero but no one else appeared to see Jim at all. Everyone's concentration had been on Harry. Jim had a difficult relationship with his father, which had deteriorated since Harry's diagnosis. One recurring event that Jim found particularly difficult was when his father came to say goodnight to the boys (who slept in separate rooms) he would say 'goodnight' to Jim, who would then hear his father in deep conversation with Harry.

Jim has been seen by a psychologist at one of the London teaching hospitals and his experience of this left him with the ability to know what was expected of him in a one to one situation. However, within our sibling group he came into his own, the other children *saw* and *listened* to Jim, agreeing with him about the unfairness of their situation.

Jim's drawings of himself tended to resembled pin-men, and he felt he was always shouting with no one hearing. One very significant drawing was his heart. He described how he felt it was being smothered by what had, and was happening within his family, and that there was in fact very little of his heart left that was visible.

From one of the work sheets he was asked to complete:

- I am the kind of person . . .   who worries when my brother cries because he only cries when something terrible happens
- People always say I . . .   Am a brave boy because of my operation
- My mother . . .   Is sometimes mean but is mostly kind and supportive
- It seems difficult   When my family is split up
- I worry . . .   When everyone is worried about Harry
- It's . . .   Hard to say I'm a tough boy because I worry a lot
- Say I'm sorry . . .   When I hurt someone

Jim wrote on the white board the following:

- I like football
- I am the kind of person who worries a lot
- My mother is very kind
- I think fathers don't express their feelings
- When I first found out my brother had leukemia I didn't know what was going on
- My friends didn't understand

He had additional problems of not being able to understand that he hated and loved his brother at the same time. In Jim's case the word hate was not an over-reaction. He really did hate his brother, for the disruption Harry had brought to his life. He felt that slowly he, as a individual, was disappearing, and he had no control over this. Also, there were times when Jim even disliked himself for loving his brother. In Jim's eyes he had saved his brother's life, he was a hero, but this had made little or no difference to how other people, including his parents, viewed him. He was still almost invisible and unimportant, which further complicated his fear that if, following the operation and at some time in the future his brother died, would he? After all, his brother had *his* bone marrow.

The impact of sibling bereavement

Bereaved siblings appear to have a higher risk of psychiatric disorders in later childhood and adult life, with a greater tendency towards depression in cases where the death was traumatic (Black 1996). Twin studies show levels of sibling grief of similar – and in some cases even greater – intensity to that of bereaved parents or children bereaved of a parent (Bryan 1995). It is likely that the nearer the deceased child was in age to the surviving sibling, the greater will have been the sense of identification and, as a consequence, the more fundamental the challenge to his or her capacity to make sense of the world (Segal *et al.* 1995). The death of older children – or of children who died even before the sibling was born, may create severe identity problems (Powell 1995). The longer term effects of traumatic loss within the family appear to be more anxiety, greater dependency, problems of individuation in later adolescence and difficulties of letting go in early adulthood (Bradach and Jordon 1995). Hogan and DeSantis (1992) suggest that the death of a sibling is one of the most traumatic and least understood crises that adolescents can encounter.

Immediate and shorter term reactions include school problems caused by poor concentration and increased aggression (Pettle and Britten 1995), or paradoxically, intensified school involvement as an escape from home problems (Kandt 1994). Many siblings describe intrusive thoughts and visualizations during the day, and sleeplessness or disturbing dreams during the night. There may be an increased fear of their own death, feelings of uselessness and lowered self-esteem, isolation, exclusion, self-blame and guilt (Lauer *et al.* 1985). There is also evidence of pronounced and rapid mood swings (Kandt 1994) and oscillation between apparently different stages of grief (DeMinco 1995). Many siblings described a sense of no longer being cared for, a loss of attention, loss of normal routines, loss of confidence, loss of sleep and lack of understanding of their feelings by peers or from teachers (Hindmarch 1995).

A longitudinal study of adolescents conducted between seven and nine years after the death of a sibling from cancer (Martinson and Campos 1991) concluded that about one in six adolescents still believed their siblings' death continued to have a major negative impact on their lives. Some siblings, even nine years after the death, still avoided the subject of their dead brother or sister for fear of upsetting their parents. Sibling death has been linked to depression and to behavioural problems in later life (Blinder 1972; McCown and Pratt 1985). Hogan and DeSantis (1996) suggest that there is not only an increased sense of vulnerability on the part of the surviving sibling, but also feelings of guilt about being alive and happy.

It is vitally important, however, to stress that these negative consequences are not inevitable. A number of studies show that it is how the family as a whole copes with a child's death that determines the quality of the surviving siblings' adjustment (Heiney 1991). Full access to information, opportunities to share feelings openly and closeness of family relationships all contribute to their chances of making sense of the death and appreciating what it means to them and to their lives. Studies by Lauer *et al.* (1985) demonstrate the positive consequences for siblings of being involved in the home care of their terminally ill brother or sister. Work by Hogan and DeSantis (1992, 1994) suggests that bereaved siblings' grief appears to be expressed more openly if they perceive their social networks as loving, respectful and caring towards them. Working with The Compassionate Friends, they also identified the importance to siblings of family conversation and activities that confirmed the 'continuing' relationship between the family and the deceased child.

Black (1996), Bradach and Jorden (1995) and Rubin (1996) each argue that it may not simply be the death itself as much as the damage done to the particular family system that ultimately determines the longer term effects on siblings. How each parent copes with the death in particular appears to be a central factor in surviving children's capacity to adjust successfully. Pettle and Britten (1995) argue that early recognition of children's grief and opportunities for exploring and expressing it can prevent longer term psychological problems. Researchers into sibling bereavement describe a variation in outcomes similar to those identified following parental bereavement. While the death appears to leave some siblings more vulnerable to social and psychological problems, others seem to achieve a greater maturity and enhanced sense of the value of life. Bereavement *can* bring families closer together as well as driving them further apart.

The role of social support and opportunities for making sense of their loss are important factors in helping determine whether bereaved siblings become what Robinson and Mahon (1997) and Hogan and DeSantis (1994) call 'resilient' or 'vulnerable' survivors. It is valuable at this stage, therefore, to summarize the range of circumstances that seem to contribute to successful sibling adjustment, and draw conclusions about the best ways of offering appropriate support.

Problems of adjustment for bereaved siblings

Problems of adjustment arise from a number of different sources. As already noted, sibling grief is complex and multilayered. In addition to the direct loss of someone who may well have been dearly loved and who shared a central part of the sibling's 'life world', the surviving child may have been deprived of someone whose presence played a key role in defining his or her sense of self.

Loss of security, of a sense of permanence and of innocence will each figure in the changes to which the bereaved sibling has to adapt (Wass 1991). Belief in parents' definition of the world and in their ability to make things all right is shaken. Children who have until recently seen death as part of the entertainment industry now have to face it in personal terms. They become aware of their own vulnerability and perceive distraught parents as proof of adults' inability to protect them (Kandt 1994). They may be shocked by the depth of visible distress in one or both of their parents. They may sense as much as see this turmoil directly – parents may hide it and the children's developmental stage may not have equipped them with concepts to adequately process these events. They may not, as yet, possess the vocabulary with which to speak about their feelings (Hindmarch 1995). Information on which greater understanding might build may also be denied 'in their own interests'. Parents appear to mistakenly believe that holding back details of the death and its causes spares surviving children further pain (Black 1966). At the same time, adults also appear to consistently overestimate the amount of information they have passed on to their children, having neither the patience nor the emotional reserves to ensure that explanations have been heard or understood (Pettle and Britten 1995).

Balk (1990) suggests that when older children and young adults are bereaved, the experience might dramatically increase an already existing crisis of adolescent identity formation. Lack of self-esteem and feelings of life's pointlessness might increase, as may the kinds of risky behaviour generally associated with teenagers. Relationships between parents and adolescent offspring may be ambivalent in the best of family circumstances, and fear of stigma and self-conscious reliance on peer approval might also conspire to prevent them from facing or voicing painful feelings. The twin crises of adolescence and sibling loss have been identified by Hogan and DeSantis (1996) as a form of 'double jeopardy', each being difficult enough to cope with on its own, but in combination producing unanswerable questions about personal worth, identity and the meaning of life. Rubin's research into the impact of the deaths of adult sons in the Arab/Israeli conflict found examples of parents who, years after their bereavement, still appeared to have a closer, better relationship with their deceased than with their surviving sons (Rubin 1996).

Surviving children may lose the attention of their parents who, however hard they try not to exclude them, find it impossible to treat the rest of the family as they did before. Healthy brothers and sisters may feel shut out from the intense dynamic between terminally ill children and their parents. Information about the illness may be withheld, familiar routines of 'home' may be disrupted and the entire family appears to be preoccupied and emotionally fragile. After the death, siblings may find themselves either left out or the object of intensified anxiety and over-protection. In time they might become the object of the aspirations parents had for the lost child, or the survivor who can never live up to what the dead child was or what he or she could have become.

Developmental and psychological problems

Smith and Pennells (1995) describe how children express grief differently to adults, yet note how crucially dependent on them they are for exploring, confirming and checking out their gradually dawning realization of death and its irreversibility. It is one of the chief ironies of sibling grief that the very people on whom the child is most likely to depend for successful adaptation are themselves the least emotionally equipped to recognize or deal with this need. Yet, as we have noted above, children's ability to cope appears to be directly linked to parent's ability to cope.

At the heart of this successful adaptation lie opportunities for open and effective communication. Black (1996) argues that even very young children have relatively well-developed concepts of death, and with support they can, in time, come to accept that it is physically permanent, irreversible, has a cause and is universal. This becomes easier as children's conceptual and language skills develop. Under fives may still see death as temporary. Wass (1991) points out that, to this age group, many aspects of life still seem magical, and irrational connections between events and outcomes can all too easily be made. Lewis and Schonfeld (1994) argue that many children, like some adults, see events in terms of 'immanent justice' assuming that whatever happens must be a consequence of someone's actions – good being rewarded, wrong being punished. Hence, when a death occurs, for whatever reason, it is all too easy for parents to overlook children's feelings of total responsibility because of a particular act or thought they believe 'caused' this retribution. However, most young children will possess some knowledge of death based on its numerous depictions on television. Wass argues that following bereavement young children will experience a wide range of fears such as being left alone, being punished, fear of the dark, and fear of ghosts and monsters.

In the case of older children, they may have a more detailed and macabre knowledge of death, showing fascination for horror films, comics and video games with gory death featured regularly. Following bereavement, this familiarity with media images of death may bring home all the more profoundly their own and their parents' mortality, and feed imaginations where information is lacking or the manner of the death was especially distressing.

The physical appearance of adolescents and young adults can lead them to be treated as if they were fully mature. Parents and family friends may assume they will shoulder some of the responsibility their grieving parents have temporarily set aside. Kandt (1994) argues that society is uncomfortable dealing both with death and with adolescence. As a consequence, few people feel competent or willing to become involved with adolescent grief.

DeMinco (1995) characterizes adolescence as a contradictory period where young people want to be heard, but are unwilling or unable to express their feelings. She argues that anger is an empowering emotion, helping compensate for feelings of fear and helplessness, but its use serves to distance adolescent survivors further from their parents and other adults. Though they may want to know about death and grief they are unwilling to ask for, or receive, intimate support:

> Expecting easy, open conversations about feelings with young adults is unrealistic. Extremes of confrontation and silence are more likely as they explore new emotional territory and readjust relationships with peers and adults.
>
> (DeMinco 1995: 184)

Balk (1983) suggests that one of the consequences of this characteristically adolescent mixture of anger, detachment and denial is a particular form of 'lingering grief' where they are reluctant to reflect on what their dead brother or sister meant to them. Lewis and Schonfeld (1994) argue that many children do not possess the conceptual ability to process their grief reactions, and so carry their search for a satisfactory explanation for the death into each new developmental phase. They argue that this 'unfinished business may accompany them well into adulthood and beyond' (Lewis and Schonfeld 1994: 617), and that these complex feelings might be evoked whenever there is a new crisis or on particular anniversaries associated with the dead person.

Kandt (1994) argues that adolescents generally lack the life experience that teaches them they can survive trauma. As yet they have not experienced the insight that no matter how bad events seem, eventually they move on and can, in time, seem more manageable. If they think about death at all, adolescents may possess an unrealistic and romantic attitude towards it. At this point in their lives they are generally more preoccupied with educational or career choices and with problems of establishing and keeping their own intimate relationships outside of the family. Brothers and sisters are part of the home landscape from which they are trying to escape. To have to face the reality that life ends, and that it can end for young as well as for old people, may be very difficult.

Systematic study of bereavement in adulthood has focused on the death of a partner, a child or a parent but rarely on siblings. Our own limited work suggests that the death of a sibling both in childhood and beyond can have long-lasting implications for psychological well-being, for the establishment of intimate relationships, and for a sense of life's meaning throughout adulthood. It is also likely that sibling bereavement during adulthood has greater impact than is generally recognized. For many adults, their own occupational and family career tends to fill up much of their lives. As a consequence, the meaning that a brother or sister holds for self-identity can be easily taken for granted. It may only be their death that foregrounds the role they actually played in anchoring a sense of roots and shared personal history. Their loss may produce feelings of isolation that seem at odds with continuing demands of bereaved people's own normal family life. Equally, family bereavement also tends to be conceptualized in terms of the primary family – so the grief of bereaved adult sisters and brothers comes very secondary to the deceased's own partner or children.

According to some writers (Erickson 1980; Colarusso and Nemiroff 1981) a critical stage of later adult development involves reconciliation with the meaning of one's own life, and sibling bereavement may compound challenges already initiated through the death of a parent, redundancy or retirement, or children gaining their independence. Elder people, perhaps more isolated in modern societies than they might have previously been, may also have relied upon the knowledge that brothers or sisters figured among – and still shared – some of their earliest and fondest memories. Deaths of these siblings not only mark the countdown to one's own death, they also mark the dwindling of those with whom one's early life can be recollected. Childhood stories become harder to tell when no one is left who shared that early landscape.

Social and relationship problems

Hogan and DeSantis (1994) stress that 'bereavement is a social network crisis'. They argue that sibling identity, quality of family relationships and life-stage of the family as a whole must each be taken into account when explaining variation in bereaved children's and adolescents' adjustment, and in deciding on appropriate forms of support. Corr and Corr (1996) argue that *questions of meaning* are central for adolescents confronted with death. Raphael (1994) notes that adolescent issues of growth, sexual maturation, independence and identity provide the backdrop against which death has to be made sense of.

The more family members talk about the death, the greater the chances of meaning being created. Younger children, with less coherently developed models of the world may also be faced with major challenges of meaning. The ability to process thoughts, contradictions and fears are a closely related issue. *Opportunities to talk* about the death may be affected by willingness or reluctance to communicate openly either by the parents or by the children (Schwab 1997). A common problem for younger children and for teenagers may be an inability to talk about the death and its consequences long enough to begin to construct meaning for themselves.

Parents may be unwilling or unable to share their feelings and thoughts, and very reluctant to discuss the details and causes of the death. This may be especially so with miscarriages or stillbirths that occurred before subsequent children were born. In turn, adolescent children may themselves be embarrassed or uncomfortable about being open with parents who do want to talk. Increased parental anxiety may lead to over-protection. Gentry and Goodwin (1995) note that among the many problems leading to anonymity in the modern world, the drifting apart of the extended family reflects the decline of an important source of support. Hence the relationship between grandparent and grandchild, providing such a rich source of frank discussion, may also be absent or harder to enact.

Bradach and Jordan (1995) argue that experience of a traumatic death in the family can have important effects on later adolescent's ability to achieve a sense of personal independence. Pettle and Britten (1995) suggests that parents may place an 'intolerable emotional burden' on surviving children. These findings suggest that the quality of the family's adjustment as a whole will affect siblings' capacity to make sense of the loss and of its implications for their own sense of self.

Following the death of a sibling, children lose a companion and a rival. They lose someone with whom they identify, someone they admire, someone they love and someone they hate. The closer the relationship between the siblings – the more their life-space was shared – the greater will be the loss of their own identity. Robinson and Mahon (1997) suggest that in comparison with other family relationships, such as that between a parent and child, siblings experience one another from within a relatively egalitarian relationship. Hogan and DeSantis (1996) suggest that resolution of sibling grief will therefore depend on the extent to which the deceased brother or sister was relied on to mark the boundaries of the survivor's own life. In the case of twins, this life-space will have been virtually identical, and each could have relied almost exclusively on the other to reinforce the boundaries of their shared world (Bryan 1995).

Some children react to the bereavement very quietly. Some are withdrawn and there may be major behavioural changes. Raphael (1994) makes the point that they may even take on a pseudo-adult type of behaviour in order to be 'grown-up' and master the pain of the loss and particularly to deny the helplessness that they equate with being a child. Although differing patterns of response have been identified, children's grief may not be recognized and their understanding of death may be complicated by the attempts of others, especially parents and family members, to protect the child. Protection can be experienced as 'exclusion' and the child feels shut out. The family can draw attention away from their need to grieve and frequently refuse to accept that they need to be part of the parents' grief. Gorer (1965) suggests that 'British parents find it embarrassing to talk to their children on subjects of deep emotional importance and they try to hide their own deep emotions from their children's observation'. The responses to a sibling's death must always be viewed from within the family network, and the way the family copes at the time of death will strongly influence the individual child as will the strategies the family adopts to establish a new structure to replace the broken one.

Following the death of a sibling, surviving children's grief can be complicated by rivalry for parental love and attention within the family. Some relationship networks appear little affected by the death. There may be some distress but feelings are often covered up and grief hurried through. There appears to be a swift return to 'normality'. The siblings in this instance learn to keep their own feelings to themselves. This internal management of grief may continue into adult life unless opportunities are presented where they are encouraged to explore their feelings about the death (McCown and Pratt 1985). Raphael (1994) suggests few adults in this position find the opportunity to share their longings, feelings, memories and regrets with others, even those they trust most deeply.

Cultural factors

Feelings of guilt and rehearsal of imaginary chains of events that justify self-blame, even in the face of evidence to the contrary, appear to be a central and recurring characteristic of sibling grief. 'Siblinghood' as a cultural role has received little attention compared with motherhood or even fatherhood, yet the unspoken bonds of responsibility and mutual destiny can be discovered in myths stretching from biblical legend such as Cain and Abel through fairy tales like Hansel and Gretel, to more contemporary themes in stories and dramas such as *The Catcher in the Rye*, *Stand by Me*, *The Waltons* and *Eastenders*.

In many respects, in spite of parents' formal responsibility for the protection of their children, siblings share the 'backstage' insights that can only come from being in the same, relatively egalitarian boat (Robinson and Mahon 1997). This discourse of fraternal obligation goes back to the first morality tale, 'Am I my brother's keeper?' and is reinforced through popular films such as *Rainman* and *American Flyers*.

Hindmarch (1995) offers the following example of this often overlooked cultural imperative. 'Look after your sister' was a regular mantra spoken by James's mother, internalized and played out (if not always willingly) by James. When, at the age of 11, his eight-year-old sister was killed in an accident, he silently accepted all the blame, even though he was not present when the tragedy occurred. Attempting to spare his feelings, James's parents avoided talking about her death, thus reinforcing his belief in his guilt, and adding further to his sense of responsibility for their distress. He became very anxious for the safety of his mother and younger brother and worried whenever he was out of their presence. Hindmarch makes the point that, from an adult perspective he was so obviously not to blame, no one thought to reassure him. Getting through to these secret feelings and finding a way of allowing James to express them was accomplished only because his teacher was able to spot his particular difficulties.

This silent guilt may be reinforced not only by parents' distress, but also by their preoccupation with the dying or dead child. The surviving siblings can feel unloved and unwanted, noting with meticulous detail, the withdrawal of their parents into their own conversations about the deceased child, their feigned interest in the surviving child's day at school, the lack of concentration in what they are telling them, the drifting gaze. 'It should have been me' is a frequent sentiment, spoken with a mixture of exasperation, guilt, rebellion and jealousy, noted by researchers and encountered many times in our own work (Hindmarch 1995).

This self-denigration may be reinforced if siblings' early experience of death breaks down their sense of security and permanence. Surviving siblings are forced to contemplate their own mortality in a more personal way than when a grandparent or even a parent dies. This is because parents and grandparents, no matter how deeply loved, and no matter how fundamentally relied on, are nowhere near as close in the chronological 'backstage' sense as siblings. The nearer they were in age, the more closely they travelled together through the unique landscape of their particular home and parent(s), the more obvious is the realization that not only 'should it have been me', it quite easily 'could have been me'.

According to William Miller (1998), legends, myths and folklore demonstrate deeply embedded assumptions in our culture about the nature of personal duty and the distribution of fortune. When bad things happen to others, our twinges of guilt arise partly from a belief that fortune's cake is finite and that we should, in some way, have arranged it to be cut more fairly. Those to whom terrible things have happened must have had such a tiny or non-existent share because ours is too large. This mythical, almost unconscious thinking – dismissed by adults as irrational – may be one of the causes of parents and other potential supporters totally missing the burden of guilt carried by children and adolescent (maybe even adult) siblings for many years after the death.

Peer groups and popular cultural views of death

In addition to these internal problems, many siblings, especially during adolescence and young adulthood, may not be helped by their vulnerability to the perceptions of their peers. As argued in Chapter 1, bereavement marks the family out as different, and many teenagers will go to great lengths to avoid drawing attention to problems in their home life.

During the teenage years and beyond, young people are engaged in 'foraging' for an identity that, on the one hand feels comfortable to live with, while on the other can be projected with confidence and pride in the new situations that adulthood imposes. Hindmarch (1995) argues that they need to demonstrate independence and personal control just at the time when they feel least secure in their rapidly changing abilities and physical appearance. Peer groups and role models from the popular media often exert a disproportionate influence on their emotional reactions to bereavement (DeMinco 1995). In addition, changed circumstances within the home such as parental conflict, over-protection of surviving children, angry outbursts and disturbing shows of emotion, can emphasize how much the death has 'spoiled' familiar routines at home. This may add to their resentment of the deceased sibling and accelerate the normal (but generally emotionally difficult) processes of detaching from parents, home and other siblings.

The part played by brothers and sisters in this identity 'foraging' should not be overlooked. Older siblings can provide valuable role models that younger ones attempt to emulate or, conversely, they may exhibit traits the younger ones work hard at avoiding. Sharing parents' idiosyncrasies, yet competing for their attention, nursing resentments over real or imagined unfairness of treatment, yet confiding intimate experiences denied to parents, their own personal growth and development is intricately bound up with that of their siblings and the unique contribution each makes to the family's dynamic. The death of a sibling, whether during childhood, adolescence or adulthood, radically affects this dynamic, forcing all the survivors to renegotiate their relative positions. Even though parents might be long dead themselves, a sibling's death can resurrect vivid memories and emotions, some of which have lain unnoticed within the core of the survivor's self-identity for many years.

Problems of sibling adjustment in families where a child has a life-threatening illness

For families where there is a child with a life-threatening illness, relationship stresses increase as the illness progresses (Doka 1996). The focus of the family is concentrated on the ill child. Siblings can come to feel more and more invisible and isolated. In our experience, brothers and sisters of children with life-threatening illnesses who become ill themselves – with colds or other childhood ailments, are frequently sent away from the family to be cared for by grandparents, aunts and friends in order that the ill child is kept safe from infection. While this appears sensible, for the siblings this can be yet another indication that their parents are only concerned with one severely ill child.

Following diagnosis, the parents' whole world is likely to be taken over by disbelief, disorientation and intense fear of the future. Their time is taken by consultations, by hospital stays and sometimes distressing medical treatment. As time goes on the parents may become absorbed by the ill child, the effects of their treatment, and anxiety about possible outcomes. They become 'experts' in the illness, acquiring familiarity with drug regimes, medical language, nursing processes and all aspects of the treatment (Ball *et al.* 1996). Within the acute hospital setting, many shoulder immense responsibility for ensuring their ill child receives the 'best' service, holding up the ideal of the London teaching hospitals such as Great Ormond Street. These parents are far from blind to the time they spend away from their other children. They know that on occasions they are unfair, and that their well children are sometimes used as scapegoats within the family. However, no matter how much awareness the parents have, the well children are highly sensitive to feelings of blame and lack of worth. Parents are often understandably too tired and absorbed by the continuing pressure and anxiety of remission and regression of the illness to do anything about their deteriorating relationship with their other children.

Even though many parents work hard to treat the ill child as 'normal', their relationship with the well sibling cannot remain the same. No matter how the parent(s) attempt to maintain the *status quo*, the extended family, health care professionals, schools and charities work against them, albeit for the best of motives. However much parents try to insist that all their children must be treated equally, the ill child is still the focus of attention. In our experience, gifts – such as computers – given by charitable organizations can become a source of resentment and sibling rivalry. The ill child may either not allow their brother or sister to use it or it becomes a source of bribery. Holidays are offered to the family, usually to places like Disney World, either in Paris or Florida and everyone is aware that if it was not for a child having cancer they would not be there. As I have heard many of the mothers state 'You have only to say my child has cancer and people put their hands in their pockets'.

From diagnosis the child who is in need of special care and attention will change the family dynamics, and fragmentation of one sort or another is likely to occur within the family unit. This can happen on many levels, but the parents – especially the mother – will work at presenting a happy, united front, when in fact their grip on many aspects of their previous lives, including their marriage, may be weakening. Assumptions that young patients belong to 'happy, balanced families' will not assist health care professionals in working effectively with either patients or their families.

For siblings, the whole world can easily come to revolve around a brother or sister with a life-threatening illness. Within sibling support groups we have organized, children between the ages of 9 and 14 often complain that they feel as if they have been stamped with a label proclaiming their brother or sister has cancer. Like their parents they too are medical experts, knowing, for instance, the names of drugs, when their sibling is neutropenic, and what is expected of them in an emergency. At school, quite often teachers will ask about the ill brother or sister, but no one asks about them. Mums will often expect the well child to take their brother or sister with them to play with *their* friends. Sometimes siblings feel they need to prove their worth by becoming 'super siblings', taking everything in their stride, being selfless and providing love and support for their ill brother or sister. Yet much of our experience with these children and young people confirms they harbour an underlying and highly ambivalent sense of anger at everyone within their family for the unfairness of their situation, and at the expectation that they will put their life on hold for the ill brother or sister.

No matter how angry the siblings are, there is often a silent collusion with the parents in respect of the possibility of relapse and death. In general, parents' unwillingness to talk openly about this possibility allows them to imagine that the well children do not know the illness could result in death. Unfortunately, in most cases this is far from true. The siblings are almost tormented by the fear that their sibling may die. Young children have talked to us about secret rituals that they carry out to keep their family and themselves safe. For example, one 13-year-old boy touched three cars then a lamp-post, one 11-year-old girl placed her right hand by her side and touched her leg with each finger then clapped. These personal superstitions and imaginary antidotes provide support for them to think and talk about death outside of the controlled environment of their family.

The double tragedy of life-threatening illness is that, understandably, many parents can only face one overwhelming set of problems that come with the diagnosis. The fear, effort and stress created in willing their child to be well and in leaving no stone unturned in seeking treatment for their illness, relegates previous, and gradually intensifying, problems with other children to a background position.

Case example 3.2

At six, Sam was the eldest of three children. His youngest brother, David, was born when he was four. Philip, the middle child was then two years of age. Less then two weeks following the birth of David, Philip was diagnosed as having leukemia and was admitted to hospital where he spent the next few weeks receiving treatment. During his stay in hospital his father stayed with him while Sam stayed at home with his mum and new baby. From that point on, Sam was overshadowed either by his baby brother or by his brother with the life-threatening illness.

Some months later Philip went into remission and treatment finished. Sam's mother sought help as Sam was by now showing difficult behaviour and a deep-seated anger. He attended three sessions and had no difficulty in telling us that, yes, he *was* angry at his mum, but he really was only trying to find out what was happening to Philip, and that he felt very sad at being left out. He said that no one cared for him and that he always seemed to come last. At home, Philip had first choice of videos to watch and when everyone went upstairs with the baby or to Philip's room he was left downstairs on his own. Sam appeared to wait until his brother was in remission before his feelings showed up as difficult behaviour.

That one child in a family is in need of special care and attention will certainly change the family's dynamic. The most important insight provided by a group of adolescents who each had a sibling with cancer was 'don't shut me out, I am part of this family too'. Holding back information and anxious feelings is certainly intended to protect well siblings and prevent them from becoming upset. In fact it is both difficult and inappropriate to attempt to conceal the true situation from siblings. Well children may, in turn, feel unable to disclose their own feelings for fear of upsetting their parents all the more. Much energy can be wasted in playing the 'protection game', and it often serves to add to the already confused emotions experienced by siblings of children with life-threatening illnesses.

Support for siblings of children with life-threatening illness

Adults, especially parents, may lack patience with children's reactions to the care of a sick brother or sister. Sometimes their attempts to express fears, anger, resentment and confusion are not well articulated. Responses such as 'what have you got to be upset about?', 'stop being selfish', 'think about your poor sister . . .', or 'would you want to change places . . . ?' are wholly understandable but, nevertheless, guaranteed to increase feelings of resentment, isolation and lack of attention or understanding.

In our experience, these children welcome honesty above everything else. Often much of the anxiety they experience results from fear of the unknown and lack of preparation for what might come. Sibling involvement in family discussion is invaluable, and information, plans, hopes and fears may need repeating regularly to check if they are hearing what is being said, and are being given a chance to ask questions and express their own feelings. These family discussions may need reinterpreting over time as children grow older and their comprehension matures and as the status of the illness changes.

Siblings may well benefit enormously from opportunities to be involved in the care of their ill brother or sister. By parents acknowledging the difficulties the family as a whole faces, by trusting them with their own uncertainties about the future, by passing on as much information as is available, well siblings can remain at the heart of the changing family dynamic and can continue to contribute to its shape and character.

Our practical experience of working with siblings of children with life-threatening illnesses indicates that parents may sometimes need outside support in fully recognizing the depth of exclusion their well children can feel. Mutual support among siblings from different families, opportunities to tell each other their stories of the resentments, feelings of devaluation, anxieties about parents and deeply mixed feelings of fear and jealousy over their ill brother or sister help reduce their sense of isolation and allow them to recognize general patterns that all families may follow during such a crisis. The involvement of a concerned adult, with knowledge of the illnesses and of typical responses of families to it, can help with offering explanations for these feelings.

Case example 3.3

Sally had spent considerable time in the sibling support group explaining how she had felt increasingly isolated from her parents – particularly her mother – since her younger brother had been diagnosed with cancer. The sibling group was set up in a separate room, taking place during a regular meeting for parents (mostly mothers) of children with life-threatening illnesses at varying stages. The parents' support group worked well, and the strength of mutual self-help was very high. A number of the mothers had become very close friends, sharing much in common. In contrast, the siblings agreed with Sally that, to a greater or lesser extent they had had to watch their mothers spending more and more time with their ill siblings, had felt extra responsibility for picking up jobs around the house that their mothers were no longer able to do, had continually to answer questions about their siblings' illness and their parents' welfare, and felt they were unable to maintain their parent's attention for any longer than a few seconds at a time. The group facilitator suggested that, on returning to the parents' group, Sally should try to explain to her mother how she felt. The siblings' response was sceptical. On return, Sally sat next to her mother who was deep in conversation with another mother. Sally looked at the facilitator who beckoned her to tap her mother on the shoulder to gain her attention. Sally's mother briefly paused to say, 'Just a minute Sally, I'm talking'. The facilitator motioned Sally to move to sit so that she could make the third corner of the triangle between her mother and her friend, so as to gain eye contact. At this, Sally's mother burst out angrily that Sally should stop being so rude and wait until she had finished her conversation. Sally shrugged and moved away, and did not try again. The brief episode was familiar to most of the siblings, yet parents were often hurt and angry when presented with such examples.

Case example 3.3 illustrates the valuable role that outside support can provide. An awareness of the family system as a whole enables teachers, family practitioners, medical staff involved with the sick child, concerned friends or relatives and so on an important opportunity to identify disintegrating relationships with well children. They can help, first, by enabling siblings on the receiving end a chance to express their feelings in a reassuring environment and maybe alongside other children who might be having the same experience. Second, they can support the healthy siblings in reintegrating themselves back into the changed family dynamic through helping parents become aware of their feelings, by encouraging greater involvement both in information sharing and in caring for the sick child, and in diverting some of the parents' attention to the more normal concerns that children and adolescents will have in their day-to-day living.

Support for bereaved siblings

Lewis and Schonfeld (1994) argue strongly that parents and other health-care providers can be supported through offering clear information on how children might react to a brother's or sister's death and by offering approaches to help them explore and express their feelings. They must be assured that they are not responsible for the death, or for their parents' distress or apparent irritation with each other. Parents must be made aware that apparently thoughtless statements or lack of emotional distress do not reflect a lack of grief. On the contrary, everyone involved with bereaved siblings must be continually reminded of the depth and complexity of their grief, and the very long periods during which it may remain hidden and unprocessed. Enabling parents to appreciate this, while they themselves are facing the biggest emotional challenge of their lives, requires sensitive and long-term support (Jurk et al. 1980). Like adults, children differ in their ability to deal with bereavement, but the presence of a number of support-ive social networks in which they feel safe to explore thoughts and feelings can substantially help their own individual resources (Ward 1996).

Wright et al. (1996) argue that hospice-based support groups for bereaved siblings can help overcome the lack of importance often accorded to their grief and support the secondary losses that arise from their parents' preoccup-ation with the death. As we have argued above, many factors may conspire in preventing them from expressing their feelings and in encouraging others to listen to them. By emphasizing self-empowerment and offering opportun-ities for their experiences to be shared and validated, Wright et al. suggest surviving children's sense of individual loneliness can be overcome.

At the same time, recognizing that others are encountering similar prob-lems helps them gain a greater understanding of the family dynamic in which they are caught, as well as providing an alternative social network from which to draw support:

> A year ago I became involved with a self-help organization for people bereaved by suicide. I discovered other people who had similar feelings to me. I stopped feeling like a freak, imagining that, for this to have happened, I must surely come from a dysfunctional family. I also started attending a group for bereaved siblings and this was good for me too. Bereaved siblings often feel they have the burden of taking care of their parents, so it's good to speak to others with similar experiences.
> (Riddoch 1998: 10)

Wright et al. (1996) describe the setting up of groups of between six and eight members, structured around clearly focused and time-limited themes.

The support of other similarly aged children and the attention of under-standing adults willing to share the problems they face appears to contribute substantially to creating personal narratives and a greater sense of control over lives that have been so substantially changed (Bright 1996).

Conclusion: resilient siblings, intimate relations and the importance of social support

In this chapter we have suggested that siblings may have long-term diffi-culties with grief resolution because they may not be able to express their feelings and they may have problems being heard even if they could express them. The importance of finding support from someone who not only can establish intimate relationships with young people when they are at their most unlovable, but who also is willing to become involved in highly charged and potentially conflict-laden family relationships is vital (Wass 1991). The chances of finding such a special person are not great. Nevertheless, from the insights provided by Hogan and DeSantis (1994), it appears that many siblings do progress from a highly vulnerable position to one in which they can develop and mature as a result of the death.

Initial losses are profound. Physically and socially there is an empty space where the sibling used to be. In addition, substantial parts of their relation-ship with parents, innocent beliefs about the stability and certainty of the world, aspects of their identity part-formed from life-space shared with the sibling, are all damaged or lost entirely. There may be a greater vulnerability to illness, a greater sense of anxiety and helplessness, guilt at their own life progressing 'as normal', depression, sleeplessness, feelings of apathy and pointlessness, isolation and distance from others and a desire to be reunited with the dead sibling. Some or all of these experiences can lead to thoughts of suicide and higher-risk or self-destructive behaviour. All too easily these feelings may be overlooked or interpreted as additional 'awkward' behaviour.

Hogan and DeSantis, however, recognize critical opportunities within this range of initial feelings for personal growth and the development of greater resilience. They argue that recognizing the irreversibility of the loss and realizing they need to get a grip of their own lives lies at the heart of this shift in resilient siblings' perspectives. This growing sense of personal control arises within the context of having to 'forage' for an identity in the new landscape where the brother or sister no longer physically exists. In supporting parents, in ruminating on the possible meanings the death might have for them, some siblings appear to shift from the ego-centrism that characterizes childhood, adolescence and early adulthood to a greater sense of ultra-centrism.

Hogan and DeSantis argue that it was the search for meaning that stimu-lated the siblings they interviewed into greater self-awareness of what they had gained through their suffering. From regretting wasted opportunities and the apparent pointlessness of their sibling's existence, they began to construct 'inner-representations' of their dead brother or sister, often having internal conversations with them, catching up on news they felt they would have wanted to know about, asking them advice on new challenges and using this inner representation to guide their behaviour. The ability to create this 'invisible presence' – often unacknowledged to parents or friends – and the belief that one day they might be reunited, is seen by Hogan and DeSantis as critical in siblings' progress from the status of vulnerable to resilient survivor.

A capacity to find meaning through suffering, to appreciate the vulnerability – and therefore the preciousness of life – to become sensitive to the suffering of others and to support them in it, all appear to reinforce a firmer belief in one's own self. Increased optimism, maturity and spirituality characterized the resilience found by Hogan and DeSantis among a number of their sample. These young people showed a greater willingness to ask for and to give help, a greater closeness to the rest of the family and a capacity to share their own feelings about the death.

The pre-existing family relationships, and the reaction of the parents to their child's death, appear to have a strong bearing on when, and how strongly this shift takes place. In family relationships where the expression of grief is acceptable, where feelings about the death, its causes and about the deceased's earlier life are welcomed and capable of being openly expressed, where different meanings can be explored and collectively shared, and where each family member is able to give and accept support from the others, adjustment is likely to be more easily achieved. Where there are conspiracies of silence, where information is withheld and emotional expression is discouraged, where surviving siblings are ignored, overly protected or substituted for the deceased child, and where different family members grieve in radically different ways but are unable to explore each's differing interpretation of their bereavement, siblings' adjustment is likely to be slower and more difficult to achieve.

Summary

Checklist for bereaved siblings

Wass (1991) lists a number of important messages that young children need to hear following a sibling's death:

- their brother or sister did not die on purpose, they could not help it and did not intend to leave them (in cases of suicide this message will have to be reinterpreted and the following one emphasized even harder);
- the death was no one's fault – but especially it was not the fault of the surviving sibling; (care must be taken to spot any hidden conviction that they were responsible – even if only in some magical way);

- when someone is dead, nothing more can be done for their health or well-being; they can never come back;
- the brother or sister who died was not angry with the surviving sibling, and loved him or her very much (even if he or she rarely showed it);
- the surviving sibling will always be loved and cared for;
- it is OK to cry and to be angry;
- it is OK to laugh and have fun too – it does not mean you do not care or that you are not sad.

Practical ways of supporting bereaved brothers and sisters

Balk (1990) lists the following practical measures that parents and other potential supporters might consider when thinking about how surviving siblings – especially older ones – might be feeling and coping with their bereavement.

- Have they been fully involved with the events of the death – care of the child if they died from a terminal illness – or opportunities to share in recounting these events if they were not a part of them? (This may be especially valuable for very young children or for children who were born after their sibling died.)
- Have they been involved as fully and appropriately (depending on their age) with important mourning rituals that help them recognize the finality of the body's disposal and with the emotional pain of letting it go?
- Do they have any unanswered questions? Do any new questions arise later and have they been encouraged to ask them, or may they sense a real awkwardness in bringing it up again?
- Has age-appropriate language been used to give them information about the cause of death, about what happens to the body, about the uncertainty/certainty of what happens to the person after they have died? (How consistent are cultural messages heard outside the family with those given at the time of the death and funeral?)
- Have parents shared how bad they feel themselves with their surviving children? Have they demonstrated it is OK to feel bad and to let other people know? Have they been told – implicitly maybe rather than explicitly – that they have to be brave for someone else?
- Have they been allowed a chance to share how bad they feel with someone they respect and care for outside of the family circle?
- Have they had to act as a carer or referee for their parents or for other siblings? How many roles previously fulfilled by parents or the deceased sibling have they quietly taken upon themselves?
- Has anyone thought to ask about earlier bereavement in the case of difficult and challenging behaviour in childhood, adolescence or young adulthood (or even later adulthood)?

4 Connections and disconnections: ways family members deal with lost relationships

Introduction

Most people, from whatever culture, appear to exhibit similar initial emotional reactions to the death of a loved one, but the way they express and deal with these reactions varies enormously (Hagman 1995; Parkes *et al.* 1997).

This chapter recognizes the *diversity* of the ways bereaved parents and siblings cope with loss. In this chapter we sketch out how many influences in modern societies combine to produce different, distinctive 'forms' or patterns of adjustment. We focus on factors that affect how family members perceive and attempt to deal with their bereavement. Each member's orientation towards their grief has implications for the kinds of support they look for, for the willingness of others to offer it, for their ability to continue to fulfil other social roles, for their capacity to reflect on their relationship with the deceased, and for their ability to maintain a sense of purpose and well-being. We will examine the range of social and emotional connections that may be damaged or broken by bereavement, and the ways in which surviving social connections may influence the bereaved person's ability to adjust to this damage (Lofland 1982).

Diversity in adjusting to loss of a child

Differences in family members' grief responses owe much to the cultural diversity of so-called 'post-modern' society. To understand why no one conceptual model is sufficient to explain grief, two characteristics of modern societies have to be borne in mind:

1 most are multicultural, encompassing many ethnic groups with different beliefs and traditions concerning death and the destination of the deceased;

2 these societies are technologically advanced, changing rapidly, are socially complex and, compared with traditional communities, relatively
   anonymous.

Mainstream modern culture contains many contradictions. Diluted Chris-
tian beliefs, popularized versions of other major world religions, fascination with the supernatural and scientifically inspired scepticism compete for
attention through mass education and popular media. An individual sense
of continuity and security is increasingly difficult to maintain, and relies
more and more on the media for a sense of belonging to an 'imagined
community'. Increasing divorce rates, geographical mobility, unemployment,
globalization and mass consumerism challenge the old certainties, fragment
personal identities and hasten the decline of stable local communities. Dominant values now stress individualism, personal choice and the importance of
self-fulfilment (see Chapter 2, p. 49).

So, although increasing interest is shown in different ethnic beliefs about
death and patterns of mourning (Irish *et al.* 1993; Parkes *et al.* 1997) far
less attention has been given to the cultural diversity within mainstream
society itself. Modern citizens are likely to possess fewer deeply held spiritual beliefs, to be surrounded by more expert but contradictory advice, to
live in weaker more anonymous communities and enjoy less security in
their personal relationships. Moreover, familiarity with death, knowledge
of its causes and awareness of popular bereavement theory has grown, while
the need and the ability to face up to personal mortality and the potential
loss of close family appears to have declined. Living longer, modern citizens
tend to live for the present (Mellor and Shilling 1993).

Even the nature of the family cannot be taken for granted. Ender and
Hermsen (1996) draw attention to the problems faced by Army Casualty
Assistance Officers in supporting non-traditional families:

> No longer can a common set of cultural understandings be assumed.
> Rather, helpers may now be asked to perform their duties in terrains
> and contexts that are very diverse linguistically, culturally, racially,
> emotionally, and sexually. The failure to address the post-modern family
> during the bereavement process may contribute further to feelings of
> victimization on the part of the deceased soldier's family.
>
>   (Ender and Hermsen 1996: 572)

Grinwald (1995) suggests that stepfamilies will soon outnumber nuclear
families in the USA, with other western societies following this pattern.

Problems of meaning

Hence 'modern' belief systems may turn out to be inadequate when called on
to make sense of the death of a child, particularly in cases of accident, murder,

suicide or cot-death. Stroebe *et al.* (1992) suggest that more 'traditional' beliefs not only enabled parents to 'place' such deaths within a broader meaning structure, they were also likely to be shared within extensive support networks. However, most western cultures now encompass a range of contradictory 'truths' about the nature of death. Incompatible beliefs about the 'spirit', its extinction or survival exist side by side. Science and religion offer competing explanations of the meaning of death and its consequences for survivors. In the West, psychology reflects modernity's dependence on rationality. Tendencies to equate grief with sickness allow it to be portrayed as a temporary mental disorder that can be worked through on the way back to normality. The stages used to describe this adjustment can be very helpful for some bereaved parents to use as a map for judging their own progress, but for others it is meaningless and a source of increased isolation.

Non-western technologically advanced societies may still hold on to non-scientific beliefs, and their own philosophies contribute to a popular global culture. The meanings given to suicide, for example, could not be more different between the West and in Japan where ancestors are still a central part of their imagined community (Klass 1996a). Our understandings of grief must respect the diversity of meanings likely to be increasingly found within most culturally plural western societies. This 'post-modern' view recognizes that a diversity of beliefs compete for the individual's attention, reflecting the principle that all truths, scientific or otherwise, can only ever be expressed in metaphor and are relative to the context of the culture that holds them as real. All explanations of death and grief, therefore, will be influenced by the cultural assumptions that filter the evidence on which they are based (Klass *et al.* 1996).

Individuality and insecurity

Explaining variation in many family members' response to loss must therefore begin with the *individualized*, essentially private nature of each person's bereavement experience. Rather than living the whole of their lives within one traditional universally shared culture with an all pervasive system of beliefs and behaviours, individuals increasingly have to discover their own meanings from within a confusing and rapidly changing menu of consumer 'lifestyles'. Nothing is dependable. Changing relationship patterns, serial monogamy, cohabitation as an alternative to marriage, increasing numbers of lone-parent families, fluctuating patterns of employment all increase the individual's personal responsibility for making sense of their own lives and reduce the power of any one overarching cultural philosophy to answer challenging existential questions. Social support in the post-modern society is likely to be focused on fewer people, to be less durable and to offer less certainty of meaning around big questions of life and death (Gentry and Goodwin 1995).

Identity therefore, rather than being fixed within class, occupation or geographical location, is better described as an ongoing 'project', created through what Giddens (1991) calls a 'reflexive self-narrative'. Here, stable identity is actively maintained through continually reordering past memories to fit ever changing present circumstances. So, in any modern family, the death of a child might be interpreted rationally by one member (life must go on/these things happen), while for another it could be interpreted spiritually (I know she is there somewhere), while for a third, it could simply reinforce the nihilism found among some adolescent groups (life's a bitch then you die).

Hence, one of the major challenges facing bereaved people is to place some sense of order on their experience. Systems of thought – whether they are traditional religious beliefs or professional models of bereavement counselling – may provide mental maps for locating apparently meaningless events and unfamiliar thoughts and emotions. However, access to these systems may be very different from person to person and from neighbourhood to neighbourhood. One devout Roman Catholic mother we interviewed, supported strongly by members of her Irish community, had no difficulty in placing her dead daughter among the angels, 'looking after the rest of the family' as many others in her family's history had done. Another mother – the wife of a lay-reader who experienced little support from her local community – entirely lost the faith she had previously held. For one professionally employed mother we interviewed, Worden's tasks of grieving, explained to her by a hospital social worker, were useful in helping account for the difficulty she had in controlling her emotions at work. For another mother who worked in a factory, her single visit to a counsellor confirmed that 'he hadn't the faintest idea what he was talking about'.

Social connections and attitudes to bereavement

This section explores how individual responses to bereavement may be influenced by the position that bereaved parents and siblings occupy within a social and cultural milieu. Differences in coping with grief can be explained in terms of:

- the quality and diversity of bereaved people's relationships both prior to the death and following it, the strength of the expectations surrounding their social roles, and the power of shared sentiments to help them make sense of the death;
- the perceived uniqueness of the relationship with the deceased child. This connection between each family member and the deceased is central to explaining differences in coping;
- the openness of the family and its characteristic ways of communicating will have been a feature of this link between deceased and bereaved people.

The family system will continue to affect the degree to which individual members share and explore their immediate feelings about the death;

- the extent to which this lost relationship was depended on for the bereaved person's sense of personal identity and meaning in life. The degree to which it defined their life-world will affect the amount and type of support sought from, and offered by others;
- the interpretations that each is able to draw on to make sense of their loss will, in turn, be affected by the beliefs and attitudes both in the wider culture and within the various sub-cultural groups to which each family member belongs;
- the nature of the death, social attitudes towards it and the degree of publicity surrounding it can have a dramatic affect on each family member's ability to find a credible meaning and reconcile it with previous assumptions about the life they were living.

Broad versus narrow social networks

Sensitivity to their own needs, and perception of other people's feelings are affected by the social milieu to which each family member belongs. The extent to which a parent or sibling is obsessed with or distracted from their sense of loss may be influenced by the strength or weakness of their connections to other people outside the family.

Must life go on? Are there still massive demands placed on mother or father in other roles such as at work or caring for an elderly relative or a new baby? Are adolescent brothers or sisters in the middle of important school exams, or struggling with an intense romantic relationship? Do some family members have good close friends they can pour their heart out to, or buddies they can temporarily take time out with from the intensity of family emotions? Social networks can be viewed as a spider's web, with emotional stability and a sense of personal identity connected to – and supported by – a whole number of threads, whose other ends are attached to people who know and care for us or give us a purpose for being. When a thread suddenly or painfully breaks, the whole web shakes, and other threads are broken as we fall. Where only a few threads made up the web in the first place, or where we were held exclusively by the one thread that is now broken, there may be little remaining to hold us up.

The emotional and intellectual demands made by full-time employment, educational study, a close-knit extended family or supportive community all offer potential anchors for the threads that make our daily lives purposeful and satisfying. Where these connections are extensive they may offer opportunities for 'distraction' from grief, they may provide a greater range of relationships in which to explore the effects of loss or to escape from them, or they may be more actively used by the bereaved person to place the lost relationship within a wider social context.

Uniqueness of the relationship with the deceased

Differences in grieving among family members may well reflect the range of connections that existed – and continue to exist – between each of them and the deceased. The individual relationships connecting the child to each of its parents and to each of its brothers or sisters are 'special' and unique. Roles of father, mother, son, daughter, brother, sister are defined and differentiated both by the culture and by the working through of the family's own unique development. Nadeau (1998) identifies the variety of unique stories each family member will be able to create about their own relationship with the dead child, but she also notes some of the difficulties they may experience when they begin to compare these stories with each other.

Each surviving family member is likely to have bonded to the deceased child in different ways. Her age, her closeness (emotionally and chronologically) to her siblings, her birth order (or only child status), her gender and the stage her parents are at in their own life-cycle all affect the meaning the death will have for them and influence the different ways in which each survivor will attempt to adjust to it. The child will also have held a different symbolic significance for each member. The more fundamental the relationship was to the bereaved person's sense of identity, the more the deceased child fulfilled an important *raison d'être* for their lives, the greater will be the loss of self following their death (Forte *et al.* 1996).

Open versus closed family systems

Differences in patterns of family communication will determine whether or not a particular member's unique sense of loss is explored and shared. The extent to which families have established habits of listening to each other's storymaking will influence how willing they will be as an audience, helping individuals translate painful emotions into personal narratives.

Is everyone given a voice or does the most distressed member gain the most attention and support? Can the family share their feelings and explore what the death means for each of them, or are they reluctant to express their thoughts for fear of upsetting others. Families that tolerate different views, accept a range of emotions among its members and deal with conflicts constructively are more likely to be capable of negotiating new connections that accommodate the loss of one of their members.

Cultural blueprints

Additionally, to a greater or lesser extent, each family member will experience a number of cultural expectations about what they should feel and how they should behave. Assumptions about motherhood, masculinity, adolescence, childhood, mortality and grief are all firmly established in the minds of family members well before they experience bereavement. Models for behaviour abound within popular television programmes and the community's expectations of individual bereaved family members are made known in a variety of ways. Has the bereaved mother longed for this first baby, struggled with infertility and anticipated motherhood to the exclusion of all other relationships, or has she integrated her motherhood into a successful and continuing career? Is the elder daughter already assumed to be looking after the domestic chores while her mother is taken up with her own personal sense of grief? Do family friends ask the husband how his wife is but rarely check to see how he is coping?

The amount of social support offered to different family members, the help they receive in making sense of the death and the guidelines laid down for mourning vary from culture to culture and from neighbourhood to neighbourhood. In most societies, the gendered division of labour places different expectations on men than on women. Similarly, in particular cultures, religious beliefs and traditional ways of expressing grief can provide shared meaning, local supportive networks and clear conventions for mourning.

The nature of the death

Finally, the cause and nature of the death itself may be a major factor both in the meaning that can be made of the family's loss, and the degree to which it is capable of being shared with other people. Unexpected, violent or difficult deaths can create extreme emotional reactions and recurrent intrusive thoughts. Social relationships may be affected for many years, sometimes indefinitely. 'Good' deaths, anticipated in advance can help grieving and offer family members greater opportunity to share feelings and thoughts about the deceased.

For many survivors, these difficult deaths produce two principle obstacles to support and conversation about the bereavement. On the one hand, such deaths are likely to trigger social awkwardness and embarrassment, preventing bereaved family members from seeking outside support and reducing the likelihood of others offering it. On the other, these same tensions can preoccupy parents to the exclusion of their surviving children who will also be experiencing the same sense of shock and ambivalence.

Where police, courts and news media are involved, or where the cause of death, even if unpublicized, remains a source of embarrassment or guilt, then fonder memories, which might help the growth of a more comfortable relationship with the deceased, become very difficult to recall. In Chapter 1 we noted the way in which stigma can spoil an individual's self-identity, and how grief can be understood as bereaved people finding ways of repairing or rebuilding their self-identity. In the same way, the identity of the deceased can be enhanced or socially 'stigmatized' by the manner of their death.

Suicide or deaths that can be attributed to risky behaviour can produce negative social reactions. Bereaved people can feel – often with good reason – that others blame them or the deceased themselves for not prevent-ing their death.

Normal feelings of anger, guilt, remorse and unreality may be exaggerated in such cases, and whereas bereaved parents and siblings in any event might be reluctant to seek support, finding someone capable of dealing with the intensely complicated reactions following suicide and murder become almost impossible. Family communications, similarly disrupted following more 'natural' deaths, also are likely to become stretched to breaking point as each member casts around for explanations, sources of blame and self-reproach.

To the isolating effects of 'normal' grief can be added a sense of betrayal, a need to attach blame, an obsessive desire for revenge and a need for an explanation. Such bereaved family members can lose their connectedness not only with the ongoing routines of everyday life but also with their memories of the relationships that existed before the death – both living and now deceased. In terms of biographical remembering, time has stopped in the moments leading up to the death and in the subsequent confused failure to make sense of why or how it happened.

A cultural context map of grief: self-identity as revealed through bereavement

To summarize, when parents or siblings experience bereavement they are already surrounded by networks of relationships and less easily identified systems of beliefs and expectations. Some are well integrated with others who share clear attitudes towards the nature of bereavement and what should be done to cope with it. A majority of the population of modern societies, however, may be far more isolated from such communities of belief and, until it happened, have given little thought to the possibility of their child's death and even less to how they would cope in such circumstances.

It is possible to simplify differences in strength of belief and social integ-ration into four typical categories (Douglas and Calvez 1990; Riches and Dawson 1997):

1 A 'moral majority', who share the values of consumer-oriented individu-alized mass society, and who are cocooned from preoccupation about personal mortality by careers, advanced medical services, a culture of youthfulness, relative affluence, the anonymity of urban living and high levels of engagement in a selective world mediated through television and other forms of technology. Death is distant and bereavement a tempor-ary illness to be worked through. Normality should be returned to as quickly as possible.

2 'Moral minorities', who, because of marked differences of social position and experience – ethnic traditions, disability, poverty and so on – not only fail to share the values of the majority, but also find themselves in

collective opposition to them, holding different attitudes and beliefs about themselves and about the nature of the world they live in. While in traditional cultures, death is ever present and mortality a feature of life's point and limitations, in modern societies, death (except of the elderly) is a minority experience for which bereaved people are unprepared, changing forever their views of themselves and the world in which they live. Such insights may be made sense of and reinforced through discovering others in the same minority position.

3 'Isolated outcasts' who believe in the same values as the majority but whose personal circumstances prevent them from being fulfilled. Bereavement denies them the chance to act out those roles that gave their life its only meaning. Excluded and out of step, personal identity collapses in the contradiction between their view of themselves and the reality they are forced to inhabit. Theirs is the intimate loneliness of being left 'utterly alone' (Stroebe *et al.* 1996).

4 'Innovators' and those whose active rejection of the values of the moral majority enable a fresh and creative view of themselves and the world in which they live to emerge. Writers, artists and others for whom solitude and a sense of being cut off from others acts as a stimulus rather than a threat fall into this category. As with moral minorities, their influence on the mainstream culture may at times be significant. Grief produces a deep challenge to previous assumptions about majority values, and suffering, rather than leading to despair, leads to the creation of a new identity and new ways of seeing both the world and their surviving relationships (Tedeschi and Calhoun 1995).

The death of a son, daughter, brother or sister places bereaved people in a position where one or more of these alternative ways of seeing the world appear to explain their feelings of grief. The death also foregrounds the bereaved person's sense of self and has direct consequences for their perceptions of other family members and of the communities in which they live and work. Figure 4.1 offers a summary of these four cultural positions applied to perceptions of loss and attitudes towards bereavement.

The vertical axis represents the strength or weakness of beliefs held within the bereaved person's cultural milieu for making sense of death. It also reflects the degree to which their life is seen through familiar social roles. This axis marks social *regulation*: the extent to which the bereaved person sees these cultural explanations as fixed and inescapable. The higher up the axis one travels, the less negotiable social roles and duties appear to be. The horizontal axis represents the degree to which thoughts and feelings arising from bereavement are familiar and shared by others. This axis reflects social *integration*: the extent to which individuals' views and values are confirmed by a community who share the meaning of death and bereavement. The further along the axis one travels, the greater is the sense of being known

Figure 4.1   The four cultural positions in response to bereavement

Fixed meanings about life and death

Disconnection/isolation
- self overwhelmed by grief
- 'normal' role identities extinguished
- pre-occupation with loss
- grief as a destination
- marriage 'given' but irrelevant

Social repair
- quarantine of bereaved self
- 'normal' role identities re-emphasized
- active denial of loss
- grief as a threat
- marriage 'given' and relevant

Weak or no   Strong
social support   social support

Personal-reconstruction
- self re-evaluated through grief
- 'normal' roles and familiar relationships re-appraised
- integration of loss
- grief as a journey
- marriage as part of individual renegotiation

Bereavement culture
- self identifies with other bereaved parents
- bereaved self in opposition to 'normal society'
- development of sub-culture around loss
- grief as a relational bond
- marriage as part of collective renegotiation.

Negotiable meanings about life and death

and understood without having to explain, of being cared for and not having to shoulder responsibilities alone.

Each category reflects a different kind of 'coping style' for dealing with the challenge of the severed relationship. Each 'style' has implications for remaining relationships with other family members and with surviving social roles. At the same time, each distinctive 'style' can be related to the impact of the death on the bereaved parents' or siblings' sense of personal identity. Each strategy has major implications for how they create meanings around the death; links directly to the nature of the connection they maintain with the dead child; and depends to a degree on the social and cultural resources they have available, and on their perceptions of the relevance and value of these resources.

Exclusion from normal living – no way back, no way forward

Stroebe *et al.* (1996) distinguish between *social* isolation, resulting from lack of involvement in a network of relationships, and *emotional* isolation, resulting from absence of close emotional attachment. They note that the former leads to feelings of marginality, while the latter results in feelings of utter aloneness. Anthony Storr argues that the death of someone close to us threatens our sense of reality at a deep level:

> these unique and irreplaceable relationships act as points of reference which help us make sense of our experience. We are, as it were, embedded in a structure of which unique relationships are the supporting pillars. We take this so much for granted that we seldom define it, and may hardly be conscious of it until some important relationship comes to an end . . . recently bereaved people often feel, at any rate for a time, that the world has become *meaningless*.
>
> (Storr 1997: 14)

Rather than coping with grief, this first category typifies those bereaved parents and siblings who are overwhelmed by their grief. They have lost both the social and emotional connections that gave their life meaning. Being unable to move back into fonder memories of their relationship with the child, or forwards into rewarding relationships with other family members or friends, they appear to be stuck, 'knocking on the door of an empty room'. One mother we interviewed described being 'in a glass bubble with the rest of the world carrying on as though nothing had happened'. At first, potential supporters feel socially awkward and later become frustrated at the bereaved person's apparent 'refusal' to shake themselves out of it. In some cases, the intensity of their grief may appear obsessive and their reclusiveness becomes a defining characteristic of their way of dealing with the loss.

Even four years after her brother's death, one bereaved sister said, 'If I want to talk about Tommy, I go to see my Nan. I still can't talk to my mother because – I guess – I know it will upset her. She still hasn't begun to get over it yet'. Here, grief continues to disconnect this bereaved mother from all but superficial contact with others. Initially, everyday routines in which the deceased child played a central part filled her thoughts with his absent 'presence'. For many parents in this position, the only significant connection remaining is with the emptiness the child once occupied – at the table, in their bedroom – but more crucially, in their inner landscape. Hence, linking objects – clothes, toys, school work – become incredibly precious and may serve as a substitute for the child's physical presence for many years.

Lost meaning

The beliefs and attitudes of mainstream culture pertaining to their pre-bereavement role overwhelm all others – particularly those that equate success and personal fulfilment with parenthood and happy family life (Braun and Berg 1994). But because this culture fails to account for child death, the lost roles of parent or sibling become all embracing. Self-identity collapses because the only relationship on which it rests is the one that is lost. Other relationships seem unimportant or cease to matter at all. Moreover, grief cannot be shared because no one else understands the uniqueness of this lost relationship.

Memories of the deceased's life cannot be comfortably recalled because the pain of the death itself cannot be overcome. Where the deceased was an only child, a twin, a victim or in some way a 'special' child, feelings of abandonment and loneliness may be particularly acute. Conversations that might have offered an opportunity for distancing these feelings and working back to earlier fonder memories are avoided. Other family members, attempting to make sense of their own grief, sooner or later give up trying to help or understand. The isolated mourner comes to personify for other members the bleakness that has descended on the family and they may, for their own psychological preservation, look outside for alternative sources of comfort.

Case example 4.1

'Aloneness' is emphasized by the loss of the 'ordinary'. One mother noted that her husband used to go fishing every weekend, but stopped after their son died. He had not felt like he wanted to go, and the friends he used to go with had long since given up asking him. Another father cycled every weekend with his son in their local club. After the son's death, this routine stopped and within a few months, contact with other club members tailed off. Most painfully, another mother described how her neighbour, whose children played with her own during their younger years, sleeping at each other's houses while the mothers developed a close relationship around baby-sitting routines, had barely visited since her son died. At the same time, she felt enormous pressure from her sister to be 'extra, extra normal' because she herself had four children. The sister's approach was to carry on as if nothing had happened. This added to her sense of being alone with her grief.

Unfinished business

On the other hand, some lost aspects of the relationship might have been far less positive, and the loneliness felt by some family members may come from deep regret, frustration or even anger. In focusing on the absence, they ruminate on the lost opportunities for resolving conflicts, overcoming resentments or fulfilling obligations they had never got around to. Possible better futures in which they either understood the deceased better or were better understood by them, forgave them or were forgiven by them, are also lost. Feelings of guilt and resentment might be further increased by the perceived responses of other family members, and ambivalence felt towards the deceased might continue to be played out in these surviving family relationships. This might be particularly so in cases of accident or suicide in which one partner or sibling accepts responsibility for not having prevented the death, or of having contributed to it in some way.

This mental disconnection from other relationships and the routines of everyday living may be increased by difficult deaths that have no rational explanation. Here, the bereaved person's grasp of everyday reality may be violated so badly that all they can focus on is the *manner* of the dying. Where the nature of the death was sudden, shocking, violent, lacking in sense, or drawn out and difficult, bereaved parents may have great difficulty in reaching back beyond this awful event to earlier memories of their shared lives with the deceased child. Their assumptions about the point of their own lives is undermined and contrasts with the now apparently trivial concerns of the everyday world. Such deaths create a painful emotional barrier separating them both from the past life they shared with the deceased and from any future life they might share with surviving family members. Children and adolescents who have fewer past memories to return to and who can easily be overlooked or excluded from what is going on can suffer particularly badly from a loss of meaning and personal role (Barrett 1996). The public and sensationalized nature of some of these deaths – such as from accident, disaster, suicide or murder – can increase both the difficulty of making sense of the death and the isolation felt by parents and siblings. Failure to find or successfully prosecute murderers, unsuccessful attempts to force organizations to accept responsibility for negligence, or cases of disappearance where death has never been established provide self-evident examples of unfinished business that can easily trap the bereaved person in forever trying to obtain crucial information without which the last chapter of a book can never be completed.

Moreover, where circumstances are difficult to explain, either because there is little sense to them – such as with SIDS – or because they are socially stigmatized – such as with AIDS or suicide – there may seem little point or encouragement in seeking support from others. Where the cause of death was intentional as with suicide, murder or terrorism, or the result of negligence or human error, as in road traffic accidents and 'man-made' disasters, preoccupation with guilt, blame and with seeing justice done serve to cut the bereaved person off from normal everyday social contact. Preoccupation with the enormity of the loss, or with the event of the death itself, can result in the bereaved person finding most 'normal' social situations very difficult to deal with. This can be compounded by the heightened discomfort others experience in trying to find words that might be appropriate to such unusual and distressing circumstances. Whereas bereaved parents and siblings might in any event be reluctant to seek support, finding someone capable of dealing with the intensely complicated reactions following suicide or murder become almost impossible.

Family communications, disrupted following more 'natural' or predictable deaths, are also likely to become stretched to breaking point as each
member casts around for explanations, sources of blame and self-reproach.
Such bereaved family members can lose their connectedness not only with
the ongoing routines of everyday life but also with their memories of the
relationships that existed before the death – both living and now deceased.
In terms of biographical remembering, time has stopped in the moments
leading up to the death and in the subsequent confused failure to make
sense of why or how it happened. One mother whose son was stabbed to
death said in her interview:

> I sat there in the courtroom during the re-trial – some 18 months after
> my son was murdered – and I thought, 'They haven't just killed my
> son, they have killed my family'. We were ruined. There was nothing
> left for us.

On the one hand, such deaths trigger social awkwardness and embarrassment, preventing bereaved family members from seeking outside support
and reducing the likelihood of others offering it. Suicide or deaths that can
be attributed to risky behaviour can produce negative social reactions and
appear virtually impossible to explain to others. The bereaved person can
feel – often with good reason – that they blame them or the deceased
themselves for not avoiding their death. On the other, these same tensions
can also preoccupy parents to the exclusion of their surviving children who
will also be experiencing the same sense of a spoiled life and future.

The impact of undiluted grief

This intimate loneliness has been described in the work of a number of
researchers. Stroebe and Schut (1995) contrast rumination on the loss with
a restoration orientation in which a return to 'normal' living provides time
off from grief. They argue that inability to temper thoughts of the loss with
the concerns of everyday life can lead to psychological problems. Davies
(1988) argues that the strength of this intimate loneliness relates directly to
the amount of 'life-space' the parent or sibling shared with the deceased.
Gilbert (1996) suggests that the stronger and more exclusive the attachment to the lost child, the deeper and longer lasting is the loneliness arising
from its loss. Forte *et al.* (1996) argue that individuals who invest their
entire sense of social connectedness into one relationship, experience far
greater difficulty in adjusting. If the child represented 'everything' to the
parent or sibling, its death marked that 'fateful moment' when all that
mattered in life was lost. The age of the child and its gender are both likely
to offer clues about the amount of life-space shared with each parent. The
birth order of the deceased and his or her closeness to other siblings like-
wise helps identify both the intensity of the relationships and the degree to

which the deceased played a major part in the bereaved person's mental landscape. Contrary to popular assumptions about children's lack of continuing grief, similar effects have been identified among those whose parents had died. Normand *et al.* (1996) described a minority of children who apparently 'did not know how, where, or whom to reach out to' and whose grief, even two years after the death was marked by its 'pervasive sadness'.

Parents who respond to bereavement by cutting outside social networks and withdrawing into themselves appear to run a higher risk of ill-health and mortality. Stroebe *et al.* (1996) concluded that other social relationships, no matter how supportive, are limited in their ability to buffer the stress of grief if the bereaved person feels emotionally isolated. They argue that the risk of mortality is highest among survivors whose remaining social ties are weak and who feel totally alone with their grief. This perception of loneliness may be exaggerated when other family members appear to count the loss as less profound – as can happen with still-birth, the death of a severely disabled child, or when the deceased was part of a particularly special relationship unique to one family member – perhaps the mother's youngest son, a twin, a father's only daughter. Brabant and Forsyth (1997) argue that some of these relationships provide parents with many profound sources of meaning – deep emotional satisfaction, a symbol of personal worth, numerous benefits of friendship, reciprocated love, respect, a sense of purpose and continuity, and a touchstone of normality.

The intensity of grief reactions and subsequent feelings of isolation appear to increase when the bereavement is unexpected or the death is in difficult circumstances (Wortman and Silver 1989; Spratt and Denny 1991; Stroebe 1994). Lack of time to prepare for the impending change, lack of understanding of the circumstances of death, inability to see justice done by their loved one, seeing themselves – or being seen by others – to blame for the death, can all contribute to preoccupation with the loss. Desire to maintain social relationships other than those linked to the deceased decline or disappear entirely. Martinson describes this process as 'building a wall' and offers the following mother's account from her data:

> I often wonder why I'm still here . . . I'm very bitter and angry . . . I feel like everyone's against me, like I'm not an equal anymore. It's easier to stay away. Sooner or later you find the only thing you have to hold on to is yourself.
>
> (Martinson *et al.* 1994: 23)

Parents and siblings are particularly vulnerable to problems in later life where the death was violent or socially problematic (Murphy 1996; Pfeffer *et al.* 1997). Seguin *et al.* (1995) found that early childhood losses resulting from suicide appeared to be a factor in later marital and parenting problems, producing a cycle of increased vulnerability in the whole family. Bradach and Jordan (1995) found that families where a traumatic death had occurred suffered greater and more lasting relationship problems than conventional families. Lang and Gottlieb (1993) found a strong relationship between suddenness of the child's death, the intensity of the mother's grief, loss of intimacy, including sexual relations between the parents and problems of adjustment. Each parent experienced 'guilt movies' – flashback memories relating to the child's life – which they felt unable to share with their partner. Lehman *et al.* (1989) describe distinctive long-term effects of a child's sudden death including 'shadow grief' – a greater sense of vulnerability and acceptance that life could never again return to normal. One mother we spoke to who saw her son's body at the road accident site suggested that in no way could she see her life as anything other than full of pain. Her loss had become the centre of her universe. All other relationships counted as nothing. She said that for her, the greatest challenge was to find ways of *incorporating* this sense of almost total disability into the routines of the normal world that were expected of her. The emotional exhaustion and sheer physical effort this involved is hard for others to appreciate.

Bereavement support services may overlook the fact that a high proportion of parental and sibling bereavement is the result of sudden and 'problematic' deaths. Quoting the National Centre for Health Statistics, Murphy (1996) points out that in 1992 in the USA accidents were the leading cause of death among 12–28-year-olds, and that murders among 14–17-year-olds are expected to rise sharply over the next decade. She also notes that between 1968 and 1985 suicide rates nearly tripled among 10–14-year-olds and doubled among 15–19-year-olds. It is worth looking at some of the particular difficulties presented by these 'problematic' deaths, especially as they can relate both to family patterns of adjustment and to the emotional and physical well-being of the bereaved individual (Bowling 1987).

Undiluted parental grief and surviving children

Parents withdrawal into their own loneliness and preoccupation with the lost relationship has implications for surviving children's grief responses. In our own study, one bereaved mother whose eldest son died at the age of nine from a brain tumour, gave an account of her relationship with her surviving two younger children:

> I feel really sorry for them sometimes. I know I hold back. I know I shouldn't. But I can't help it. I could never go through that again. I can't allow myself to get so close.

These surviving brothers and sisters not only lose a sibling, they also lose the support that the previous family routines might normally have provided. At what, possibly, is an important formative period in their own development, bereaved children and adolescents have to deal with the responses of their parents as well as with their own grief reactions.

Winnicott (1969) argues that 'secure attachment' offers children the basis for developing stable, autonomous identities. He suggests that one of the primary conditions for independence in later life is the capacity of children to be 'alone' in the presence of the mother. This balance between personal initiative and unconditional parental support is difficult enough to achieve under normal circumstances but is likely to be even harder following a sibling's death (Storr 1997). The death of a close sibling can upset the security the child has previously experienced, and postpone the sense of a 'secure attachment'. Erratic parental contact during the dying and after the death – quite possibly a mixture of neglect and overprotection, coupled with an awareness of increased marital tension – can create problems in later adolescence and adulthood. Study after study record siblings' resentment when they are excluded from information about what is going on, the guilt they carry and the sense of responsibility they feel for adding to their parents' distress (Balk 1990; Hogan and DeSantis 1996).

Bradach and Jordan (1995) found that families in which a traumatic death had occurred suffered greater relationship problems. Students from these families were less independent, appeared to have more difficulty in adjusting to college life, were more likely to experience psychological distress, and felt a greater 'gravitational pull' from their homes. Hogan and DeSantis (1994) suggested that certain types of families produced 'vulnerable' survivors. Families that produced resilient survivors were open to differences in each other's grief reactions, encouraging each member to contribute to their collective understanding of how the family as a whole had been affected. These processes were seen as mutually supportive. Vulnerable siblings, on the other hand, had been discouraged from sharing their grief. Conspiracies of silence, mutual resentments, guilt, overprotection or exclusion from information characterized relationships in these families. They suffered a higher risk of illness, self-destructive behaviour and feelings of isolation and helplessness.

Surviving children may choose to withdraw as a response that avoids contributing further to parents' distress. A number of writers identify 'premature maturity' among many bereaved siblings, in which their own grief reactions are subordinated to increased responsibility for emotional care of the parent and practical help in the household (Hindmarch 1995; Stahlman 1996). Time and again during our interviews, parents either expressed regret at the ways they had neglected their surviving children, or frustration at the problems they were continuing to cause. This additional pain is often seen only from the point of view of the parents, and Rubin (1996) describes the permanent 'wound' to a family caused by the mixture of grief and resentment felt by the surviving child following the death of a 'perfect' elder brother. In our own study, one couple said of their surviving son, following his brother's death in a road accident:

he wouldn't come home for a month. He went and lived at my mum's, he didn't want to come home. He was 14 then – going on ten! He still hasn't grown up. But he has altered, he just doesn't want to be in the house with us at all . . . I said to him, 'Why are you always going out?', and he said, 'It's horrible here, you are always crying'.

If parents' grief responses encourage surviving children to cope through withdrawing and being alone with their grief, relationship problems may follow in later life. Particularly traumatic deaths, such as homicide and murder, can exaggerate family communication problems in which guilt, stigma and blame appear to make surviving siblings more vulnerable themselves to self-harm, to suicide attempts and to longer term feelings of shame and social rejection (Parkes 1993a; Silverman et al. 1994/5; Seguin et al. 1995; Pfeffer 1997). DeMaso et al. (1997) offer a particularly helpful set of suggestions to parents who are unsure about how they should support their surviving children.

The culture of everyday life – moving on, keeping busy

This second category typifies the very opposite style of adjustment in which keeping busy, clinging to normal routines and stressing non-bereaved aspects of identity provide some sense of continuity with life before the death. Accepting core values of mainstream society that work still has to be done and 'life must go on' allows everyday relationships to be used to splint the damaged parental or sibling identity. Bonanno et al. (1995) question the assumption that avoidance of grief necessarily leads to longer term psychological problems. Stroebe and Schut (1995) suggest that avoidance is a 'natural' defence mechanism, offering short-term relief. They also point to the value of distraction through maintaining links with networks outside the family. Barbarin and Chesler (1986) found that the ability to put thoughts of the death out of their mind allowed some parents to return to 'apparent' normality. This strategy was used as for controlling debilitating anxiety and despair.

While such distractions may provide particular family members with time out from grieving, others may be unable to accept this pattern as legitimate. Misreading this response as not caring may cause other family members, deep in their own grief, to feel even more isolated.

The benefits of taking 'time off' from grieving

Stroebe and Schut's 'dual process model' (1995) argues that both orientations to grief – facing the loss *and* temporarily avoiding it through being busy with other activities – may be crucial to successful adjustment. They characterize the mind set that focuses on distressing thoughts and emotions as a 'loss orientation', and the mind set that avoids painful introspection as a 'restoration orientation'. In the latter, damaged identity is supported by reinvesting in connections with everyday life. In certain cases, this reinvestment might address the loss directly by involvement in charity raising or pressure-group work linked to the cause of the death.

Stoebe and Schut's argument rests partly on observations that widows often have to learn new skills without their husbands around. At times, their minds were occupied with practical problem solving, presenting them with new views of their own competence. For many bereaved people, subsequent events often involve practical tasks that have to be actively attended to so that, however briefly, their thoughts focus on the present and the future, instead of reflecting on the pain of the recent past. These and other unrelated distractions – such as returning to work – present opportunities for 'time out' from grieving.

At the same time, they argue, working through thoughts and feelings about the death is also necessary if the bereaved person is to adjust their internal landscape. The key, Stroebe and Schut argue, is that normal or healthy grieving involves oscillation between the two orientations, with good days and bad days, moments of hope for the future and times when nothing seems worth carrying on for. Although one orientation may feature more strongly than the other, it is likely that swings between them will increase as time moves on. Their suggestion that women may need support in undertaking practical tasks, while men need more help in getting in touch with their emotions reflects feminist analyses of the construction of masculine identities.

Routines of 'everyday life' away from the family appear to provide individual members with chances to be distracted from memories of the death, and for discovering themselves in situations where they experience validation from other people. This re-routeing of personal connections around (rather than through) the death provides a continuing source of stability for the bereaved person's damaged identity.

Diluting connections with the dead

Rather than seeing this attitude as 'avoidance' of the pain of grief, it may be more useful to recognize it as an intermittent lonesomeness recurring over many years in the midst of busy lives and apparently normal relationships. Rosenblatt (1996) calls this 'recurrent grief'. Forte et al. (1996) argue that bereaved people who enjoy intimacy across a wide set of social relationships are more likely to show resilience in the face of bereavement than those who experience intimacy in only a few or individual relationships. Personal identity in this case does not rest exclusively on the role of parent. Other valued relationships help maintain a sense of self and purpose (Bowlby

1979). Braun and Berg (1994) concluded that parents who still felt there were other things to live for – especially surviving children – and who had experienced bereavement or other traumas in the past, were more able to maintain everyday relationships than parents who had never before faced the arbitrariness of life. Powell (1995) noted that, in spite of problems of over-protection with a subsequent child, a sense of family life and restored faith and purpose accompanied the birth of another baby after the devastation of bereavement following Sudden Infant Death Syndrome. Powell noted an oscillation, between normal joy in the demands of a new baby and waves of guilt and continuing anxiety about the lost one, and how these feelings compete in the thoughts of the mother, demonstrating that restoration and loss orientations may well persist at the same time in the most demanding of circumstances.

Playing the role of normal, managing grief as a backstage emotion

If the child was one among a number of significant social connections through which the parent or sibling received affection and a sense of purpose, then many elements of the bereaved person's identity may well be able to survive the loss, helping to 'shore up' the damaged aspect of their identity and offering them alternative sources of self-esteem and social purpose (Stroebe and Schut 1995; Forte *et al.* 1996; Riches and Dawson 1997). By not talking about their loss, or by limiting conversation about it to 'backstage settings' – family or very close friends – a sibling or parent can retain a number of other 'normal' social connections outside the family. Grief over the lost relationship can be therefore managed in public, minimizing the risk of losing control at socially embarrassing times and allowing an apparent return to 'normal living'.

However, even among apparently busy people where isolation from normal everyday living is not a feature of their bereavement, periodic intrusive feelings of intense loneliness still have to be managed (see Chapter 1). Playing out the role of 'normal' is likely to be very common given the overwhelming evidence of everyday social pressures to get through grief as quickly as possible. One mother, bereaved two years previous to our interview, described 'putting on her face' for the day before she went to work: 'I've just got about eight hours – or more accurately, seven hours fifty-nine minutes. Then it just goes. I'm terrified I'll meet someone one day and collapse in a fit of tears.'

This sense of being utterly alone, even within the context of a loving family, and arising because of the uniqueness of their lost relationship, can for many parents only be dealt with – if at all – in a very safe and authentic relationship. Because the child was irreplaceable, and many of the parents we interviewed commented on the 'special' significance that the relationship held just for them, sharing their grief even with marital partners may seem impossible. They are aware that to communicate this exclusivity could easily increase the hurt and resentment felt by other family members. Even when not spoken, this reaction may be resentfully identified but rarely spoken about by surviving children. For example, one mother we interviewed was in full-time employment, had a good marriage, and kept in touch with her other adult children. She praised the support given by her general practitioner and the other parents of children on the same ward as her son. Nevertheless, she still gave a clear account of the piercing intermittent isolation she felt, even with a loved and loving husband:

> When it comes to talking about memories of our son . . . that's where I stop. I won't talk about Tom. I'll say a sentence . . . And when I get really upset he'll (my husband) say, 'let me put my arms round you'. And I can't because I'm looking at a mirror image of me and the pain on his face is just so awful . . . and also I know I'm asking him to put things right and he can't . . . and it's not fair to ask him.

This example illustrates that even where reactions are tempered by a network of supportive relationships, grief is still 'a very individual journey' and creates a barrier to sharing warmer memories of the life (Martinson 1991). Desire to protect other family members, exhaustion from the sheer effort of keeping up a 'face' to present to the outside world, and reluctance to conjure up painful personal memories, may therefore combine to prevent family members from sharing the specialness of their own loss. In time, they may overcome this reluctance to share their feelings about the death and recollect happier memories. The problem in this case is that neither she, nor her husband, appeared on the surface to need support. Yet in certain ways and at regular intervals, memory of their loss isolates each from the other and from those close relationships they maintain at work and in the wider family.

Case example 4.2 illustrates how the ability to play the role of 'resolved griever' may be linked to the factors we identified earlier: the social connectedness of the parents, the strength of other role demands on their time and attention, the manner of the death and opportunities available to make sense of it.

Case example 4.2

Whereas after Tom's death, Brenda still had two surviving daughters, Peter was David's only child. Both boys died in their 20s. Whereas Brenda's son had left home two years previously to study at university, David's son had lived at home before he died. David acted as coach for Peter's competition cycling career. Where Brenda was able to nurse Tom through the last two weeks of his brain tumour, and she was with him when he died, Peter was killed unexpectedly in a road traffic accident. Where Brenda had discussed Tom's wishes with him and had helped him achieve many of his ambitions before he died, David was still in a legal fight with the lorry driver to prove that Peter, as a young motorcyclist, was not to blame for the collision that killed him. Where Brenda held onto Tom's body until they were ready to let him to go, David was discouraged by the police from seeing Peter's body, suggesting that they were better remembering him as he was before the accident (the implication being that he suffered terrible disfigurement in the accident). Whereas Brenda had to return to a full-time, demanding professional career, David, already off work with a chronic illness before Peter's death, had given up the idea of ever returning. Both he and his wife claimed that life was no longer worth living.

Working around the pain – masculinity and disconnecting from grief

The ability to maintain everyday connections after bereavement appears to be partly linked to gender, and Stroebe (1998) suggested that men may have problems in connecting with those parts of their identity that are damaged by the lost relationship.

Cook (1988) identified some of the strategies bereaved fathers use to maintain control over their grief. She suggests many men develop the skill of compartmentalizing their thoughts, shutting down memories that bring distressing emotions in their wake, filling their minds with other things – maybe projects like fund-raising or litigation against those perceived as being to blame for the death. They also do other things that actively distance themselves from the home and from reminders of their loss – working harder, drinking more, even having affairs. Cook also found that these bereaved fathers used rationalization to 'place' the death in a broader framework.

Like Das (1993) – working on the Bhophal disaster – Cook found that men rationalized personal loss into more general evidence of broad political, religious or philosophical explanations of life and fate whereas the mothers tended to see their sons' deaths as evidence of the basic pointlessness and chaos of the world. Chapter 2 considers in more detail why the experience of mothering might produce a different level of interpersonal sensitivities than fathering.

Finally, she found evidence of men suffering in similar ways to women, but letting go only in highly controlled ways in the privacy of their car, or inside their garage or garden shed where wives and others could not see the extent of their distress. Cordell and Thomas (1990) and Schwab (1996) found bereaved fathers in their samples who resented feeling they had to be strong for their wives, but who, nevertheless, uncomplainingly did their best to keep their feelings to themselves, concentrating on the more visible distress felt by their wives. This playing out of the role of strong dependable male suggested that not only were they offered little support by others, they also felt strong cultural obligations to see that the family did not fall apart following the child's death.

Other writers, Hart (1996), Chodorow (1978) and Rubin (1983) for example, see this emotional control as a skill men learn as boys when struggling to detach themselves from their mother's emotional control. They argue that this 'learned disconnectedness' – the shutting down of emotional sensitivity – is the cost many men pay for rejecting those traits and behaviours that might identify them with their mothers and female identity. Seidler (1991) argues that the ability to be hurt but to hide it, to be heroic and dispensable, to retain control, to be strong for others, to be successful in competition and to see comradeship as preferable to intimacy, are classic masculine traits – yet are increasingly expected of successful career women. Cook, like Das, sees men's 'suffering' as being characterized by stoicism and a view that 'life must go on'. Campbell and Silverman (1996) found many men used replacement as a strategy for dealing with the death of their wives. Over half the widowers in the USA remarry within 18 months – regardless of the length of time of their marriage.

Finding a way back – into the culture of bereavement

The third category represents parents and siblings who develop new relationships with others who have been through similar bereavements and are well placed to understand their feelings. Having found no answer to their knock, their understanding of the empty room and the child's life that occupied it is helped by others exploring it with them. Contact with The Compassionate Friends or with others who willingly share their need to grieve the dead child or sibling may have come initially because of the inadequacy of mainstream sentiments for making sense of the loss or providing evidence that the depth of their grief is appreciated. These new connections allow a special kind of 'visiting' in the old country neighbour sense. Time to pause, being understood and sharing the same landscape are core characteristics of many rapidly disappearing traditional cultures. Modern values and the demands of the clock provide few opportunities to reflect on what bereaved people have lost or time to build a new identity. Communities of bereaved parents and siblings promote values and beliefs about mortality and the nature of the dead that are very much in opposition to those of mainstream society. These communities offer for many a sanctuary where they can talk proudly of their dead children, cry about their deaths, share their dreams and nightmares and swap endless reminiscences without the fear of being thought morbid or crazy. Research into self-help groups has indicated the value of communities of bereaved parents in helping transform the relationship with the deceased so that it can continue in the minds of bereaved parents (Klass 1996b) (see, also, Chapter 1).

Writing the last chapter – connecting with those that knew the deceased

This category also includes parents and siblings who are able to utilize existing relationships to share memories of the deceased. Membership of any community that knew and cared for the dead child, or who are genuinely interested in getting to know them, increase bereaved person's opportunities for accepting that the death is part of a broader pattern and moving further back into memories that become a source of warmth and pleasure (Marwit and Klass 1995). Tony Walter's biographical model of grief (1996) stresses the intellectual (as opposed to the emotional) processes that might also be part of Stroebe and Schut's loss orientation. His argument emphasizes the importance of sharing memories of the deceased with others who knew them in order to produce a completed picture of the deceased – a 'comfortable memory' – with which the bereaved person can live.

Here, rather than sharing emotional pain, grieving is seen as a cognitive activity in which bereaved people who knew the deceased jointly review the life that was lived and help each of them 'write the last chapter'. Such reminiscences, as well as working through events leading up to the death and the funeral, involve earlier shared family events and the discovery of aspects of the child that was unknown to parents, but quite possibly known to siblings and to school friends or teachers. The creation of these family stories about the deceased are part of that 'privilege' (as one bereaved mother noted) of learning through others what a special person your child was. Radley (1990) has drawn attention to the value of physical objects such as photographs and artefacts in encouraging conversations about the past, and we have discovered in our own research that children's school work, old toys, family portraits and holiday snaps are not only a crucial link with dead children but also a source of continuing conversational remembering among family members and friends (Riches and Dawson 1998a).

However, obstacles to this shared reminiscing may be quite substantial. Such conversations may be so distressing to other family members that they never get spoken. The nature of the death may be so painful or socially disturbing (suicide, murder) that all intellectual efforts are exhausted by trying to explain the event of the death itself, causing a block to discovering warmer memories of the life that was lived up to that point. The extent to which family members, friends and acquaintances are available and willing to help write the last chapter is dependent very much on the patterns of family relationships, wider social networks and cultural assumptions already in place before the child died.

Reconnecting with the dead – finding a place for the deceased

Dennis Klass's contribution (1996b), though similar to Walter's in its stress on continuing relationships with the deceased, differs in two important ways. First, it focuses on the role played by relationships with people who did *not* know the dead child, but who have themselves experienced a similar loss. Second, it more literally explores the place where the deceased child might be envisioned *now*. Where Walter sees adjustment as creating an ongoing relationship with a shared memory, Klass sees adjustment as successfully transforming the lost physical relationship into an abstract internal one.

At one level, this might translate as a spiritual search – either through clairvoyants, more conventional religious movements or personal faith – for a place (heaven, the other side, watching over me) in which the child can be pictured. It may be created around more concrete objects or places that are symbolically associated with the child – the cemetery, their room, photographs or toys, places they loved to walk or play. At another level, the presence of the child can be shared in communities of bereaved parents such as exist within The Compassionate Friends. In contrast to the culture of mainstream society, conversations about deceased children in which details of their looks, personality, school accomplishments, favourite foods, and endearing ways are seen as normal and encouraged. Photographs are exchanged, diaries, stories and poems are passed round, and the deceased children play a central part in collective discussions about how parents can survive such loss. Also, unlike Walter, Klass admits the importance of emotional pain and the contribution that more 'experienced' bereaved parents can make in helping the recently bereaved identify milestones they will have to pass in working through their suffering.

Klass described how many deceased children come to exist as a 'presence' in the minds, lives and conversations of their parents. Hogan and DeSantis similarly discovered large numbers of brothers and sisters who strongly believed that one day they would meet their deceased sibling again. Both researchers found evidence of inner conversations with the dead child – siblings in particular – taking time to bring them up to date with recent developments in the family and in their own lives. The contrast between this emphasis on continuing bonds and Bowlby's (1980) emphasis on detachment is quite marked. On the one hand, grief work is seen to be a precursor to facing the reality of the death prior to letting go and moving on. On the other, it is seen as the necessary translation of the child's physical presence into an abstract one in which the relationship, rather than being given up, is transformed into something that can be held onto.

Opportunities to share thoughts and feelings about the death, memories of the life, and details of the child's idiosyncrasies – with people who knew them and with people who are interested in coming to know them – are crucial to both Walter's and Klass's views of grief and adjustment to loss. Hence, friends and other bereaved parents and siblings can play an important role in helping to create a place for the deceased within the psychic and social lives of surviving family members.

Innovators – finding a personal way back and a new way forward

This last category includes parents and siblings whose suffering has forced them to 'stock-take' many aspects of their lives. Neither mainstream culture nor the cultures of other bereaved parents offer acceptable meanings for the death, and neither set of social relationships provide comfort for the damaged identity. Personal survival and a refusal to give in to despair result in a close examination both of personal grief and of surviving intimate relationships – beginning a journey of individual growth and change (Rando 1991). Their exploration of the empty room has led them on a solitary journey, outside of the house. Looking back they see themselves, their family and the life they led in a new light. For some, it leads to eventual return and renegotiated, often closer, ties with family members. For others it leads to a new life, new priorities and a greater sense of personal independence. Here, although links with the past are remembered, many of these prior social connections are re-evaluated. Adjustment to loss involves the bereaved person in a major identity transformation. They have not merely struggled to adjust. Their suffering and highly personal exploration of the significance of the death acts as a catalyst for a fundamental review of life's meaning and their role and purpose within it:

> Changing oneself often means rising above oneself, growing beyond oneself. The death of a child, especially an only child, presents the kind of suffering and challenge to self that creates an existential crisis – a search for the meaning of human existence. Attig (1996) calls this a need to relearn the world.
>
> (Talbot 1997: 45)

Connecting with the loss – working through the pain

The humanistic approach to personal development emphasizes resilience and the individual's capacity to learn from distress. Maturity and intimacy are gained on the road to 'self-actualization' and gained through the capacity to connect with one's own emotions. Coming to face the inevitability of loss and discovering that a legacy is left in the identity of the bereaved person offers an opportunity for personal growth and a clearer appreciation of surviving relationships.

The bereaved person's sense of emptiness and their knowledge that no answer will come from knocking at the door produce in them a sense of solitude rather than isolation. Both isolation and solitude have in common a sense of distance from other relationships that might provide meaning or offer distraction. With bereaved parents or siblings who experience a developed sense of solitude however, rather than remaining stuck waiting for the answer that will never come, they face the pain of entering the empty room and allow themselves to remember when it was occupied. Intense emotional release may be achieved through the ability to visualize and replay memories of the deceased. If other family members are able to enter this room then these memories can be compared and shared.

Memories of the lives the deceased child touched and influenced may be rehearsed and re-evaluated, especially those with other family members. In cases where the marital partner's relationship with the deceased child was weak or characterized by conflict, such re-evaluation may lead to weakening or breaking of the marital bond. In this way the bereaved person's search for a meaning goes well beyond the empty room and beyond the house and the family. A number of parents we talked to browsed through a number of possible sources for an answer – self-help groups, clairvoyants, religious and spiritual beliefs. This activity, largely private and characterized by the gaining of information and occasional support from particularly significant individuals – a hospital chaplain, or a social worker at the children's hospital who briefly became a 'true friend' for example – was an intellectual search driven either by dissatisfaction with others' ways of coping or by a reluctance to share with them their own unique relationship with the deceased child.

Drawing on the work of Joanna Macy who runs workshops on despair and empowerment, New (1996) suggests that:

> despair 'lurks subliminally beneath the tenor of 'life as usual' (CF health-as-normal-functioning). Yet this emotion is culturally taboo and 'the refusal to feel takes a heavy toll' on our capacity for joy, our perception and our ability to think, for we process out anxiety provoking data, which is feedback we urgently need in order to take intelligent, effective action . . . The distance between our inklings of apocalypse and the tenor of business-as-usual is so great that . . . we tend to imagine that it is we, not society, who is insane.
>
> (New 1996: 156)

Hence solitude may be a healthy response to those outsiders and family members who unwittingly exert pressure to get over grief as quickly as possible. Lee (1994) gives an example of one employer who expected a bereaved father to be operating as 'normal' within ten days of his child's death. One of the fathers we interviewed, whose daughter had been murdered, was expected to take his annual leave during the trial. He also noted that they could no longer switch on the television, as virtually every drama or film involved a murder. These pressures create in some parents what Lee describes as a 'healthy sense of outrage'. Their resistance to the implication that their child did not matter creates passions of anger that 'encircle them as a kind of camouflage' and cut off their desire to be part of 'normal' society. They need to know that their child's life has made a difference, and a successful search for meaning may result in previously taken-for-granted family or work identities being modified or entirely rejected.

Hence, other family members may come to be perceived as strangers who have, as yet, failed to grasp the profound implications of the death for 'business-as-usual'. One bereaved mother described how she felt isolated from her husband, and no longer able to perceive herself as having a sexual or intimate relationship with him:

> what you want from your partner is to be cherished and loved . . . and probably courted. I can remember saying to my husband, 'I want to be courted' . . . and he couldn't do that. He hadn't the reserves to do that.

Storr (1997) criticizes the belief that mental health and personal identity are dependent on the achievement of intimate social relationships. He argues that a number of people value solitude, using it as a basis for reflection, introspection and interaction with ideas. C.S. Lewis is an example of someone who led a very private life, was socially awkward, yet was capable of profound emotion, high levels of creativity and enormous insight. For some people we interviewed bereavement appeared to produce a kind of enforced, self-contained solitude rather than feelings of isolation. The meaning of the death is achieved through discovering that their relationship with the deceased has left a legacy within their own identity. Instead of the empty hole, they come to see the world at least partly through the dead child's eyes. The deceased's character, their aspirations, ways of seeing the world and the life they lived – no matter how brief and no matter how difficult its end – come to be seen, in time, to have left a lasting impression on the bereaved person. In the word's of Kaplan's (1995) moving book 'no voice is ever wholly lost'.

Growth through suffering

Tedeschi and Calhoun (1995) describe the self-affirmation that some people experience as a positive long-term consequence of their suffering trauma and bereavement. Looking back over the months and years of coping with the worst event they could have possibly imagined, they come to recognize strengths they did not know they possessed and to appreciate aspects of the world they had never previously noticed.

These bereaved people feel more emotionally mature, less egocentric, more self assured, more discriminating in who they allow to influence them, have a greater sense of compassion and wonderment at the fragile but precious nature of life. Their relationship with others is fundamentally changed. A parent's or sibling's philosophy of life may be rethought giving him or her:

> a clear sense that his life path had shifted dramatically. The crossroads could have led him to despair . . . yet he struck out on the opposite

path . . . and now understands his life and lives it in a more meaningful way.

(Tedeschi and Calhoun 1995: 39)

Among the studies of parental and sibling bereavement can be found a number that identify these positive outcomes (Hogan and DeSantis 1994; Lee 1994; Stahlman 1996):

Just as being in love can make the world look different through heightening our awareness, so the state of being in grief can make things look different too. With grief though, it is more the ability to see 'into' or 'behind' things.

(Lee 1994: 47)

This last orientation towards grief is a mixture between solitude and a willingness to rethink the nature of the world. A principle characteristic of this way of dealing with grief is its use as a source of creativity (Gordon 1978). Whether the bereaved person set about a search for meaning through studying psychology and the theories of death and bereavement, whether they explore various religious beliefs or simply recognize contributions they can make to supporting other bereaved parents through writing or talking about their own experiences, significant aspects of their subsequent lives appear to become an active 'memorial' to their dead children in a world whose nature is forever changed. Rather than accepting the meaning offered by others, or collapsing into a position in which no meaning can be found at all, these parents and siblings use both the death and the life of the deceased as a central narrative, giving meaning to their own subsequent choices and decisions.

In our research we have encountered many people whose successful 'career changes' relate directly to their struggle to come to terms with their personal loss. Shelley Wagner, whose poems celebrating her son's life and exploring every detail of his death through drowning, has become a nationally acclaimed writer in the US and Colin Parry, whose contributions to our understanding of the problems in Northern Ireland, has become a well-known broadcaster in the UK. Numerous other examples exist of bereaved parents and bothers and sisters who have translated their lost relationship into a creative and valuable outlet.

It is more than possible that these changes are not seen by bereaved people themselves in such a positive light and, whether or not our analysis is of any use to therapists or counsellors, it could easily be perceived as insensitive by bereaved parents and siblings. In response to a draft of this chapter, one bereaved mother whose son took his own life said,

I know they say that something positive can come out of struggling through these experiences, but I can't see it. If I live to be a hundred, I know that not one good thing can ever possibly come out of his death.

Implications for bereavement support

This chapter reflects a shift in viewpoint from a modern to a post-modern conception of death and bereavement. This shift has substantial implications for counsellors, therapists and bereavement support workers (Stroebe *et al.* 1992). In place of a perspective based solely on rational assumptions that bereaved people need to achieve autonomy and independence from the deceased through accepting the reality of their loss, counsellors may have to recognize that 'successful grief resolution' takes many forms.

Bereaved people in most western societies have access to a range of explanatory perspectives, including the 'romantic' view in which continuing rather than severed emotional ties help transform their relationship with the dead and allow some sort of continuing bond. In many cases, therefore, counsellors may need to find ways to help the bereaved person 'hold on to' their loved ones, as well as in others helping them to say goodbye and accept that in time they may leave their loved ones behind (Walter 1996).

An important implication of this insight is that *within the same family* different members may legitimately seek to deal with their grief in radically different ways. Indeed our previous argument suggests it is almost inevitable that gender differences will produce at least some tension between husbands' and wives' strategies for dealing with grief, and that generational differences will similarly result in differences between children and their parents.

Bereavement support of a single family, therefore, may have to work with a range of styles of grieving that might at times appear contradictory and that might have directly negative effects on the family's well-being as a whole. In order to take these differences into account, bereavement support might involve some or all of the following activities:

1 helping find others who can share stories of the deceased in order to create a memory that can be lived with comfortably (Walter);
2 helping find others for whom the experience of losing a child or brother or sister is familiar and who are themselves happy to engage in conversations about the deceased on a regular basis (Klass);
3 helping the bereaved person find ways of facing and dealing with the emotional consequences of losing a child or sibling (Cook, Stroebe);
4 helping the bereaved person find ways of re-engaging in meaningful relationships that help them take time off from grieving (Stroebe, Forte *et al.*);
5 helping the bereaved person find information or belief systems that offer a way of making sense of the cause of the death and of coming to terms with what it means for their own beliefs;
6 helping bereaved family members understand that differences in their grieving does not mean some cared more than others for the deceased;
7 helping family members recognize that their own ways of grieving may be blocking the chances of others sharing their feelings within the family;

8 offering support for individual members who are never likely to overcome years of family miscommunication.

Summary

- Traditional societies tended to have clear universally shared beliefs about
  death and appropriate social roles for the deceased and for bereaved
  family members. In late modern societies, reluctance to acknowledge personal mortality, plural often contradictory beliefs, unclear and changing
  roles and greater individual autonomy present bereaved people with a
  range of choices about how to make sense of grief and how to adjust
  appropriately to a lost relationship.
- The belief systems of modern societies may be particularly inadequate for
  making sense of the death of a child or for providing networks that
  support bereaved parents and brothers and sisters.
- Individual choice of strategy for managing bereavement may depend on a
  combination of factors: the significance of the lost role for the bereaved
  person's personal identity; the uniqueness of their relationship within the
  family system; the range of other valued relatively undamaged roles still
  available to the bereaved person; the family's ability as a whole to allow
  different interpretations of the loss to be shared; the cultural explanations available for explaining the death and the strength of social expectations about each member's bereavement behaviour.
- Variations in response to these factors may be summarized into four
  typical strategies: loss of meaning, loss of support and exclusion from
  normal living; retaining the meanings of everyday life and finding support in returning to normal as much as possible; rejecting 'the normal'
  and finding new meanings and new support from others who share the
  same experience; rejecting 'the normal' and searching alone for meanings
  to explain both the death and the different world it has produced.
- Loss of meaning and exclusion from others is likely to leave the bereaved
  person stuck with thoughts of the death and feelings associated only
  with the emptiness of loss. Intense or ambivalent relationships with the
  deceased, relationships where few others shared so much of the deceased's
  life-space as the bereaved person, no prior awareness of the fragility of
  human life and unexpected or difficult deaths all contribute to problems
  of meaning and preoccupation with the empty space left by the deceased.
- Such responses in one individual can lead to other family members pay-
  ing more attention to the difficulties posed by this response than to their
  own feelings of loss.
- Normal everyday living can offer opportunities for distraction and reaffirmation of self-identity outside of lost family role. Grief may be handled
  within this by privatizing distress and 'playing out' familiar non-bereaved

roles. Some individuals may be more skilled in playing out these roles. Some may be exposed to greater pressure than others to play them.

- Bereavement may provide an opportunity for seeing self and the world from a radically different perspective. New meanings about life and the value of existing relationships may be created having major implications for family and career.
- Searching for meaning may involve new relationships with others who knew the deceased (family and friends) or with similarly bereaved parents' or siblings' groups who willingly share memories of the deceased child. Cultures of bereaved parents and siblings place mortality at the centre of their belief systems and have an uneasy relationship with the culture of everyday normality.
- Each category is a cluster of tendencies not a prescribed stage or path. For grief assessment, the framework as a whole can be used to check out the absence of often overlooked social and cultural supports. 'Progress' in adjusting to grief may involve shifting from one category to another, in oscillating between two or more, or in remaining relatively permanently within one for the rest of the bereaved person's life.
- Conventional grief theory could be interpreted (see Figure 4.1) as helping the bereaved person shift from top left (lost meaning and social exclusion) to top right (the culture of normality). At the very least, this framework draws attention to the importance both of cultures of bereavement (bottom right) and the ways that solitude and reconstruction of self and world view (bottom left) can lead both to personal adjustment, positive outcomes, but also to more uncertain family relationships and to very different engagements with the culture of normality.

Difficult deaths and problems of adjustment

Introduction

In the previous chapter we argued that where the death is sudden or difficult, parents and siblings are particularly vulnerable to problems in later
life (Murphy 1996; Pfeffer *et al.* 1997). Hazzard *et al.* (1992) suggest that
parents of children who die suddenly are more vulnerable to despair and
score more highly on measures of anger, guilt and loss of self-identity. In
this chapter, we explore why social stigma resulting from its circumstances,
the arbitrariness or injustice of its cause and the bereaved person's inability
to prepare for the death, may each contribute to problems of adjustment.

No way forward, no way back

In cases where the nature of the death was sudden, shocking, violent, lacking
in sense, or drawn out and difficult, bereaved parents and siblings may have
great difficulty both in reaching back beyond this awful event to earlier
memories of their shared lives with the deceased child, and in moving forward through adjusting their lives to accommodate the fact of the death. It
seems totally senseless and inexplicable. Nothing can give it any meaning.
No warm or peaceful memories can rise to the surface of such troubled
thoughts and fierce emotions. Barely controllable anger, frustrated disbelief,
intense and recurrent guilt, a craving for revenge, for justice, for time to be
put back so that things can be put right mingle with self-blame in isolating
individual family members from each other and from outside support.

Klass (1996b) and Walter's (1996) 'new' directions in grief and Stroebe
and Schut's 'dual process' model (1995) each offer clues as to why bereaved

family members might become preoccupied with the manner of the death, experiencing difficulties in sharing memories that allow them to develop a more comfortable relationship with their deceased brother or sister. For many survivors, 'difficult' and sudden deaths produce major obstacles to finding support and initiating conversations about the deceased child. On the one hand, unexpected deaths – especially violent ones – present a deep psychic challenge to the bereaved person's assumptive world (Parkes 1993b). For the death to have any meaning at all, quite fundamental beliefs about the nature of the world, about the bereaved person's place within it and about the point and predictability of all existing relationships, have to be turned upside down. To begin to even apprehend such a death – to acknowledge that it actually has occurred and is not simply an awful waking nightmare – may require a lengthy rethinking of ingrained assumptions about personal identity that the bereaved person has neither the intellectual nor emotional reserves to accomplish (Tedeschi and Calhoun 1995). Moriarty *et al.* (1996) discovered very high levels of hostility in both parents following the sudden deaths of their children. By converting disbelief and lack of explanation into anger, couples may increase their own relationship problems through using each other as targets for their frustration:

> I couldn't stand him near me. I said to him, 'Why wasn't it you?' I have said the most horrible things to my husband . . . because he was the only one I could take my anger out on, he was the only one I could go to . . .
>
> (Riches and Dawson 1998b: 152)

At the same time, such a death may also trigger major social discomfort, preventing bereaved family members from seeking outside support and reducing the likelihood of others offering it. These same tensions can preoccupy parents to the exclusion of their surviving children who may also be experiencing the same sense of disorientation. Their effects may also discourage surviving children from attempting to explore their feelings about the death and its consequences with parents or friends.

Notoriety and shame

We have argued elsewhere (Riches and Dawson 1998b) that some people's deaths – like their lives – can become famous or notorious. Where police, courts and news media are involved, or where the cause of death, even if unpublicized, remains a source of embarrassment or guilt, then fonder memories that might help the growth of a more comfortable relationship with the deceased become very difficult to recall, and any sense of a positive future becomes impossible to contemplate. No explanation can ever make sense of the death. No world can ever be achieved that matches the turmoil that has become the bereaved person's way of life. Their most private relationships and personal emotions appear to be public property, always available for gossip or airing, throughout the first year or even longer, and then on each anniversary of the death or whenever a death in similar circumstances is reported.

In Chapter 1 we noted the way in which stigma can spoil an individual's self-identity, and how grief can be understood as the bereaved person's attempt to find ways of repairing or rebuilding their self-identity. In the same way, the identity of the deceased can be so badly 'stigmatized' by the manner of their death that the bereaved person's future life can appear forever 'blighted' by the sensationalism that surrounds it, and by its resurrection every anniversary and on every occasion a similar event occurs (Arlidge 1997; Walter *et al.* 1995).

Clive Seale (1995b) has described how a 'heroic' death through terminal illness can help bereaved people make sense of and come to terms with their loss. Similarly, Rubin (1996) demonstrates how parents can attach patriotic meaning to the loss of sons who died fighting for their country. Conversely, where the death is notorious or senseless, the reverse effect appears to operate. Suicide or those deaths that can be attributed to risky behaviour can produce negative social reactions. The bereaved person can feel – often with good reason – that others blame them or the deceased themselves for not preventing their death and they are prevented from exploring more helpful meanings through the sense of 'shame' that is attached to the death (Seguin *et al.* 1995).

Normally temporary feelings of anger, guilt, remorse and unreality may be amplified and drawn out in such cases. To the isolating effects of 'normal' grief can be added a sense of betrayal, a need to attach blame, an obsessive desire for revenge and a need for an explanation. Such bereaved family members can lose their connectedness not only with the ongoing routines of everyday life but also with their memories of the relationships that existed before the death – both living and now deceased.

Murder and manslaughter

Grief resolution is particularly difficult for the parents and siblings of murder victims. Parents are likely to become preoccupied with the need to make sense of their loss in terms of achieving 'justice' for their murdered son or daughter. Police procedures, the operation of the courts, coroner's office and the mass media can all substantially disrupt opportunities for sharing the news of the death, for taking some sort of control over the disposal of the body and for beginning to share each other's feelings of how the loss is affecting them (Riches and Dawson 1998b). Perception of the Criminal Justice System's inefficiency or apparent consideration of the accused over the victim can further add to intense feelings of rage and a need for revenge (DeVries *et al.* 1994). Conrad (1998) describes how intense but understandable emotional reactions following a predicted death contrast with the extreme and chaotic trauma resulting from a sudden, particularly difficult and essentially senseless cause of death.

It seems likely in such cases that parents will only begin to cope 'well' with their grief after some considerable time has passed, certainly measured in years rather than months. Indeed, it may be many months before those responsible for the death have been caught and arrested, and a number of cases result in re-trials, acquittal or failure to prosecute through lack of evidence. In the meantime, a search for information about the death, post-mortems, controlled access to the body and legally required interrogation of all close relatives postpone opportunities to say goodbye to the deceased, to begin to face life without them, and to start to rebuild dislocated family relationships. Throughout this lengthy period in which any 'writing of the last chapter' is postponed, feelings of outrage, recurrent intrusive visualizations of their child's last moments alive and preoccupation with seeing justice done create turmoil both in the bereaved's inner landscapes, and in their relationships with other family members (Rynearson 1995).

We have argued that surviving siblings are frequently overlooked at the best of times. The intense anger likely to be felt by family members, lack of information over the manner of death, the fear of triggering further distress in each other, and the need to keep pushing for justice or revenge focus attention on the cause of the death. This preoccupation reduces shared memorializing of earlier, happier times. It encourages surviving siblings to keep their own feelings to themselves, either shouldering as much responsibility for keeping the home running as they can, or keeping out of the way of their parents whenever possible.

To these responses can be added the fear and insecurity children will feel for their own safety, often showing up in the form of nightmares or intrusive visualizations of the death itself. They lose their trust in others (Pynoos and Eth 1984). Many lose their belief in the police and the law to protect them and to bring their bother's or sister's killers to justice. They also lose their belief in the basic 'goodness of human nature', having to face the truth that someone chose, for whatever reason, to take the life of their sibling (Parkes 1993a). They may also accept some responsibility for this death, stringing together whole catalogues of implausible events that they might have engineered so as to avoid the circumstances that led up to the death.

Road traffic and other 'avoidable' accidents

We include this category for two reasons. First, death by dangerous or reckless driving or driving under the influence of alcohol or drugs overlaps with manslaughter and murder – especially as far as the perceptions of bereaved family members are concerned (Sprang and McNeil 1998). In some ways, the involuntary thoughtlessness of the act that preceded the death is even harder to explain than a premeditated killing. Second, the procedures of the police and courts may create similar experiences for be-reaved families to those of a murder case – particularly the growing realiza-tion that retribution is going to be neither as swift nor as severe as the bereaved person felt they had a right to expect. Lehman *et al.* (1989) note the greater strain that such a death appears to place on marriage relation-ships, and the long-term challenges for grief resolution it presents to both parents and surviving children.

As with murder and manslaughter, preoccupations with the cause of the death, with blaming the driver who was involved with the accident, with the police who fail to produce sufficient evidence to correctly place blame on this driver, and with coroners or magistrates who identify the deceased as having some responsibility for the accident can all get in the way of the family sharing longer term memories of the life of the deceased. As with murder, the suddenness of the loss is intensified by lack of information about the last few seconds of life and intrusive visualizations of what might have happened. As with murder, press coverage may add to the 'notoriety' of the death, and local publicity may add to the bereaved family's difficulty in sharing feelings and getting back to fonder past memories. Although too big a subject to deal with here, large-scale disasters reflect all of the above problems, though magnified through media attention many times over (Arlidge 1997).

Case example 5 1

Jessie was a young woman in her early 20s, whose younger sister Adele, 19-years-old, was killed in a horrific car crash approximately four years prior to seeking support from a bereavement service. The car overturned after hitting a tree and burst into flames. No other car had been involved, and the younger sibling and her companions were trapped inside and burned to death.

Jessie found difficulties with many issues around her sister's death including the fact that the story had been reported in the national newspapers. Feelings of intrusion into her personal grief at that time, not being able to see her sister's body, and feelings of guilt still caused her problems. Jessie had created a scrap-book full of the reports from both the local and national newspapers. This was used as a starting point for Jessie to go through her perception of what had happened that night. Although she accepted that her sister was dead, she found it very difficult to move beyond the awful nature of her death and the guilt she felt about her life without her.

The irony was that her feelings rested not on anything she had done before the death, but on the realization that her own life was continuing and she was apparently coping well without her sister. Ironically, she felt her confidence had grown since her sister's death. Although she had been the eldest, Jessie had lived in her sister's shadow. Adele had been the bubbly one, the confident popular girl with lots of boyfriends. In contrast Jessie had had difficulty in attracting boyfriends, felt she had low self-esteem and little confidence, and had been bullied at school (for which she received counselling). Being close in age, the two sisters had spoken of how they would not be able to survive without each other, how they had planned a double wedding, and planned to live as close to each other as possible. They had intended to have babies at the same time so that their children could grow up as they had done.

After her sister's death Jessie knew she had changed. She had become more confident, more assertive and was in a stable relationship. The loss of their planned fantasy life together and the realization that she was in fact surviving without her sibling, had given Jessie intense feelings of guilt about her present life, and what appeared to be a successful future without her sister.

Lehman *et al.* (1989) suggest that many siblings experience long-term anguish in which meanings are hard to discover and a personal sense of purpose is lost. In two of the cases they examined, the impact was so great as to be implicated in surviving siblings' suicide attempts. They concluded that following sudden bereavement through a road traffic accident, there appeared to be a high degree of strain placed on all family relationships, leading to a greater likelihood, on the one hand, of relationship breakdown, and on the other, to closer and more valued family ties.

Suicide

Of all the causes of death that challenge parents' and siblings' attempts to give it meaning and find a way back to fonder memories, the taking of someone's own life must be among the most difficult. Yet, in the USA, it is the third leading cause in adolescents and young adults after accidents and murder, and is among the top ten causes of death throughout western society. These figures may be an underestimate as coroners are reluctant to bring in a verdict of suicide if there is some possibility of accidental overdose, car crash, drowning or fall (Berman 1986; Comer 1995). '. . . survivors of suicide experience an especially severe form of bereavement that differs both quantitatively and qualitatively from other forms of bereavement' (Silverman *et al.* 1994/5: 41).

Families that have experienced the suicide of one of their members appear to be vulnerable to a disproportionate number of additional problems. Silverman *et al.* (1994/5) report higher levels of divorce, separation, relationship conflicts, alcoholism, illness prior to the suicide itself, greater difficulties in coming to terms with the death, more vulnerability to illness and accident, and therefore more likelihood of reinforcing the sense of failure and negativity that may be created in the family's history of itself. Ten per cent of those whose suicide attempt is unsuccessful will try again within the next 12 months, and evidence suggests these individuals are the ones whose earlier attempts are paid least attention to or evoke most anger in their families (Coleman *et al*. 1996). After death through suicide, there appears also to be a higher chance of surviving family members attempting suicide or other forms of self-harm than for any other cause of bereavement (Silverman *et al*. 1994/5).

Seguin *et al*. (1995) argue that grief following suicide is likely to be particularly difficult to resolve because of exaggerated feelings of guilt, embarrassment, rejection, self-reproach and social stigma. Although bereavement following suicide shares many of the psychological reactions that occur after other unexpected deaths, long-term adjustment may be even more complicated. On the one hand, attempting to make sense of the death inevitably increases the survivors' sense of personal responsibility and sharpens anger with the deceased. On the other hand, the social stigma of suicide is likely to increase bereaved family members' reluctance to seek social support and to further isolate them from each other. The cultures of many western societies – with their legacies of religious sanctions against suicide – increase the degree of shame felt by families of those who take their own lives. Silverman *et al*. (1994/5) stress the role of anger and ambivalence in this complicated grieving, with family members feeling an overwhelming sense of failure, of having nothing of any value left to give, and consequently feeling incapable of talking through feelings of the death, never mind working beyond it to more relaxed memories of their earlier lives together. Finding a meaning through which to contextualize the death may be virtually impossible.

Siblings bereaved through suicide may suffer very similar reactions and feelings to those bereaved through murder. Pfeffer *et al*. (1997) note that, in common with their parents, they may obsessively work through detail after detail of the events surrounding the death and the days leading up to it. They may well experience powerful intrusive visualizations of the last moments, sleeplessness, nightmares and other symptoms associated with so-called post-traumatic stress disorder but, in addition, all these personal responses are liable to be caught up with additional anxiety, frustration or anger over their parents' reactions.

Case example 5.2

When John's elder brother put a rope round his neck and stepped off a ladder on the landing of his house, he had already asked John if he could borrow three thousand pounds to pay off one of his many debtors. Two years older than John, Pete was 34 and had always been the spendthrift of the pair. As John put it 'If Pete wanted anything, then he had to have it – like yesterday!'. Pete's lifestyle had led to the breakdown of his marriage, and though John had done his best to support his elder brother, he frequently was frustrated by his unwillingness to 'stick at anything'. John on the other hand had worked hard and put money aside for part of the costs of fertility treatment he and his wife were aiming to undergo, following many years of unsuccessful attempts to start a family. Their own mother had taken her life when both boys were young, and they had been raised by their grandmother, so John had found it particularly difficult to refuse his brother's request for the loan. However, as he said, for once in his life he lost patience with Pete and told him he would have to sort his problems out himself. We spoke to John two years later, and he still did not believe Pete had intended to kill himself. He had developed a complex and detailed account of that morning, combining facts with guesswork that had become a complete theory of why Pete's death was entirely John's fault. Pete had telephoned John to ask him to come over. John, still angry at having to refuse Pete's request for the loan, stopped off on the way over for a haircut. Meanwhile (he discovered later) a mutual friend had gone round to see Pete, knocked at the door, and hearing no reply, gave up and left. John said that he was certain Pete had been waiting for him on the top of the ladder, and probably stepped off when he heard the knock, knowing that if John heard no answer, he would use his key to let himself in and discover Pete in time to save him. Hence, it was John's failure to go straight round, and the coincidence of the second visitor, that (he believed) had led to Pete's death. Though intellectually he might sometimes suspect he was not entirely to blame, emotionally, John's guilt for his brother's death, his sense of failure in preventing him getting into debt and from ruining his marriage, the particular feelings of resentment that led him to stop off at the barber's before going to Pete's house, and his failure to spot the likelihood of Pete attempting to take his own life in the light of their mother's suicide, all were combined by John into an elegant but self-destructive explanation of his brother's death. These emotional obstacles to John's warmer recollections of their early lives together were made even more insurmountable by the nagging fear that, given their family history, John's growing depression might lead him too into taking his own life.

Worden (1981) argues that the mixture of anger and guilt experienced by siblings needs to be appreciated, particularly as their own sense of mortality is highlighted. He suggests that their grief may be complicated by a fear that they too may be capable of taking their own life, and this is not easily expressed in the strained family relationships that may accompany death through suicide.

AIDS related deaths

Klein (1998) argues that grief resulting from acquired immune deficiency syndrome (AIDS) related death is unique, possessing the complications that arise both from a highly stigmatized condition, and from the multiple losses that bereaved partners, family members and friends experience. AIDS and human immunodeficiency virus (HIV) have their own specialized language and terminology. The need for clear information contrasts with the extreme prejudices and ignorance associated with societal reaction to the condition.

Seeking support and understanding in the case of an AIDS related death may expose bereaved people to some of the feelings experienced following suicide. Only with very close and intimate relationships can they express their feelings without risking an unsympathetic or embarrassed response together with a sense of stigmatization by association. As with suicide, bereaved siblings may much prefer to deny, avoid or hide their feelings from others in order to escape finding themselves sharing aspects of the stigma that accompanies the condition (Doka 1989).

There have been few medical conditions prior to AIDS that have so fundamentally challenged comfortable social assumptions about sexual behaviour, sexual orientation, drug use and health care practices. Klein notes that the survivors of AIDS related deaths rarely find relationships in 'mainstream' culture that can validate their grief, and modern society is ill-equipped for providing consistent long-term support for the growing number of individuals bereaved of parents, friends, children and siblings through AIDS related illnesses.

Such bereaved people may have particularly complex support needs. They will already have expended considerable time and emotional energy during the course of their loved one's AIDS related illness. In coming to terms with news of the diagnosis, in coming to terms with the social or sexual context in which HIV was contracted and in the roller coaster of fear, despair, hope, and finally intensive physical and social caregiving in the final stages of the illness, they may end up in a form of intellectual disorientation and emotional numbness following the death. This may be compounded by their experience of other AIDS related deaths in and among the sufferer's friendship network, leading to what Cherney and Verhey (1996) describe as 'emotional burnout'. Here, they may be unable or unwilling to deal with other losses in their life, appearing to others as callous and indifferent.

In common with many survivors of death following murder, manslaughter or death by dangerous driving, people bereaved following an AIDS related death frequently suffer a deeply disorienting attack on their previously held view of the world. The apparent senselessness of the multiple losses preceding and accompanying a distressing death, discrimination and abandonment by many people who might have been expected to be supportive, and the sheer international scale of the numbers dying may produce intense anger, alienation from normal everyday routines and an inability to share more comfortable memories of the deceased's earlier life events.

Klein notes that suicidal feelings, fear of forming new relationships, family conflicts and symptoms similar to post-traumatic stress disorder have been identified among people bereaved as the result of AIDS related illnesses. In addition to losing someone they love, they have also had to watch them lose society's respect, their physical and emotional well-being, their familiar personality, and additionally suffer the consequences of discrimination. Sharing such deep feelings of depression and hopelessness may set up significant barriers to longer term biographical remembering and transformation of the relationship with the deceased child or sibling.

Miscarriage, stillbirth and neonatal death

A major problem facing mothers and fathers of infants that die before they ever really 'lived' is that friends, family, medical staff and even parents themselves may fail to appreciate that their grief is the result of the death of a real, existing person (Thomas 1995; McGreal *et al.* 1997). Puddifoot and Johnson (1997) argue that mothers who miscarry need as much family support as parents of older children, yet the absence of a family history in which these others have come themselves to know the infant can lead to assumptions that the loss is less significant (Lovell 1983). This is particularly so in cases where the father has failed to develop any sort of relationship with the unborn baby.

At the same time, Worth (1997) argues that fathers do increasingly share in their wives' antenatal experiences. Being able to feel the baby's movements and sharing plans for its future contribute to their own bonding with the unborn infant. Developments in medical technology that allow a father to hear the monitored heartbeat and observe scan's of the baby's outline in his wife's uterus add to the sense of fatherhood and changing identity (Murphy and Hunt 1997). Hence, both partners can suffer a particular sense of loneliness because of the mismatch between the extent of their inner adaptation and their outward appearances. However, continuing cultural expectations on fathers to support their wives tend to inhibit them from expressing this distress and they are far less likely to be perceived by others as needing support (McGreal *et al.* 1997). Puddifoot and Johnson (1997) concluded that fathers' emotions were particularly confused following miscarriage, perceiving themselves to be in the double-bind of having to repress their own feelings in order to support their wives. In our own research, a number of mothers who had experienced miscarriage or stillbirth commented on the lack of support they received from either medical staff or wider family. With the former, the failure of medical technology combined with a severing of their identity from the other mothers with whom they shared antenatal visits and, with full-term babies, labour wards. One mother said,

> I felt as if they were ashamed of me. I went in through the same door as all the other pregnant women, but had to come out through a back entrance. The doctor told me that something had gone wrong. I had to

wait ages, then they gave me another appointment to come back to 'tidy up the odds and ends'. I was devastated.

Another mother commented on her husband's embarrassment at her inability to come to terms with her miscarriage. Although she knew he was upset, he not only seemed incapable of talking to her about it, he tried to prevent her from talking to other people. She said that because they had no baby to show, he felt they could not expect anyone to understand how she felt. Her mother's response was very similar. Everyone appeared to conspire to downgrade her sense of grief and to imply she was 'making a fuss'. As so many women have angrily commented, 'their response was, you can always have another'.

This failure to acknowledge that any child has ever lived may make acceptance of the death very difficult. The reluctance of most hospitals to perform a post-mortem and hence to offer clear medical explanations for the stillbirth or miscarriage adds to problems of giving meaning to the death. Detailed projections of the baby's future life, growing up and adulthood may be shared with no one, not even the partner. Yet the loss of these future plans and of the parental identity that both parents may already have internalized need to be acknowledged, then relinquished, for adjustment to take place (Theut et al. 1990). Such adjustment is complicated if the mother becomes pregnant again, with her fear of becoming too attached to the unborn baby intermingling with ongoing grief over the death of the previous one:

> Encased in the foetus's death is a cherished image of the child-never-to-be. A major task is to create open, hopeful vistas for surviving children, both born and unborn. The 'work' goes on for months and even years.
>
> (Taner Leff 1987: 112)

Infants who are born but live only for a few hours, or who live for longer periods but only with the help of intensive medical and nursing care present their parents with the heartbreak of grieving a brief life that is shared by no one else except the hospital staff. It may also be a life that cannot be shared because of the clinical distance that intensive care inevitably puts between infant and parents (Murray and Callan 1988). One mother at an annual gathering of The Compassionate Friends mentioned how guilty she felt in comparison with parents whose children had died after many years of life, when her baby had lived only for six hours. The role of nursing staff, and of other parents with similar experiences, is crucial in witnessing the fact of the life, in helping share enthusiasm and concern for the person that the infant might have become, and in confirming the overwhelming significance of what has been lost. The long-term effects of such a loss must not be underestimated (Theun 1997). One 85-year-old mother we interviewed still retained deep feelings of loss, guilt and frustration over the death of her newly-born daughter, her husband's refusal to find out where she was buried and his reluctance to talk about her.

Where a mother has chosen to have her baby aborted, the social stigma of the nature of the loss, an inability to share grief or experiences with others, the strong likelihood of lack of support from the baby's father, and ongoing ambivalence about the choice made can exaggerate all the above problems. In any event, grief of parents whose babies die before or at birth seems to be less socially legitimate than grief over infants that live long enough to gain a social identity of their own. So, the sense of isolation and loneliness felt by women who have undergone abortions may be seen by others as totally illegitimate, and the daydreams they may have over how their baby might have grown up had they lived are rarely shared by anyone. One woman we interviewed commented that her friends and husband had no knowledge that she had had an abortion as a 16-year-old girl, that her parents never spoke about it, that she had lost touch years ago with the baby's father and that our interview with her was the first time she had ever told anyone the name she had given to her daughter. She also recognized, looking back, how vulnerable she had been to the social and family pressures that led to her deciding to go through with the abortion.

Infant deaths and Sudden Infant Death Syndrome

Many of the problems identified above do not occur in the case of infants that are brought home and who live for periods between a few weeks and 12 months. They have achieved an independent existence and have a social role outside of the immediate family, confirming the couple's (or single parent's) new identity in the interactions of health visitor, neighbours and friends. The suddenness and lack of medical explanation of the death of this apparently healthy infant therefore makes Sudden Infant Death Syndrome a particularly difficult event in which to find sense or meaning (Aadalen 1980; Carroll and Shaefer 1994).

Intense feelings of guilt and the search for a cause of the death may emphasize marital differences in dealing with grief whatever the cause of the infant's death (Dyregrov 1990; Hunfield et al. 1996). These differences may be compounded because fathers are shocked not only by the death of the infant, but also by the intensity of their wives' grief (Torrez 1992). Cordell and Thomas (1990) argue that many fathers give up their own need to grieve in order to support their wives and hold on to what appears to be a desperate situation. Cornwell et al. (1977) sensitively portray the sense of intense despair and profound anguish felt by many parents following bereavement through Sudden Infant Death Syndrome, noting that even when a subsequent child is born, this grief can recur throughout their lives. They also note that mothers may be particularly vulnerable. They may not have returned to full-time work, and so are socially isolated following the death – their network of fellow mothers only serving to emphasize what they have lost. If they have returned to work, the cultural imperative that mothers care for and nurture their children may make their sense of guilt and failure even stronger. If it is their first baby, they will have had to work hard to adjust to the new parent role and will have found much of their life-space filled with the demands of feeding and caring for the new infant. Where these tasks are shared with the father, he too may find major difficulties in making sense of the sudden and inexplicable loss of these intense and emotionally charged new routines. Where the relationship with the baby is uncomfortable, and where its presence is resented – however silently or reluctantly by either parent – the subsequent sense of guilt and regret may be difficult to share or come to terms with.

Death of a child with developmental difficulties

We include this category of death in this chapter for a number of reasons, in spite of evidence that some parents bereaved of disabled children gain new perceptions of themselves and of the world as a result of their experiences (Milo 1997).

Grief that arises following the birth of a child with learning or developmental disabilities requires a particular form of adjustment with which this book has not attempted to deal (Fortier and Wanless 1984). However, evidence suggests that such adjustment often places considerable strain on marital and other family relationships. It can promote particular patterns of family relationships that emphasize the link between the parent(s) and the disabled child sometimes at the expense of other relationships both in the family and in the wider community.

Following the deaths of these children, parents whose life-space has been almost exclusively tied up with their care, and whose view of the world has adapted to cope with the stigma or sympathy of mainstream society, may find major problems in living in the 'normal' world without the special child upon whom their own identity has been sometimes built (Copley and Bodensteiner 1987). Alternatively, where such a death is perceived as 'releasing' the rest of the family to live their lives more 'normally', guilt and resentment at a society that assumes this reaction to be appropriate can also create problems of sharing experiences of the death and creating stories of the relationship that has been lost.

Complicated grief as limbo – caught in marginal social roles

Each of the above examples illustrate how bereaved parents and children may experience difficulties in adjusting to a lost relationship because the manner of the death excludes them so profoundly from opportunities to either share their experiences of it – and hence to comprehend it, make sense of it and adapt their identity – or to reconnect with aspects of 'normal' living that might distract and move them on to some 'semblance' of more normal living.

The example of miscarriage and stillbirth is an exception to this, particularly when subsequent children are born and raised successfully. However, this is only a partial exception, showing that intermittent grief and intimate loneliness, sharply intruding many years later into apparently normal lives, may result from aspects of the bereaved person's identity still remaining stuck in incomprehension at their loss. This phenomenon is particularly acute in the rare cases of the birth of twins where only one survives. Parents are both mourning and engaging in new parenting at the same time (Bryan 1995). The surviving twin is a constant reminder of the loss, and parents can only too easily come to idealize the one that died, or, in avoiding conversation about them altogether, create an ambivalent presence with which the surviving twin struggles to relate without having any real understanding of its nature.

Disenfranchised grief, resulting from others failing to accept the severity of the loss, or social stigma, resulting from the notoriety or sensationalism of the circumstances of the loss, can each attach aspects of the bereaved person's identity irrevocably to that period of despair and confusion in which their internal world failed to match the realities of their awful new circumstances. Miscarriage and stillbirth cruelly reverse the months of adaptation to identities of new parenthood, leaving an empty space in the womb, the nursery, the couple's conversation. Sudden death gives no warning or opportunity for parents or siblings to prepare for the empty space that inexplicably appears in their daily routines, their joint histories and their sense of themselves. Stigmatized deaths and deaths in the full glare of the media reduce opportunities to explore meanings of the loss and to come privately to terms with how it will affect their families and sense of identity. Social and cultural resources in these examples can serve to trap bereaved family members within a particular marginal role, acting as markers that separate the culture of everyday modern living from the more threatening possibilities of arbitrary, unacceptable or inconvenient dying.

Difficult deaths and problems of long-term adjustment

Murphy (1996) investigated parental stress following the violent deaths of their young or adolescent children and found long-term problems arising from both impaired ability to manage emotions and poorer capacity to make effective decisions. Cognitive and emotional functioning were apparently reduced over an extended period of time owing to preoccupation with the manner of the death and an inability to adapt their view of the world to accommodate such traumatic experiences. From her own exploratory studies

Murphy concluded that such parents were at an increased risk of separation, divorce, illness and economic loss because of the high levels of distress that persisted for years. Health and personal relationships deteriorated and further losses confirmed their sense of despair and loss of control over a malign and cruel world.

Murphy describes a community support programme designed to target both cognitive and emotional problems, and loss of social support. Using very small groups of similarly bereaved parents, support was offered based around a problem-solving approach. Focusing on parents' experiences, information and skill development were offered in a number of problem areas: managing emotional and cognitive responses, monitoring personal health, repairing parenting skills, improving marital relationships, dealing with legal difficulties and managing expectations for the future. The approach offered both direct teaching and group-based discussion and aimed to compensate for loss of feelings of personal control and for the loss of wider relationships resulting from their inability to re-connect effectively with everyday routines.

Mahan and Calica (1997) examined perinatal bereavement and concluded that professional support should focus on providing information about the cause of death and about the nature of the emotional and cognitive problems parents might well be experiencing. Noting how most families' ability to process information and make decisions is badly impaired by grief, they stress that all communication by professionals should be limited and appropriate at the outset, with generous opportunity to answer questions as they arise. All decisions that can be postponed should be, and essential information should be written down for parents to re read later. They argue that over a long-term period parents should be encouraged not to fear being thought of as ignorant or annoying by professionals who could provide further information, recognizing that recurrent thoughts and growing anxiety may revolve around baseless or incorrect beliefs about the death and its causes. Mahan and Calica also stress the importance of supporting the family as a whole, including surviving children and helping parents to use simple but unambiguous language in explaining what has happened to their brother or sister.

Summary

- Complicated grief may be at least partly the result of social and cultural factors as well as individual psychological ones.
- Inability to comprehend the fact of a death may be increased by its unexpectedness, its arbitrariness, violence and lack of rational explanation.
- Lack of opportunities to explore the meaning of such deaths and to externalize personal feelings and confused thoughts may be increased by the notoriety and shame attached to the cause of death or manner of dying.

- Circumstances that increase the likelihood that others will fail to appreciate the impact or significance of the death may add to a sense of loneliness and personal isolation.
- Finding distractions and opportunities to 'move on' to more normal routines may be postponed when circumstances surrounding the death remain unresolved.
- Adjustment of family routines to accommodate the lost relationship may similarly be postponed in cases where individual members are caught up either with attempts to gain 'justice' for the deceased or a sense of personal responsibility for their death.
- Difficult deaths may be so much a part of wider cultural 'myths' that they structure part or even all of some bereaved people's long-term identities into a marginal social position. These individuals may serve as 'markers' serving to set a boundary between predictable everyday living and the threat of disaster, disorder and personal tragedy.

6 | Things that help: supporting bereaved parents and brothers and sisters

Introduction

The previous chapter explained how it is possible to understand differences in adjustment by examining the cultural perspectives through which bereaved people view their experience of loss. We suggested that self-identity, social context and the meanings given to bereavement can frame perceptions of grief in four distinctive ways:

1 as an insurmountable barrier forever preventing return to normal living (identity disintegrates through isolation and exclusion from everyday social relationships);
2 as a painful, unwelcome but ultimately manageable challenge to normal living that may subside with the passing of time but will never disappear (repair of identity through continuity with everyday routines punctuated by intense but varying periods of loneliness);
3 as a motivation for seeking out others who appreciate bereaved parents' or siblings' unique and permanent sense of loss and who share their frustration with an everyday world that cannot cope with child death (rebuilding identity from within cultures of bereavement);
4 as the opening of a fateful window through which self and the world can never be viewed in the same way again (a trigger for individual identity reconstruction in searching for a world that can be lived in without the deceased).

We suggested that the dominant perspective through which parents or siblings perceive their bereavement may be influenced by how much their identity depends exclusively on the deceased, the nature of the death, the extent to which their social and cultural milieu help them make sense of the

death, their opportunities to maintain contact with everyday routines outside the home and the potential of their intimate relationships to support
them in their adjustment.

In this chapter, we examine the experiences bereaved family members
have themselves identified as helpful in coming to terms with their grief. We
illustrate how practical forms of support can shift grief from the first, highly
disoriented position in which only loss, despair and intimate loneliness is
felt, to one of the other three positions that indicate the return of some
order and direction in the thoughts and activities of the bereaved person.
Many of the ideas come directly from the bereaved parents and siblings
with whom we have spoken in the course of our work and research over
the past four years.

Things that help – little ladders, big levers

Bereaved parents and siblings identify a range of things that have helped
them when overwhelmed by the first of these perspectives. For most, the
period during and immediately after the death feels unreal and out of time.
It may last only briefly or it may extend over months, even years. It may
be escaped only to return at certain times even more powerfully. Shock,
numbness, confusion or even a 'ghastly euphoria' have been mentioned as
characteristics of the disorientation parents and siblings experience at the
death (and to a lesser extent at the diagnosis of life threatening illness) that
frequently gives way to a sense of inconsolable loneliness.

Things that help can be divided simply into two levels of support – those
'little ladders' that help them hold on and maybe climb temporarily out
of the despair in which they appear to be stuck, and the bigger 'levers'
that help them move on to discover ways of surviving and of repairing
or reconstructing an identity that better matches their changed circumstances (Wellman *et al.* 1988). These two basic types of support reflect
the key themes of this book – coping with a sense of intimate loneliness
and adjusting to a new reality without their child or brother or sister.
Sharing the profoundness of their grief and providing practical help can
give parents and siblings little ladders that enable them briefly, and in
small measure, to overcome their sense of being totally alone. A genuine
sense of being heard and understood can develop in the context of close
friendships and authentic respectful relationships. Here, support is not a
one-way transaction from an unknown 'helper' to the bereaved person
but a mutual expression between two or more people who each deeply
loved and miss the deceased, or who deeply care for the bereaved person.
It is also important to note that only from an intimate knowledge of the
bereaved family's routines can practical support or genuine understanding be given.

Bigger levers, through which bereaved people regain some sense of control over their lives, may be provided by new meanings that help them shift their perspective. Information helps place the death and their feelings in a more manageable context. Things that help make the death more 'real' and provide it with some context – even if it can never 'make sense' in rational terms – may provide a firmer basis from which to begin the process of adjustment. Information might, in time, offer some reassurance that no more could have been done. It might give a clearer picture of the events that led up to the death. It might offer some insight into what is to come and ways that others have survived it. Acknowledgement by others of what they have lost and how their identity is affected might help them feel less alone in coping with the major challenges that must be faced in daily routines, family networks, meeting other people and within their own waking and dreaming thoughts.

The creation of a new reality, both through conversation with others and within the bereaved person's internal self-narrative, are central in adjusting to these changes (Giddens 1991; Nadeau 1998). Shared stories of the death and memories of their earlier life help reduce disbelief at the loss and support them in searching for new kinds of connections with the deceased (Klass et al. 1996). Photographs, clothes and possessions belonging to the child and places with which they were associated play a key part in these conversations. So-called 'linking objects' – places and physical evidence of the life that was lived – help bereaved people hold on to their memories of the deceased, help confirm the reality of the life they lived and help develop insight into the continuing impact those lives have on the living (Riches and Dawson 1998a).

This sharing of memories and personal feelings can only take place within emotionally supportive social relationships. Family and friendship networks can provide settings for talking and thinking about the deceased as well as for more practical support when household routines break down. Hence the quality of these everyday patterns directly affects the pace and direction of adjustment. They strongly influence the willingness of each to express their feelings and share their memories. At the same time, self-esteem and a sense of purpose might be also maintained to a certain extent by the roles, responsibilities and social contacts bereaved family members have outside the home.

A continuum of support

These little ladders and big levers come from what Parkes calls 'a spectrum of support' (Parkes 1996). At one end, special friends, both of the bereaved person and of the deceased, can help grieving in direct unplanned ways such as offering emotional support following the death and during the funeral, demonstrating through personal grief that bereaved people are not alone in their love for the dead child, helping celebrate anniversaries of the child's death and birthdays and witnessing the value of the child's life. At the other end of the spectrum, qualified professionals and trained volunteers also may have a key role to play. Information, reassurance and mental maps of the road bereaved people are travelling can help re-establish some order in their confused thoughts and emotions.

Somewhere in the middle of this spectrum, help given by other bereaved parents or siblings may provide insights that plot a way through the worst experiences of their grief. Groups and individual relationships that recognize the need to grieve and do not set time limits, that willingly encourage remembering, that provide bereaved people with opportunities for continuing to relate to the deceased, and that offer role models of how others have survived, can help enormously in exploring and managing confused thoughts and feelings. In the same way, with particularly difficult deaths, support is often gained from being among others whose relatives died in equally sudden, painful or traumatic circumstances. Anger and frustration at the injustices of a society – or an event that caused or allowed such deaths to occur – find a voice and political outlet in cultures that help their members by contradicting the values of mainstream society. Validation from such groups may be crucial for a particular member if others in the family deal with their grief in entirely different ways.

Whoever offers support, the value of communication in acknowledging the death and in trying to make sense of it, the comfort provided by sensitive social relationships and the wider confirmation that bereaved people are not alone – or losing their sanity – are vital elements in exploring their needs and developing strategies for meeting them.

Little ladders – support around the dying and death

Tedeschi and Calhoun (1995) draw conclusions about useful support from their own clinical work with people who have faced traumatic and deeply disturbing experiences. They note that bereaved people need help not only in learning to adapt to these events, but also in recognizing that their struggle to survive has actually changed them in positive as well as negative ways. That such awful experiences might have some positive outcomes may be very difficult to appreciate until considerable time has elapsed, and such insights cannot be communicated directly. They have to be experienced, and for some parents and siblings, such personal development may only ever be perceived by others and not by bereaved people themselves. Hence, support may take many forms and may be useful at very different times in the lives of bereaved parents and siblings.

Tedeschi and Calhoun stress that adjustment is rarely swift or straightforward. Usually it is slow, uneven and frequently blocked by a preoccupation with the death and by attempts to postpone its consequences. This observation supports the conclusions of Stroebe and Schut (1995) that bereaved people need at times both to 'move beyond' the death itself and get on with living in the here and now, as well as finding the solitude for exploring their loss and its consequences. We have already argued that the nature of the death, the manner of its communication and preparedness for it, and the support available during its immediate aftermath, may strongly affect family members' ability to comprehend what has happened and face its implications. Support in 'apprehending' what is happening in these early periods appears to be a foundation for later successful adjustment.

Telling bad news and facing death

The problems experienced by medical staff and emergency services in communicating bad news – of the diagnosis of a life-threatening illness, of a fatal accident, murder or disaster – are widely acknowledged (Taner Leff 1987; Taylor 1988; Von Bloch 1996). The implications of how parents and siblings come to hear and understand such news are far more important for later adjustment than is often recognized. Somehow, knowing the extreme and inevitable distress that such communication causes appears to add to the need to get it over with as soon as possible, to encourage relatives to guess themselves what the news-bearer is trying to say, and to withdraw early to allow them 'privacy' with their own thoughts.

Von Bloch (1996) notes that relatives will find such shocking news almost impossible to take in initially, and that denial and disbelief are a 'natural' defence against the pain of full realization. She stresses two key qualities in communicating bad news in as helpful a way as possible. First, because of the time taken for the information to sink in, medical or emergency staff should acknowledge they may need to remain with, or be accessible to the bereaved relatives for some time. Second, they must be able to give information and answers to subsequent questions in as clear, detailed, unambiguous and direct a manner as possible. Throughout, appreciation of the family's torment and the uniqueness of their loss must be demonstrated. This might take the form of sincere expressions of regret, acknowledgements of the extreme pain they must be feeling, explicit care for their physical welfare and appreciation of their need to share their distress in privacy. Extreme reactions, ranging from uncontrollable weeping through to overt hostility should be anticipated and prepared for. Such training and support of medical and emergency teams still appears to be woefully inadequate (Swisher et al. 1993).

It is not possible to prescribe hard and fast rules about viewing the body, particularly in cases of extreme mutilation or disfigurement. However, Von

Bloch supports our own research findings – that parents and siblings are more likely to regret not having seen the body, than regret seeing it and wishing they had not. Again, the role of medical or emergency staff in preparing relatives for what they will see, giving them clear information on which they can make a decision and leaving time for them to really think through whether or not they do want to see their child is more important than setting out with the intention of preventing them from such a visit to 'spare their feelings'. Many parents reported that no matter how awful their children might have looked, they could not have been worse than the fantasies created in their own imaginations.

At this time of dawning recognition of the enormity of what faces them, bereaved family members need further help. They need a contact number and someone to visit personally for further answers to the questions they have not yet thought of. They need to know exactly what will be happening to their loved one's body during the next few hours and days, along with sensitive explanations if a post-mortem is required. They also need to know their rights of objection to a post-mortem and their opportunities to be represented at this operation. They need reassurance that any further handling of their child's body will be accomplished with respect and dignity, and they need to know when and where they can continue to visit it. They also need to be sensitively informed of any requests the hospital might have for organ donations and told, as many hospitals do in writing, of the legal procedures they need to follow in acquiring the death certificate, registering the death and making arrangements for the funeral.

Though it maybe outside the responsibilities of medical staff, ensuring that a close family friend is on hand to support parents and siblings in the hours after receiving this news might further help its comprehension, providing a slightly more objective audience with whom each family member can work through their thoughts. Not knowing how to fill this period from death to funeral, when time appears to have stopped and all the bereaved person's natural responses are to do something yet there is relatively little to do, reflects a crisis of bereavement peculiar to late modernity. In traditional cultures, the family's close involvement in washing and laying out the body, receiving and catering for visitors who come to pay their respects and share the mourning, and the clear rituals that have to be accomplished prior to the burial or cremation, structure this time in ways that fit culturally shared beliefs. In stark contrast to this, modern bereavement can increase the isolation felt by family members. In extreme cases – as with procedures following murder or suicide – families may be separated for interview before they have even begun to absorb the news of their child's death. Such isolation around this initial apprehension of the death may add to the already major problems of acceptance arising from the nature of the death itself (Riches and Dawson 1998b).

Comprehending death and enduring its consequences

The value of talk, especially within a controlled and caring relationship has been referred to frequently in the previous chapters. Its value in helping bereaved parents and siblings turn the nightmare into a more manageable, if tragic reality, cannot be stressed enough. Work with people experiencing symptoms of so-called 'post traumatic stress disorder' illustrates how debriefing in a safe and supervised setting enables some sense of control to be regained (Tehrani and Westlake 1994). We outlined in Chapter 1 the theory that language and conversation is a primary medium through which human beings create the reality of their lives, ordering and simplifying a welter of experiences into predictable boundaries and recognizable labels. Hence, it is clear that the greater the sense of loneliness felt by the bereaved person and the more others avoid them, the more unable or unwilling they are to put their thoughts and feelings into words, then the greater is their chance of becoming mentally stuck within the enormity of the death itself. Their inability to comprehend what has happened – their understandable urge to close their mind to the degree to which life has changed forever – means they remain 'knocking ever more loudly at the door of this empty room'. Hence, Tedeschi and Calhoun (1995) suggest that bereaved people may need help and understanding in coming to 'accept' and 'endure' their loss. We would support this principle, and at the same time draw attention to the centrality of conversation, visualization and social relationships through which such comprehension and ability to 'endure' might be successfully achieved.

Internal conversations with the self have been noted as a strategy used by bereaved fathers for coming to terms with the reality and consequences of their child's death (Cook 1988). Simply acknowledging that this is taking place may be immensely beneficial. Even tacit 'permission' to deal with their grief in a way that is not necessarily obvious to other family members may help them feel less alone and better understood. Such acknowledgements also recognize those responsibilities that they feel prevent them from letting go or asking for help. In our own research, we found a number of men who adopted particular private strategies for exploring their losses. One, for example, directed his internal conversation at his son's grave, which he visited every day. Another, who worked as a farmer, spent many hours alone in the cab of his tractor, going over the death of his young son. Neither of these men shared their internal conversations with their wives, and the depth and difficulty of each's 'endurance' was witnessed by no one. We have found a number of men who, in the intimate support of self-help groups, have finally wept when presented with this simple insight that their silent suffering *is* recognized and appreciated. As one mother, who was a trained counsellor before her son died, said:

I have changed a lot. I respect people who don't want to talk about their feelings. I accept that now. Before John's death I wouldn't have. My husband can only tolerate talking about it for a little while – then he needs to get on with something else . . . to get busy . . . to take his mind off it. . . . That is how he copes.

However, conversations with others can provide a valuable vehicle through which the 'story' of the death can be created and its reality comprehended and endured (Nadeau 1998). Walter's model (1996) of biographical memorializing illustrates the central role played by close friends of the deceased. In many of our interviews, bereaved parents have noted the importance of the deceased son's and daughter's friends in helping them 'write the last chapter'.

Case example 6.1

Talk is a vital medium for creating the 'story' of a death, and hence helping to regain control over events that make the bereaved person feel so powerless. One mother described the gradual realization that the plane crash reported in the news was the same flight her daughter had been on. She recalled clearly the support she had gained during these first few days from her daughter's close friend. Together, they produced an inventory of the clothes, jewellery, make-up, books and other distinguishing features that would help the crash investigators identify the body. This process of sharing the last journey in their joint imaginations, of discussing the disaster on the other side of the world, of crying together and sharing their love helped create the truth of her death and also a narrative of her dying. Another mother spoke fondly of how her son's close friend still sometimes sought her out in order to talk about him, 'because there was no one else he felt he could talk to'. She noted how sad yet privately special and validating such occasions were.

Similarly, close friends of the bereaved person themselves are often identified in interviewee's accounts of the support that helped them through the time immediately after the death. In many cases, parents felt that their bereavement sorted out who were the 'real' friends, and grief mingled with deep hurt at the notable absence of many people – including their own brothers or sisters in some cases – who they had previously believed were close friends. A number described the one special person who had 'been there' for them. These individuals were characterized by their willingness to return again and again to listen to the same story of the death, to cry with them, to help them face the rest of the world, and to put up with what the bereaved person saw in retrospect as awful behaviour. The indirect way in which these friends supported partners and surviving children should also be acknowledged in that they were able in many cases to gently nudge friends into noticing the effects of their 'difficult' behaviour on other family members.

Sometimes these 'friends' were new ones, acquired during the dying of the child. One mother counted her hospital social worker as that special person who had helped her through the time of her son's death. This worker remembered not only the anniversary of his death, but also his birthdays during the four years since he had died. She noted that this social worker was always there if she needed to talk and that her desire to get to know the son who died provided her with an audience for continuing to explore the implications of his death.

Facing the irrevocability of the death and coming to endure its inevitable consequences is harder, we have argued, when the death is sudden or occurs in difficult circumstances. Talk in these cases, may initially have more to do with establishing the sequence of events leading to the death, of establishing cause and blame, of exploring personal responsibility and feelings of guilt, as it is of the later process of facing the personal implications of the death. The role of conversations with professionals and other 'experts' in simply establishing what *has* happened cannot be overestimated. The reality of the death cannot begin to be created unless a complete description and explanation of its causes and nature are established.

The harder the details are for parents and siblings to acquire, the more they feel 'victims' of circumstances and procedures beyond their control. The less opportunities they have for sharing their confusion and shock with each other and with professionals who were 'at the scene', the harder it becomes to comprehend the reality of the death. The more they are prevented or dissuaded from seeing the body, the more likely they are to experience distressing fantasies and alternative scenarios played out within their imaginations.

Talk here, then, from professionals who might be expected to offer authoritative accounts of what has happened, accounts of what might happen next, and what has happened in similar circumstances, helps the bereaved person begin to orient themselves within the distressing and unfamiliar world into which they have been thrown. The landmarks provided by such individuals may be crucial in helping highly disoriented bereaved people anchor their own sense of sanity within boundaries that, for a little while, are protected by others with wider experience. Hence the role, for example, of medical staff in contextualizing Sudden Infant Death Syndrome (Cornwell *et al.* 1977) or of psychiatric social workers in explaining the increasing vulnerability of young men to suicide (Comer 1995). Such professionals may provide some kind of a mental map on which family members may plot their shifting sense of shock, disbelief, guilt and failure, as they learn to comprehend and endure such intense and complex feelings of loss.

Case example 6.2

One woman we interviewed who had experienced two still-births – the second of twins after seven month's gestation – found the only useful support came in the shape of the hospital chaplain. Few of her friends, and particularly her husband, appeared willing or able to acknowledge the depth of her despair or the profundity of her loss. Other medical staff appeared to see the event as a 'failure' on everyone's part and she felt a general conspiracy to deny her children had ever lived – and therefore could not really be grieved. In contrast, the chaplain who helped her organize the funeral and arrange for her twins to be buried in the local cemetery, demonstrated understanding of the precise emotions she was experiencing. He witnessed her loneliness and her loss of two individuals that had been a part of her for seven months, and part of her deeply desired future for many more years. His insights, not only into her own frustration at the hospital refusing to look for medical causes of the still-birth, but also into the inability of the community in general to appreciate that she had been a mother and had now lost three children, helped her feel a little less alone and guided her through the almost intolerable weeks following her losses.

Immediate support – helping bereaved people feel less alone

Conrad (1998) urges anyone who has a close relationship with the bereaved family to visit them to offer help and not to be hurt or oversensitive at the understandable responses they might experience. She notes that news of such an unexpected death will create major disorientation and confusion, with family members feeling contradictory urges to do something yet feeling incapable of doing anything. With anticipated death, the sense of unreality is still likely to be present. In some cases, the loss of a child who has been nursed for a considerable time might be as disorienting as a sudden death. For example, the wholesale commitment of parents – mothers particularly – to the treatment regimes they believe will cure their child, and their involvement with therapy, remission cycles and return of symptoms may result in a massive sense of personal failure as well as the loss of a highly charged identity bound up with their child's survival.

Conrad argues that all potential helpers should be reassured by realizing that bereaved parents and siblings have no more idea than they do about what is the 'appropriate' thing to say or do in the aftermath of a child's death. In many respects, there is nothing that can be said that will make the pain of early loss any less – while many things can certainly trigger the distress they feel and are barely controlling. Not to be afraid of such expression, and a willingness to act towards them as the good friend they have always been demonstrates honesty and a desire to help in any way they can. Help in these cases can never be prescribed – it has to be negotiated with honesty and sensitivity. The greatest mistake any friend can make is to turn their back on the bereaved person because they are afraid of upsetting them. We cannot stress strongly enough the contradictory needs of newly bereaved parents. While they are enormously hurt by people avoiding them or being embarrassed at not knowing what to say, they also have neither the energy nor the patience to attempt to explain how they feel or what they are going through. One mother said,

> The friends who rang or came round and said things like, 'I am so sorry. I just don't know what to say to you . . . but I am thinking of you . . . And what can I do?' were being honest and I found that helpful. I didn't feel so much as if we were on our own . . .

While not taking control, Conrad suggests that a good friend may be able to act in a more organized way, identifying what minimum tasks need to be accomplished to keep a household running, and what actions must be taken by bereaved relatives when someone dies. By trying to construct such a list of minimum needs, close friends can decide what they can offer to do. Conrad suggests offers of help should be specific rather than vague, and based on a thorough knowledge of the family. Writing these offers on a piece of paper with the helper's telephone number confirms their willingness to support at any time, and not just during a single 'token' visit. Although the actual help needed will vary from situation to situation, and Conrad is writing particularly about the parents of murdered children, she lists the following practical forms of help that might well apply to supporters in most circumstances where a child has died:

- as a liaison person, acting as a buffer between the bereaved person and the demands of the outside world – especially if the press is involved;
- as a telephone answerer and/or recorder of calls from other people;
- as a caretaker of young or elder family members;
- as a chauffeur or transport arranger;
- as general handyperson – feeding the pet, sorting the laundry, doing the ironing;
- finding a hairdresser who will come in on the morning of the funeral;
- offering to drive and accompany parents to inquests, to see the minister and funeral director; or even, if a close friend of the deceased, to be with them when they visit the body of their child;
- taking prepared food such as casseroles that can be frozen then microwaved;
- being there in the aftermath – available to show grief at a shared loss and also as someone trusted and prepared to listen and also as someone prepared to find out information that parents may feel unable to pursue themselves;

- being there in the long-term, helping to share the grief, guaranteeing them you will help keep the child's memory alive, recognizing that their lives can never be the same again and continuing to offer both emotional and practical support.

Conrad also warns against offering books on grief, against suggesting the bereaved person seek counselling and against any overt religious assumptions about death and the afterlife. Clichés that suggest it was part of a larger pattern, that it was God's will, or that time is a great healer are particularly hurtful and unhelpful.

Helping say goodbye

The accounts given by parents of things that helped them show the importance of being able to exercise control over the body of their dead child and over the ceremony and events surrounding the burial or cremation. In one case, a mother whose eldest daughter died at the age of 21 said she knew how to get it right 'this time' as she had, 17 years earlier had to cope with the death of her 12-week-old baby.

Because of the suddenness, the confusion of activities and emotions, and the unfamiliar protocols of hospitals, funeral directors, clergy and legal systems, parents and siblings can all too easily feel unable to exert control until long after the body of their child has been disposed of. Yet, for those who have been encouraged to take control and who have had time to think about what their child might have themselves wanted, the funeral and memorial services can provide a valuable part of the process Walter (1996) describes as 'writing the last chapter'. Raphael (1994) suggests that the funeral, and the practical necessities of its arrangement mark a turning point in facing up to the truth that a child or brother or sister is actually dead. Hence the importance of thinking carefully before excluding anyone in the family either from contributing to the arrangements or from attending the funeral (Lauer et al. 1985). As a social ceremony, it publicly marks the shift of status, both of the deceased and of the bereaved person. The irrevocable consequences the death will have for individual family members may become more comprehensible during the funeral. Simply having to deal with being among others, of having to find words to deal with other's expressions of condolence and grief, of having to remember past events and of having to consider returning home to a world from which their child's body has now gone, creates greater comprehension that their social role and identity, whether they want it or not, has shifted fundamentally from where it was. It is at this point, in the weeks and months following the funeral, that close friends are most needed and yet, according to the evidence, when they are most likely to withdraw their support.

At the same time, the funeral may also provide an opportunity for individual family members to recognize that other people too had great affection for the child they have lost. One parent said of the letters of condolence she had received,

> I didn't want sympathy or religious clichés. The letters that I found most comforting were those that showed me how much *they* missed her – how deeply they were grieving as well as me. I knew she was special, but I wanted everyone else to know it too.

The day on which the child is buried or cremated is a special day and an important part of the immediate aftermath of bereavement. It can foreshadow later appreciation of the legacy of warm memories the child has left behind. Comments from the dead child's friends, from their teachers or from others that knew and loved them, specially chosen music or remembered stories that capture their particular character traits can all contribute to an occasion in which the value and significance of the life that was lived is marked and remembered later with fondness. The planting of trees, the setting of memorial benches and other physical markers, contributions to significant charities and the sharing of stories that celebrate aspects of the deceased life can all add to parents' and siblings' recognition of the impact their loved one had on the lives of others.

Hence, the roles of friends, as well as those of funeral director, minister or officiant in a non-religious committal, are central to making this day worthy of the child's memory. The importance of prior experience cannot be emphasized sufficiently. Experience is a great teacher, but it may be too late when bereaved family members look back and wished they had done it differently. The help of other bereaved parents in such cases might be vital, and one mother learned much from the friend she gained when both were caring for their sons in an oncology unit, but whose son died ten months before her own. Equally, the knowledge and confidence of a minister or an experienced officiant capable of putting a congregation at their ease in the light of previous knowledge of the cathartic potential of funeral ceremonies can transform a dreaded and bleak event into part of the story of a valued life. Conrad (1998) speaks of the horror of the burial or of the cremation and urges close friends to give voice to their own spontaneous memories during or after the ceremony. Such immediate expressions of love and affection for the deceased help symbolize that the life was far more than this moment of the committal of the deceased's body. The story of the life can merge with the mythology of the funeral. One teenager's coffin was notable for its total absence of flowers. It disappeared behind the curtains of the crematorium with nothing on it except this music lover's well-strummed guitar, accompanied by his favourite heavy rock track belting out at a volume he would have approved of. Friends and parents still talk about this service and how he would have approved of it even ten years later.

Case example 6.3

A bereavement support worker recently gave an account of a 3-year-old child's funeral she had recently attended. The little girl, like many her age, had loved the 'Teletubbies' – a popular British children's television programme. The whole funeral had their theme running through it, with Teletubby figures decorating the tiny coffin, wreaths and cards in the shape of Teletubbies and even the music from the series being played during the ceremony. It was reported as a very informal gathering with a mixture of traditional religion and modern pop culture. In spite of this description, the worker reported how moving and effective this service had been, allowing other young children and their parents to become fully involved and contribute spontaneous memories of the little girl's life and loves. Part of the lasting 'mythology' of her life had already become the retelling of the story of the minister's resignation to the Teletubbies 'taking over' of what might otherwise have been a fairly conventional and sombre event.

Another part of saying goodbye that needs the support of someone with either insight or experience is the question of disposing of clothes and possessions belonging to the deceased. Conrad (1998) stresses the regret some parents and siblings later feel if they attempt a 'clean sweep' of everything that was owned by the deceased. The importance of these linking objects, and the role they play in helping transform the relationship with a living person into a meaningful connection with the deceased is vital. The hole left by the child's absence can be so tangible, so literally experienced by some parents or close siblings as a missing part of their own bodies, that cuddling toys, teddies and clothes, lying in their beds, sitting in their rooms among their things can all offer some form of temporary comfort. How temporary this is depends enormously on circumstances, but any supporter must remember that time in many cases may be measured in years rather than months. Considerable thought should be given to conventional reactions to this apparent failure to 'let go'. Barely touched bedrooms should not be dismissed merely as a symptom of pathological 'sanctification' of the deceased. Such familiar objects may be playing an essential role in helping bereaved parents hold on and gradually transform a vital relationship with the memory of their child.

Most hospitals have recognized the importance of taking photographs of miscarried or still-born babies, of keeping locks of their hair and clippings from their nails, and of helping parents appreciate that one day these pieces of evidence may become cherished touchstones of the short life they shared. The so-called 'treasure box' may be all that is available compared with the many possessions an older child might have had, but in many cases organizing photographs and other markers of the infant's existence helps reconstruct both their short lives and their possible futures in the bereaved person's memory (Lovell 1983; Riches and Dawson 1998a).

Case example 6.4

One mother kept a diary of her experiences throughout her pregnancy, buried her stillborn twins in a cemetery within a short walking distance of her home, planted two roses in their memory, and desperately wanted to show someone the photographs taken of them with her and her husband. Because they did not look like full-term babies she was hesitant to offer them to friends, and she felt her husband was embarrassed by her need to talk about them, as they had not lived. The role of the hospital chaplain, and of others who expressed a desire, not only to see the photographs, but to hear about all her experiences with these unborn twins, was crucial in confirming the brief motherhood she achieved. Such markers of a life, no matter how short, can, in time, be used as a source of comfort rather than of distress. Here, the work of the experienced or insightful helper, who neither forces reluctant parents to look into possible regrets nor passes over opportunities to unobtrusively collect and later share keepsakes of the baby's physical existence may be of enormous value when parents begin to look back and wish they had something more substantial to remind them of their baby.

Helping after the funeral and beyond

Newly bereaved parents often express the paradox of needing to share their sense of loss with others yet feeling almost totally inhibited from doing so. Klass *et al.* (1996) argue that bereaved parents care deeply about what others feel about the death of their child, needing desperately to know that they too are deeply moved by their own sense of loss. Yet in modern societies there is a wall of reserve and social etiquette reducing opportunities to authentically demonstrate this, and a genuine anxiety over not knowing what to say or how to respond, even among those qualified to do so (Kirchberg 1998).

Not having to explain

Hence, the fundamental need for proactive empathy – for friends and professional helpers alike to reach out to bereaved parents and siblings in an effort to communicate their appreciation of the unique distress parents and siblings are experiencing. This is not the same as saying directly that you understand how they feel – that would be impossible and is guaranteed to anger bereaved parents. But helpers' own expressions of grief and their gentle insights into how routines, family relationships and personal coping are disrupted, can illustrate that there is no requirement on the bereaved person to explain their complex feelings of loss and hopelessness. This openness to bereaved people's feelings is a major step towards being 'in there with them, rather than on the touchline, shouting instructions'. As the bereaved mother of a disabled infant who lived for 40 weeks before his death writes, it seems crucial that others know how easily hurt she could be, but how difficult it was to tell them:

> During that period of not knowing whether I wanted to tell other people or not [immediately after the funeral], I almost longed to wear a black armband just as an outward symbol of my inner fragility. I wanted people to know without having to tell them. When people don't know, you fear the comment, the joke, the association you know will strike a chord in you when you are unprepared, a chord of which you cannot control the vibrations. Memories suddenly forced on me, that took me unawares, would make me break. There was a particular Fats Domino song which I used to dance to with Will in my arms. I would dance to the rhythm and at the chorus 'You left me reeling and rocking' I would begin to rock him quite violently and he would always burst into laughter. One day I heard it on the radio. I could not control my reaction. It was the same with many other things. On the other hand, emotionally prepared, I could remember many things about Will in calm.
>
> (Boston 1981: 97)

One of the most thoughtful and affirming gestures a good friend can make is to never forget the child that died, and to recognize the need of many parents and siblings to have others remember them and initiate conversations about them. To remember both their lives and their death involves being conscious of key anniversaries and of the times of the year – Christmas for example – when their grief may be at its most acute and yet most likely to be overlooked by the 'festive' comments of others. One bereaved mother commented:

> I am always touched by a card on the anniversary of his death. Old friends remember how awful that time of year is for me . . . and remembering his birthdays. Autumn and winter are a terrible time of year. Christmas isn't a bundle of fun, and we don't want to be under pressure to put on a brave face.

Being stuck

We argued in the last chapter that long-term social isolation, inability to get beyond the event of the death, overwhelming feelings of despair and a sense of pointlessness all characterize an inability to comprehend and make the necessary adjustments for coping with the death of a child. Deits (1992) sums up the symptoms of this particular perspective in which the enormity of grief renders the bereaved person powerless to identify either personal or social resources that might help them move towards a view of self that can accommodate the loss:

- persistent thoughts of suicide that appear to be getting more specific over time rather than passing;
- self-neglect to the extent that basic survival tasks remain undone;
- avoidance of all social contact including withdrawal from other close family members;
- emergence of a recurrent pattern of one particularly intense response to grief such as unremitting depression or inability to recognize that the deceased can never return;
- the emergence of patterns of behaviour that clearly lead to serious self-harm such as alcohol or drug abuse;
- feelings of losing touch with reality are common, but the growth of long-term persistent fear of insanity, recurrent high levels of anxiety or panic attacks, invasive vivid flashbacks, unwanted hallucinations, and failure of basic bodily functions are all causes of concern and suggest referral for specialized help.

Each of the above symptoms has been identified by many of the parents we have interviewed as common responses during the aftermath of their bereavement. Deits suggests that it is the persistence and the exclusiveness of these symptoms that should alert the helper to the need for more specialist support.

We have argued throughout this book that being stuck in this particular perspective may be as much the consequence of social and cultural factors as it is of an individual's particular psychological make-up. Certainly, in addition to referring on to more specialist help, it is important to examine how the rest of the family is dealing with the grief, and the extent to which the bereaved person's own sense of identity is bound up with their relationship with the deceased. It is also vital to examine the degree to which the causes of the death and the events leading up to it have been explored with others who shared it or who have knowledge of the more general circumstances in which it might be better understood.

Acknowledging grief – the helper as 'witness'

At the same time, there are practical measures that the bereaved person can be encouraged to undertake, which may not yet have been considered. The first of these is the degree to which someone who appears 'stuck' has actually been allowed to share the detailed events of the death and previous life of their child with anyone else. We have been continually surprised by the lack of opportunities afforded bereaved parents – and siblings even less – to systematically describe what they have been through. This process of externalizing events, putting in the detail of what has happened rather than how they feel about it, is the first but often crucial stage in creating the reality of the loss. One bereaved mother, critical of so many 'helpers' who tried to get her to let go of her guilt, said gratefully of a friend who listened fully without ever interrupting or attempting to help her feel better: 'I felt completely and utterly validated. She didn't make it feel any less meaningless. But she helped me connect it . . . helped it go somewhere.'

We have been contacted by friends who express their anxiety about parents who 'still insist on talking about nothing but their child's death – even two years after it has happened'. Our view is that two years appears to be nothing in the lifetime of bereaved parents. Their needs to continually repeat and rehearse the events of the death, feelings of blame and regret, their own part in its aftermath, problems they have subsequently encountered with other people's responses and so on, should all be respected and met. This should be undertaken, not with a sense of resignation and professional patience, but with an active desire to really understand the size of the problem they are facing in translating their old stable predictable world into this new one without the child or sibling that gave it meaning. Here, the helper fulfils the role of 'witness'. Such listeners help not so much in how they respond, but in how prepared they appear to 'take the bereaved person's story' (Brannen 1993). To hear it, to acknowledge it, to care about it and to reflect its profound implications may be one of the most obvious forms of help the bereaved person can receive in terms of enabling them to shift from a position of incomprehension and social exclusion to the beginnings of acceptance and social connectedness (Riches and Dawson 1996b).

This role of witness is particularly important among bereaved family members who have real problems in verbalizing their feelings and thoughts. Neither children nor people with learning difficulties may possess concepts that enable them to process their feelings, or the language to ask for help in doing so. Providing alternative channels of exploration and communication through art, music and play is therefore essential in such circumstances (Gersie 1991; James 1995).

Sharing perceptions of grief – helper as 'mediator'

In close combination with this first witnessing activity, a close friend or professional helper should examine the grief orientations of other family members. In our own study, parents whose partners adopted very different strategies for coping often felt it was their husbands or wives who had withdrawn their support, not they who had chosen to feel excluded. Partners who threw themselves into work, into fund-raising or into any activity that took them out of the house and away from sharing their feelings appeared to add to their partner's sense of isolation and worthlessness. Similarly, parents who control their emotions for the sake of their surviving children may give the mistaken impression that they have cut themselves off, or actually do not miss the dead child, therefore unwittingly modelling a response that hides their feelings. In these cases, the helper needs to distinguish between expressing feelings and 'breaking down', allowing children into the parent's anger and sadness without the fear such conversations will inevitably lead to the parent's greater distress (DeMaso et al. 1997).

The mediation skills needed to repair deteriorating relationships may only be possessed by a professional counsellor and such uncomfortable insights may only be acceptable from a close personal friend. However, helpers who do not possess these abilities may nevertheless be in a position to organize such support. Close knowledge of the family's network is essential if a friend is to be involved, and successful facilitation of misunderstanding between partners or parents and children has to be based on first hand access to each member's story. Opportunities to rehearse and rewrite personal narratives are crucial if the family as a whole is to 're-edit' its mythology to take account of the death and their own continuing lives together (Nadeau 1998; Byng-Hall 1998).

The contribution self-help groups can make in sharing perceptions of 'complicated' grief should not be overlooked. Clark and Goldney (1995) note how family members bereaved through suicide felt less stigmatized when they were able to share their experiences with others in the same situation. Those 'further down the line' offered models of successful coping, and their insights helped newly bereaved feel less alone.

Maintaining social relationships – helping (re)connect

Even in the absence of progress towards improving understanding between individual family members – and it may take considerable time before they recognize that they need help here (Helmrath and Steinitz 1978) – encouraging the bereaved person to re-engage in other old relationships – or in new relationships – may serve to help them comprehend and endure their bereavement in a more social and externalized way.

Pre-existing friendships are among the most obvious to explore, especially if they appear to have deteriorated since the death. In similar ways to the misunderstandings that arise between partners, friends can easily be hurt or feel they are intruding when, in fact, their own inability to cope is reinforced by their friend's apparent indifference to them. The comment that they must therefore, by definition, not have been 'true' friends is one that may all too easily be accepted by the bereaved person themselves, but it demonstrates an idealistic view of friendship. Given the problems partners and children have with each other during grief, it would be surprising if friends did not also need help sometimes in overcoming the awkwardness and misunderstanding that bereavement can cause.

New relationships with individuals who want to listen, and who have the skill to encourage bereaved people to share their stories, may take the form of professionally trained volunteers, bereavement counsellors, hospital social workers or ministers. Referral to many of the self-help groups who have themselves had to accept and endure their children's deaths has, in our experience, also stimulated close and lasting individual relationships independently of any activities laid on by the group itself.

Case example 6.5

When we first interviewed Diane and Robert, two years after their only adult son had been killed in a road traffic accident, they both appeared stuck – very depressed, with little outside contact and with Robert unable to return to work. They had been to one group meeting with The Compassionate Friends (TCF) but felt 'it wasn't for them'. Only one other couple had lost an only child, and the others 'just seemed to be different . . . they didn't understand . . .' However, during the following two years they kept up their contact with this one couple, starting with visits to each other's homes, progressing to eating out and, finally, taking a foreign holiday together. Robert acknowledged that finally, at times, they could talk about other things beside their dead children and that they even managed to 'have a laugh' sometimes. This deep insight each couple had of the other's experience, and the lack of need they both had to explain themselves provided a unique support system for returning to some 'everyday' relationship patterns that provided an outlet for their need to talk of their children while at the same time presenting a future that could be structured with some sense of purpose. Robert had returned to TCF and, though still very depressed, was increasingly acting as a supporter of more recently bereaved couples.

It is also important to note that not all bereaved parents or siblings find this kind of support helpful. Reif *et al.* (1995) argue that attempts to offer social support too early following the death could be seen by some as intrusive, and that individuals who did not perceive their support network as helpful were unlikely to be able to share their feelings openly.

Doing something – helping structure time

According to Tedeschi and Calhoun (1995), helpers can begin to shift individuals who appear stuck by encouraging them to identify and set small specific goals to deal with their sense of despair and isolation. Part of this strategy arises from the view that temporarily avoiding grief, or gaining permission to take time off from it, may be very beneficial (Bonanno *et al.* 1995; Stroebe and Schut 1995; Klein 1998). This may be taken literally; both Boston (1981) and Klein (1988) note the benefits of taking a brief time out from the home that carries so many reminders of everyday losses. They also illustrate how finding a calm place where no one is likely to intrude may help them break through habitual patterns of remembering only the death into glimpses of warmer memories of the life they lived together.

Identifying small goals relating to the lost child might be a valuable first step. Writing letters to friends and relatives who sent flowers, helping with the establishment of some sort of memorial and, later, going through and labelling photographs, obtaining school work and cleaning the house or the child's room might all be short-term goals that fill time in ways linked to the deceased.

Inaction, deep introspection and loss of control of thoughts can lead to increasing belief in personal inadequacy. Physical activity has often been recognized as a response – spring cleaning, redecorating, gardening – that reconnects bereaved people with a purpose and helps re-establish a routine. Hence, among the simple goals offered, physical exercise of some sort – maybe only walking – that reminds bereaved people of their own needs to take care of themselves, can be both a diversion and a reconnection with bodily experiences that were familiar before their loss. In our own research, we have discovered bereaved parents who searched out the places their children used to go in order to walk 'in their footsteps' for a little while – so helping them remember the times before their deaths, as well as helping them come to accept the reality of their dying (Riches and Dawson 1998a).

Small goals can lead to much larger ones. Two women whose children both died in tragically difficult circumstances set up a support group for their local area. One of them explained how such concrete actions helped:

> We had to find a new way of being a family . . . of finding a new way of 'doing life'. I don't believe he is anywhere now. He's dead and nothing can ever bring him back. I can't ever have the world I thought I was in . . . that John was in. But in setting up this group I am starting to build a world that's got some connection with him. Nothing will ever make sense of his death, but doing this helps make sense of me going on living.

Identifying personal resources – helping to live with the loss

Tedeschi and Calhoun (1995) suggest significant benefits can be gained if traumatized individuals can reframe their experience of helplessness and victimization as a challenge to be met and overcome rather than a sentence to be served. It is this element of personal resilience that Hogan and DeSantis

(1996) identified in siblings who adjusted most successfully to their bereavement, and that Braun and Berg (1994) found in parents who were most able to cope with their child's death. For those parents we interviewed who already belonged to communities that knew, loved and mourned their child, and that shared strong religious beliefs about the destination of his or her spirit, it was the concrete everyday connections with neighbours, friends and extended family that reinforced a model of the world that helped them live with the death.

This positive world view presented bereavement as a challenge that could be survived, naturally integrating their loss across the community as a whole, ensuring that everyday contacts celebrated memories of the child and that weekly services reinforced her place in a collectively held world view. In contrast, a secular version of this challenge could be found in a mother who signed up for a psychology course two months after her son died, saying that she knew if she did not do something, she would 'go mad'. This course led to a full-time undergraduate programme that offered many rational and scientific models through which she could begin to understand her own experiences and reactions. In both cases, it was the routines of everyday life that acted both as a social support and as a mirror reflecting back to them their capacity to survive even in the face of their children's death.

Bigger levers – things that help shift perspectives

As previously noted in Chapter 1, Marwit and Klass (1995) suggest that, over time, the dead can be discovered, still connected to the living and playing a number of positive roles in the inner landscapes of surviving family members:

- as a role model;
- as a symbol of certain worthwhile attitudes and opinions through which the bereaved person's own values could be clarified;
- as a guide and spiritual support in times of trouble;
- as a significant and valued part of the bereaved person's own life story.

Klass, Silverman and Nickman (1996) argue that a major problem some bereaved parents initially experience is not so much denial of the death, as disassociation from those elements of it that cause pain. So, although remembering and sharing stories about the deceased is vital for accepting the reality of their death, parents may be reluctant to do so because of their fear that they cannot endure the distress it produces. Indeed the glimpses of warmer memories of the life lived together may initially be so unbearable that focusing on the death helps protect parents or siblings from the final accounting of the value of what has been lost.

Hence, help in reinterpreting the experience of a loved one's death and making sense of the impact such a loss has had on self and family may be a crucial part of longer-term adjustment. Finding ways of more comfortably recollecting their past lives and discovering their ongoing influence is a part of this reinterpretation. Information that helps restructure the meaning of death and that offers ways of understanding how others cope in similar situations is valuable. Talbot (1997) refers to 'logotherapy' – or therapy through meaning – as central in helping bereaved mothers come to terms with the death of their only children. Huber and Bryant (1996) offer a simple model of a ten-mile mourning bridge that metaphorically represents the distances parents come to see themselves as having to 'travel' during the years following their bereavement.

Helping rehearse less painful remembering

Support in finding ways to share these stories becomes crucial in helping parents comprehend the events surrounding the death, for enduring its pain and for eventually finding a place in their everyday lives for the presence of their dead child. Adjustment therefore involves not simply facing the reality of their bereavement, it includes a more positive shift in their perception of the dead and the valuable part they play in their thoughts and behaviour.

Case example 6.6

Roger agreed to be interviewed as part of our research three months after their 15-year-old daughter had contracted a respiratory illness and died unexpectedly within a few weeks of being taken into hospital. When we arrived, Roger said that Joan – his wife – was still too upset to join in but would remain in the room while we did the interview. She appeared to be watching television, but as the interview moved away from the events surrounding their daughter's death and Roger got out the photographs and her school reports, Joan turned down the television and began to join in. Both parents talked for over two hours, not about her death, but about their walks together in the hills, about her talent in the school band, about her teacher's comments about her work, about her conscientiousness and about her earlier life – details of her babyhood, infancy, growing up and friendships. The interview, though not intended to be therapeutic, appeared to have allowed both parents the chance to talk to each other and to an 'outsider' in ways that Roger had felt they had not done before.

A significant milestone in adjustment is accomplished, therefore, for some bereaved parents and siblings when they recognize that their child continues to affect their own lives in positive ways. This insight may be a long time coming, and its subtle voice may have been drowned out by the weight of negative consequences that have arisen from the death. Rubin (1984) suggests that this turning point is only possible after the death itself is accepted as a real and non-negotiable event. This milestone is marked when remembering the dead becomes a source of warmth and pleasure rather than a cause of stress and emotional pain (Walter 1996). From our research we would suggest that it may take a long while for bereaved parents to pass this milestone, and that some may never reach it.

Keeping an open mind – signs, dreams and strange comfort

Searching for the deceased is recognized as part of the difficulties bereaved people have in accepting the fact of the death. At another level, this behaviour can also be interpreted as anxiety about how and where the lost child is. One bereavement worker told the story of a mother who sent her baby's blanket to the mortuary because, although she knew she was dead, she still worried about her being cold 'in that place'. Another mother said that her daughter's absence struck her so intensely that, 'the emptiness itself had become a presence'.

In a greater number of cases than we would have predicted before we began our research, primarily among bereaved mothers, dreams, 'signs' or clairvoyant messages appeared to provide some comfort in reducing anxiety over this absent presence (Rogers and Man 1990). One mother's account described weeks of sleeplessness punctuated briefly by vivid nightmares of the graveyard where her daughter was buried. However, when we interviewed her many years later, she still was able to recall the night the same dream began, but her daughter came to her, carrying a lantern and telling her to stop worrying so much, that she was with her grandma, was quite happy and would be waiting for her mother when her time came to die. Another mother whose young son died from a brain tumour visited a clairvoyant and, though very sceptical beforehand, told us that she felt 'as though a huge weight had been lifted from my shoulders'. She did not visit this clairvoyant again and was, in all respects, a highly intelligent rational, educated woman. Yet she described how this message from 'the other side' included details of a special story shared with her son that she felt could not possibly have been known to anyone else. Again, this incident was remembered as a turning point in reducing the sense of utter desperation she had felt.

Berger (1995) as a result of investigating a number of similar incidents, calls for an open mind from helpers encountering such 'paranormal' phenomena. Fear of stigmatization clearly prevented many parents from sharing these experiences, yet Berger recognizes the comfort gained through finding a 'place' for the deceased to inhabit. This sense of presence, rather than being discounted as mere hallucination, may be a valuable strategy some bereaved parents and siblings use to cope with a world that lacks the physical presence of the deceased (Hogan and de DeSantis 1994). Similarly, Wiener *et al.* (1996) found a majority of the bereaved mothers they interviewed had dreamed of their children, heard their voices or smelled flowers or other evocative scents associated with their life. Discourses about bereaved people's vulnerable mental states are common and no doubt have a foundation in attempts by certain organizations to exploit grieving parents. However, we, along with Berger found contrary evidence that dreams, visions, spiritual messages or other signs of the deceased's presence appeared to contribute, in some cases, to greater acceptance of the death and to a lessening of psychological distress. Wiener *et al.* (1996) argue that these experiences are often overlooked, and suggest that they play a significant role for many parents in helping them remember the life that was lived rather than being a symptom of their fixation with the death. They recommend that professional helpers should enquire about these experiences, validating parents who have them and encouraging their retelling in detail.

Helping discover that the dead are significant others

Following the turmoil of loss, the deceased may be discovered still occupying a highly influential place in the mental landscape of bereaved parents and siblings. Rather than this simply being perceived as a temporary defence mechanism, or as an unhealthy idealization of the deceased, appreciating that the dead child can influence parents and siblings is sociologically no different from acknowledging the continuing influence of dead parents on the attitudes and behaviours of their living adult children. Seeing self and aspects of the world through the eyes of the deceased may clarify thoughts and help the bereaved person deal with unfinished business (Stroebe *et al.* 1992).

Kaplan (1995) argues that 'social ghosts' can often play a positive role in repairing personal identity, in providing models for action, in supporting personal values and in enhancing self-esteem and self-confidence. He describes the 'internal dialogue' one bereaved father had with his dead adult daughter (Kaplan 1995: 126). On one particular day he recalled seeing Amy's teddy bear looking back at himself and his wife when he experienced a vivid shift in perspective. In a memorable flash of insight he discovered the fact that Amy had played a key role in their lives both before and after her death. His obsession with the manner of her dying subsided and he thereafter began to recognize the countless impacts her life had had on theirs. This bear was not just a baby's toy, it was also her favourite object at 19, and might have been the gift she would have given to her own daughter had she lived. The teddy bear became a symbol of her influence on him and on his world, eventually enabling both he and his wife to share and live out some of the opinions and aspirations Amy epitomized in the years she was alive.

Klass (1996b) similarly recounts stories of how memories of children's strength of character and special relationships with their parents can directly affect their lives. For example, one father ran a five-kilometre race two weeks after his daughter was killed in an accident. He wore the number she had been allocated in the same race because of her encouragement for him to take up running. Another father overcame a long-term drinking problem because of the disapproval he knew his daughter had felt at his behaviour. Support that helps parents discover the lasting influence their children have had on them, that helps them momentarily forget the loss and remember the good times they shared, that helps them appreciate the strengths they possess as a result of being the mother, father, sister or brother of the deceased child, can help them bridge the chaos of their bereavement and reconnect with happier memories of the deceased.

Story making in communities of bereaved people

Acknowledging the influence that the dead exert does not necessarily remain at a private, internal level, nor only at the level of shared family remembrances. Klass *et al.* (1996) demonstrate some of the ways that bereaved parents continue to develop their relationships with dead children through joining bereavement self-help groups. Their research illustrates how the relationships they establish within such groups appear to provide some parents with substantial support in transforming their initial sense of despair over their lost relationship into a more lasting and positive inner representation of the child with which they can continue to interact.

Other members of the group appear to provide an extension of the relationship they had with their child. Opportunities to regularly have conversations *about* them come to replace lost chances of talking directly *to* them. The new relationships in which pride and affection for a lost child or brother or sister can be shared is somehow imbued with these same sentiments. In our experience, these shared stories range across every aspect of the bereaved person's experience, including marital problems, difficulties fathers have in expressing their feelings, the lack of support many feel from the 'normal' non-bereaved world, their experiences with clairvoyants, their use of their children's possessions to hold on to their presence, their dreams of their children and their nightmares about their deaths.

Klass notes that during the 'transformation' of this relationship with their child, emotional pain is very gradually exchanged for clearer, more comforting inner representations. A central principle of The Compassionate Friends is to encourage their members to identify less with the distress and hopelessness of the death, and more with the energy and love that was in their living child. Klass includes the following comment from one bereaved father: 'If the price I pay for loving Douglas is the pain and sorrow I now have, I still think I got a bargain to have had him for thirteen years' (Klass 1996b: 208).

Further distinct benefits can arise from membership of self-help groups, which illustrate how these particular social contacts may help in successful adjustment. Tedeschi and Calhoun (1995) note that opportunities to help others can be very therapeutic for bereaved people themselves. Videker-Sherman (1982) described this as the 'helper-therapy' principle, and argued that, for some parents, the very effort of putting their own feelings aside as they worked to support more recently bereaved people helped them appreciate just how far they had travelled in coming to terms with their own losses. At the same time, the more recently bereaved were provided with role models of others who were 'further down the line' than themselves, and received some reassurance that it was possible to survive (Videka-Sherman and Lieberman 1985). Ball et al. (1996) found parents of children receiving treatment for life-threatening illness gained considerably from the 'culture' of patients, relatives and hospital staff that exists within the treatment regimes of oncology units.

Often overlooked, is the benefit of these groups in supporting the sometimes dramatic differences in the ways men and women handle their feelings. One mother said of the ward her child was on: 'the mothers are all in the kitchen, talking like mad. I made some wonderful friends while John (her son) was in there. The men . . . they just used to hang about in the ward looking uncomfortable.' There is a space for these 'uncomfortable men' in self-help groups, often as chauffeurs initially, who sit on the fringes but who later are encouraged to help organize events, make the tea and join in with discussions. At the annual conferences of The Compassionate Friends formal speakers and informal friendship groups each contribute to opportunities for fathers to find other men with similar problems of emotional expression, for mothers to find others to complain to about their husbands, for the more experienced parents to help support the less experienced, and for dead children to be cried over and spoken about proudly, in detail and at length. The entire wall of their main conference hall is covered with photographs, newspaper cuttings, poems and other mementoes of their children's lives. Considerable evidence now exists that the relationships within these groups offer some parents the opportunity to explore possible meanings behind their own bereavement, and to find some purpose in their own lives (Wheeler 1993; Klass 1996b).

A final, and not insubstantial, contribution that this form of support highlights is the role of laughter. Tedeschi and Calhoun (1995) recognize the value of humour in dealing with adjustment to traumatic experiences, and many others – Kaplan (1995), Klass et al. (1996) and Walter (1996) – each identify the significance of being able to remember the dead with warmth rather than distress. One couple in our first interview said they felt they would never laugh again, yet, two years later acknowledged that within The Compassionate Friends they felt at liberty to sometimes 'have a laugh' because 'everyone else is in the same boat. No one ever forgets why we are here'. Where humour in the culture of everyday life may appear insensitive or disrespectful of the dead, in a culture of bereavement it has greater legitimacy – and a greater degree of privacy. Learning to remember aspects of the deceased's life that were funny, and sharing them with other family members and with fellow bereaved parents and siblings may be an important part of transforming relationships both with the dead and with the living.

Some parents who are reluctant to join such self-help groups claim, nevertheless, to benefit from their newsletters and publications. Merrington (1995) and Mirren (1995) have written very personal accounts of parents struggling to survive their children's deaths. These insights range from the deaths of infants through to the deaths of adult children, and their stories offer evidence to other newly bereaved parents that they are not alone and the feelings they are experiencing are suffered by others. Benefits also accrue to the writers of these stories. These publications become a part of the authors' biographies of their children's lives, fixing their memories in print and allowing others to discuss them and therefore get to know them, even in their absence.

Summary

The previous points may be summarized in terms of four basic principles. A flexible approach to the assessment and planning of bereavement support, and effective work with bereaved parents and siblings in late modern societies should demonstrate them.

Respect for cultural diversity

Sensitivity to alternative ways of perceiving and interpreting death, of alternative beliefs about the destination of the deceased, and of alternative approaches to the relationship between the living and the dead is essential in a late or 'post-modern' society. This principle of cultural relativity necessarily includes and respects the existence of particular cultural absolutes among the varied religious, ethnic and individualistic points of view that make up western cultures. Some of these will differ from, and maybe challenge, the beliefs of the helper, who should separate out any personally held 'absolute' beliefs from potentially conflicting ones held by the parents or siblings he or she is attempting to help.

Respect for ways of talking and for ways of keeping silent

Acceptance of the value of talk as a vehicle for reconciling inner mental representations with external realities must be balanced against the need to respect the feelings held within certain cultures that such 'private' experiences should not be shared with outsiders. In addition, there are ways of communicating other than through conversation, and methods that match the age, gender, cultural background and religious beliefs of the bereaved person should be fully explored and utilized. Any language used must be grounded within the cultural experiences of the bereaved person (Lewis and Schonfeld 1994). For example, the value of publishing 'poetry' in newsletters for bereavement self-help groups is sometimes criticized for its sentimentality, yet many members find this form of expression easier to identify with than more 'intellectual' articles. Similarly, younger children may find play, drawing or story telling far more effective in representing their experiences than direct conversation – especially with an adult.

Respect for individual coping strategies

Helpers must accept that they will encounter a wide range of feelings, emotions and beliefs in bereaved people and that empirical evidence is at best ambiguous when identifying which of these is likely to be the most 'healthy' in terms of grief resolution. This principle also acknowledges that the majority of people survive bereavement largely through their own efforts with little if any 'intervention' from trained professionals.

Respect for the reality of local social worlds

Helpers should recognize that most bereaved parents and siblings continue to live out their lives within existing social settings. The influence of already established patterns of communication within family, neighbourhood and occupational networks needs to be identified and explored. It is easy to overestimate the impact that one-to-one bereavement support might achieve and to overlook the resilience of social systems to individual change. It might be especially important to explore the shifting dynamics of marital, family and occupational relationships before the bereavement occurred and to appreciate the influence of these established patterns on how each family member sees themselves and the rest of the family.

7 | Conclusion: professional support in a post-modern world

Introduction

One bereaved mother who trained and practised as a counsellor before her adult son died summed up a view expressed by many of the parents we interviewed:

> I know they say nothing can be as bad as your son dying, but some of the things people say are really hurtful. With friends . . . I guess they mean well . . . trying to help . . . But counsellors . . . they should damn well know better.

The gap that some parents perceive between how they feel and the professional help they receive requires us to make the theoretical assumptions underlying our views of bereavement support explicit. This final chapter offers a few reflections on professional and volunteer bereavement support based on our reading and our many conversations with bereaved parents, bereaved siblings and with bereavement support workers.

The danger of simplified models of grief

This book has outlined and used a range of grief models in examining diverse experiences of grief in late-modern societies. We have explained why we believe that no one particular model is adequate to explain how individuals deal with grief across all cultures and circumstances. However, because bereavement counselling and one-to-one professional or volunteer support have a significant role to play both in direct support and in shaping beliefs and attitudes towards death and loss, we wish to stress again the need for a flexible and open-minded approach to the phenomenon of be-reavement and an eclectic use of grief models in understanding adjustment to loss. This model is supported both in the work of Coles (1989) and in a further response of the mother already quoted above:

> They've got to be willing to listen to you . . . You know, really *hear* what you are telling them. Not force you into any one way of being. Not trying to fit you into some schema of their own. They shouldn't have any fixed notions . . . they should be absolutely open to learning from you . . . you're the one that is going through it!

First and foremost, we are arguing that sensitivity to the diversity of beliefs held by bereaved people is a prerequisite of effective support. A supportive relationship must be based on familiarity with those cultural practices through which the bereaved person's experiences are made real (Stroebe *et al.* 1992). For help to be perceived as authentic and valuable, it must communicate respect for the bereaved person's own accounts of their experi-ences. To translate an insight from Basil Bernstein (1970) talking about good teaching: the consciousness of the bereaved person must first be in the mind of the helper before the consciousness of the helper can begin to enter the mind of the bereaved person. Really listening may involve forgetting preconceived notions about stages and trajectories, and it certainly must be unhooked from the 'need to make it better for them'. One bereaved mother we interviewed commented:

> I feel this so strongly . . . I could *kill*. When they use words like 'letting go' . . . they should be immediately struck off! When they ask me what I have done with his bedroom, there is the implication that I should have done something with it. I don't want to do anything with it . . . and I know they are sitting there thinking – 'oh oh . . . she can't let go'. I feel really guilty about John's death. Really, really guilty. I just want them to hear me feeling guilty. I want them to hear that I will always feel guilt for his death. I don't want them to explain to me why I shouldn't feel guilty . . .

Another bereaved mother whose teenage son took his own life read Chap-ter 4 of this book in draft form and disagreed with the suggestion that suffering could produce personal growth. She felt that absolutely nothing positive could be drawn from his death, and no meaning could ever be found that would enable her to make sense of it. Nadeau makes this same point, arguing that because some deaths can only ever be seen negatively 'a disservice is done to families when they are given the message that they should be able to find positive meaning and purpose in their lives no matter what the loss' (Nadeau 1998: 241).

Nadeau argues that counsellors who impose 'professional' models of grief may discourage bereaved people's own attempts to make meaning for themselves. More crucially, it may also prevent counsellors from seeing problems between family members in sharing sometimes hurtful differences of interpretation. Sinclair and McCluskey (1996) show how anxious and emotionally fragile behaviour in one family member inhibits the open expression of feelings by others. Complex differences in meanings between partners and between parents and surviving children may be totally overlooked in one-to-one counselling. Problems arising from these differences may be exaggerated if one family member finds a model of grief that reinforces his or her own interpretation and confirms the inadequacy of other family members' responses.

We have tried to show that bereavement counselling is one link in a chain of possible help that stretches from the 'natural' support of close-knit traditional communities through to specialist psychiatric treatment in clinical settings. Help that is perceived by bereaved people as 'expert' is one of a number of solutions to the problems they may face. Like Conrad (1998) we feel the term 'bereavement counselling' should be used with caution as it often carries negative connotations in the minds of many parents and siblings. Faith in such expertise varies enormously in modern plural societies. Some cultural and occupational groups are far more willing to explore the support that counselling offers than others.

Gentry and Goodwin (1995) argue that a major problem in post-modern society is the breakdown of supportive social networks and the increase in anonymity that accompanies it. Loss of community, the drifting apart of extended families, less secure employment, increasing divorce, single parenthood and living alone all contribute to bereaved people turning to what Gentry and Goodwin term 'commercial service providers'. Hence, while some may look to undertakers or freelance counsellors for the support they need, others may find talking to their hairdressers or bartenders a more natural source of personal support. In short, they will tell their stories to those with whom they feel comfortable:

> The most effective support tends to come from those who share a context of meaning ... rather than those with special training [...] well-intentioned statements can be seen as intrusive, especially when one person tries to help another find meaning in a loss.
>
> (Gentry and Goodwin 1995: 556)

We therefore believe that a post-modern approach to bereavement care must encompass a flexible, open-minded and multi-dimensional view of support. By considering the range of social and cultural contexts as well as individual factors, a balance can be struck between the varying 'professional' insights of clinical experience and the unique perspectives of bereaved parents and siblings. Anyone offering help should respect the view we have encountered many times in our research and practice – 'unless you have had to bury your own child you don't have a clue how I feel'.

The skills and knowledge of the 'professional' helper

In practice, the implications of such a flexible approach suggest that we should be open to the value and limitations of a variety of grief models within which a bereaved parent or sibling might come to understand the meaning of their loss. We should also recognize the power of social and cultural assumptions to create views of the world within which such models operate. How death is perceived, the degree of preparation undergone before it is experienced, its impact on the bereaved person's identity, the view of the relationship that he or she has lost and the subsequent turning points that mark adjustment into living without the deceased, are constrained and shaped by cultural values and available social contacts.

Hence, assessment of need and strategies for support have to take account of the operation of existing social networks and culturally specific views of the world. This may involve not only really listening to bereaved people themselves, but also to their family and friends, and to others who possess a deeper knowledge of their culture. The values and beliefs of the community – whether real, imagined or fragmented – within which they face the consequences of the death have to be understood, as does the language that shapes their thinking.

The role of the supporter may therefore be as much one of simply 'being there' and encouraging (maybe even of explaining and co-ordinating) existing help, or of referring the bereaved person on to other networks of support, as it is of direct bereavement 'counselling'. The quality of the relationship between bereaved and supporter, the willingness of both to learn from each other, and the intimacy of their communication may be key factors in ensuring that the support offered is perceived as helpful.

Appreciating the 'normality' of parental and sibling grief

Many researchers stress the enormous challenge to personal resilience that child and sibling bereavement produces. Emotional distress, lasting for many years, may not only be understandable, it may actually be quite 'normal'. Hence Rando (1991) identifies, and strongly argues against, a clinical tendency to 'pathologize' bereaved parents – especially mothers – by seeing lengthy or extreme grief symptoms as abnormal. She suggests that many of the problems these parents encounter are the consequence of living in a society that avoids the fact that children die regularly and in relatively substantial numbers. Paradoxically, being a bereaved brother or sister appears to attract far less clinical attention. In practice, it is more likely to be the mother than the father who is perceived as 'being stuck', yet her role in the joint renegotiation of marital, parental and sibling roles is crucial in determining the long-term adjustment of each family member. This is not helped by seeing the coping strategy of any one of them as 'abnormal'.

In post-modern societies the status of 'bereaved parent', 'bereaved brother' and 'bereaved sister' are at best seen as temporary, and are less publicly recognized than in more traditional cultures. Yet Rosenblatt (1996) suggests there is sufficient evidence to lay to rest the notion that parental grief ever ends or ever *should* end. Rando (1991) also stresses that grief for dead children may never be 'resolved' in the sense that the bereaved person may be incapable of ever fully returning to 'normal'. Rather, they may spend a great deal of time arriving at what has been referred to as a 'new kind of normal'. These new routines grow from a 'loss of innocence' that can never be regained (Layne 1996). Accommodating their experience of the fragility and brevity of all life may actually be more difficult because of mainstream culture's general avoidance of this insight. During our interviews, one bereaved father said:

> How can you ever get over it? It's like saying when your leg has been cut off, 'It will heal in time'. That's stupid. You may learn to live in a world where you've only got one leg. But you can never go back to walking about like people who've got two.

Mellor and Shilling (1993) have argued that in post-modern societies death has been 'written out' of the culture by isolating the elderly, hospitalizing the dying and creating the belief that medical science can extend our lives indefinitely. The deep and lasting distress felt by many bereaved parents and children contradicts this myth and while it may be inconvenient and even rather challenging to the majority who prefer to believe that everything lasts forever, their grief is neither unreasonable nor abnormal.

Facing death and the influence of the dead

The fact of our common mortality is one that effective bereavement supporters must face and come to terms with if they are to work alongside bereaved people, to appreciate the variety of ways in which they attempt to deal with the death of their loved ones and to genuinely help them write the story of their grief. This involves a strategic letting go of the cherished beliefs, routines and priorities, which we inevitably build to protect *our own selves* from the insight that, relatively speaking life is both short and fragile. To hear, validate and understand the struggle of others to make sense of the loss of familiar certainties and future dreams, we must ourselves be aware of our own dependence on certain fundamental assumptions about the nature and meaning of life and about what happens to us after it ends:

> When I consider the short duration of my life, swallowed up in eternity past and to come, the little space that I fill, and even can see, engulfed in the enormous immensity of spaces of which I am ignorant and which know me not, I am terrified, and am astonished at being here

rather than there; for there is no reason why here rather than there, why now rather than then.

(Bauman 1992: 18, quoting Pascal)

In the face of a child's death, Rando, along with Kaplan, Klass, Walter, Hogan and DeSantis, among many others whose work this book has drawn on, offer evidence that, in time, many bereaved parents and siblings come to believe that 'death ends a life, but it does not end a relationship' (Anderson, quoted by Klass *et al.* 1996: 17). When personal assumptions are tested in such a painful and concrete way, it should not be surprising that some parents and siblings, not unreasonably, find it impossible ever to come to terms with such a loss, while others find comfort in maintaining some kind of connection with the deceased throughout the remainder of their own lives. Whether this continuing bond is based on religious, paranormal, psychological or rational notions, such beliefs can be of enormous comfort to bereaved people. Hogan and DeSantis (1994) and Klass *et al.* (1996) present many examples of children and adults who still carry on internal dialogues with the deceased, as well as maintaining their presence within both family and in wider social relationships. Indeed, Hogan and DeSantis go as far as to suggest that long-term successful adjustment is more likely when siblings actually believe that one day they will be reunited with their brother or sister. At the same time, there is also evidence that other parents are clear that their child is gone, totally and irrevocably. They believe that death ends both the life and the relationship.

Whether possessing a religious, atheist or agnostic view, helpers should be open to their own prejudices about the nature of mortality, and to the varying ways others might or might not continue to use the dead to give meaning to their lives. Attempts by bereaved parents or siblings either to 'give up' or to 'hold on to' their loved ones should not, therefore, be seen as evidence of pathological behaviour preventing their successful adjustment.

Needs of professionals and volunteers

Time and again we have been brought up sharply by our own failure to fully reflect on the depth and endlessness of parents' and siblings' suffering. Our inability to sometimes grasp the emotional consequences of the blight that has come to their lives only serves to increase their sense of isolation. One bereaved mother who read the draft of Chapter 4 was gently critical of the notion of 'taking time off' from grieving, and expressed her frustration at the attempted support of other people:

There is nothing except the pain . . . . of knowing life is spoiled. Everything is spoiled. There is no joy, no excitement of looking forward to

Figure 7.1 One mother's perception of the long-term effects of bereavement

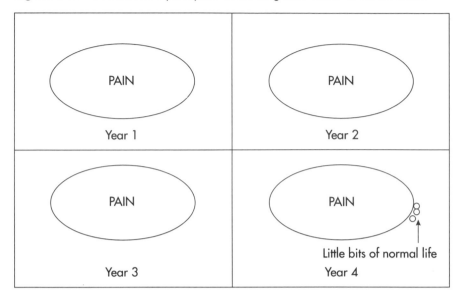

holidays ... People try to help, but everything they say just hurts. And I can't ignore it. I have to tell them. And they stop talking to me because they are afraid of upsetting me. Someone said, why don't you plant some bulbs by the side of the road where he was killed? I know that's a nice idea and lots of people do that. But they just don't know that I can't go near that place ... I still can't get rid of the images of him lying there ... in the road ...

To emphasize the point she drew her own diagram of her four years of grief (see Figure 7.1).

A therapist colleague of ours recently offered the following insight: 'The more you really hear what they are telling you, the more difficult and painful it is to keep listening.' Acting as a witness – providing a space for awful thoughts and experiences to find their way into words, helping bereaved parents and siblings by simply letting them know someone else hears what they are going through – is emotionally demanding. The personal cost of hearing and being with families who have a child with terminal illness, or who are enduring the consequences of their child's death may be easily underestimated.

Mahan and Calica (1997), for example, note that although professionals working with families suffering a perinatal death use their own unique emotional responses to help them work with bereaved people, such intimacy also has its dangers:

Repeated exposure to loss may not be emotionally healthy, particularly for persons whose personal losses were great, recent, or remain unresolved. Repeated exposure can lead to professional 'burnout', decreased sensitivity as a defence mechanism, or a skewed perspective about perinatal outcomes.

(Mahan and Calica 1997: 150)

Anyone offering help to bereaved parents or siblings will need their own support in coping with the emotions and images that their work elicits, yet all too frequently health care workers, members of the emergency services, social workers and counsellors come way down on anyone's list of those in need of care and understanding. Although supervision systems may exist, and individuals may be encouraged to seek support if they feel they require it, the professional culture of many organizations militates against acknowledging that these needs are central to maintaining a compassionate, open and sensitive service.

The benefits to such professionals of engaging in mutual support activities, whether they be supervision groups, interdisciplinary sharing of perceptions or residential conferences are stressed by Mahan and Calica. Indeed, our own experiences of these activities – both academic and professional – have mirrored what we have seen operating at conferences and support groups for bereaved parents. Relatively informal groups, with similar experiences and mutual interests, can be seen exploring events and emotions. People who in many cases had been strangers, achieve relationships of a depth and intensity that would be impossible in their everyday lives. Here, meaning-making in an accepting context is as valuable for professionals as it is for their 'clients'. This sharing of stresses, insecurities and new ideas contributes immensely to maintaining an open mind, independence from any one particular interpretive framework and a sense of emotional well-being. The ability to feel 'comfortable' with uncertainty, to accept limitations both to personal knowledge and to the capacity to help or put things right, and a willingness to keep learning – especially from bereaved people themselves – are central to professional practice in a post-modern world:

With the increasing diversity of cultures within the United States and other countries, there is a need to be receptive to alternative worldviews and to recognize there may be many different pathways to the resolution of grief [. . .] Clinicians can lessen the likelihood of intervening in ways that increase bereaved client's distress by reflecting on the assumptions about human behaviour they are using, determining if a different therapeutic approach will be more helpful when dissonance occurs, and continually checking with them to determine if they are experiencing the therapy as helpful.

(Corwin 1995: 40)

The bereavement supporter – explorer, guide or companion?

Hence, the model of professional support we offer sees the 'practitioner' as an explorer and companion rather than an expert. To be sure, some of the landscape the bereaved parent or sibling inhabits may seem familiar to us, and we may *think* the maps we already possess might help in guiding them through this territory. But it is *their* journey, not ours, that has to be travelled. Their social and cultural context directly affects their capacity to express or explore their bereavement with others – and with us. Indeed a sense of deference or suspicion may well inhibit their willingness to tell us how helpful our support is if we appear too knowledgeable (Rennie 1994).

Fundamental assumptions deeply buried within ethnic traditions, surfacing only at times of crisis, may also affect the way bereaved people try to make sense of their feelings (Corwin 1995). These alternative interpretations must be respected without the practitioner attempting to impose what may seem a more helpful (or comfortable?) way of explaining their feelings (McNamee and Gergen 1995). We have to explore these and hear their impact as a friend rather than as a critic. The bereaved parent's or child's perceptions of the death, the extent to which they are 'in touch' with or 'ignorant' of their feelings, and the significance they give to them can also be affected by the gender and age of the bereaved person (McGreal *et al.* 1997). To appreciate this, we have to listen to what is not being spoken as well as what is, without imposing our own cultural assumptions about body-language and non-verbal cues. Just as importantly, we have to remember that our own gender, age, class or race may get in the way of their ability to make us hear. We may not appear to be someone who could act either as a companion or as a guide, and our explorations may all too easily seem like intrusion (Reissman 1991).

The shape and size of the bereaved person's family, their patterns of communication and their access to other support networks are all affected by each member's cultural, educational and occupational history (Moos 1995; Nadeau 1998). Hence, not only do we have to recognize the variety of the cultural and social landmarks that shape individual perceptions of death and not only do we need to suspend our judgement while exploring the personal resources that each family member uses to deal with it, we also have to appreciate that the very relationship we have established with them is based on highly selected presentations of the self both they and we feel others might want to see. Even friends (especially friends?) 'manage' the information they give each other so as to produce the impression they would most like to make (Goffman 1971). Corwin sums up this tentative, companion-like and exploratory relationship as:

> a therapeutic stance that neither eschews specific cultural knowledge or behavioural theory out of concern for stereotyping or false 'knowing' . . . , nor overlooks idiosyncratic perceptions and interpretations

of the culture. Rather, a full understanding of another's point of view involves a process that Geertz (1983: 69) described as a 'continuous dialectical tacking' between idiosyncratic perceptions and meanings and broad characterizations of culture and grief experiences.

(Corwin 1995: 28)

Hence, an awareness of religious, cultural, class and gender differences should remind us of our own incomplete grasp of the meanings bereaved people are struggling to place on their experiences, rather than confirming the stereotypes indicated by the maps we use. Our awareness of the remarkable variation in family patterns should alert us to the power of close emotional ties in shaping feelings, beliefs and behaviours rather than helping us jump to conclusions about dysfunctioning families and unskilled communication. The maps that make us useful as a guide are always incomplete. They necessarily simplify and imply an order to things where there may be none. We must use our explanatory models with care. Our maps can only help if we know where we are. Therefore, we must first become a companion or fellow traveller – walking quietly with bereaved parents and children, whatever direction they are taking – listening to the stories of their family and the images they use to describe the ways bereavement has affected them. By becoming a companion first we may get to discover their inner landscape rather than merely rehearsing our own. In exploring the social networks and cultural landmarks that make up this landscape, we may come to orient ourselves and appreciate better the relevance of our maps and the value, if any, of our guidance.

So, our models of grief may be of some use, but they cannot replace the raw, original knowledge that each bereaved parent or surviving child possesses. It is the uniqueness of this knowledge that produces such intimate loneliness, even in the face of apparently common losses. We cannot get to this knowledge unless we listen, learn and demonstrate our willingness to be there with them. It is they – not the theoreticians – that are our teachers.

Summary – key ingredients of bereavement support

Discussions with parents and siblings, both with those who have been bereaved and those with a child undergoing treatment for a life-threatening illness, suggest certain professional skills and capabilities are necessary for professional and voluntary support to be effective. The following guidelines come directly from our work with parents and siblings:

Listening respectfully

Supporters must listen carefully to bereaved parents and siblings, recognizing that it is *they*, not the books or the theories of bereavement, who know what they are going through. They are the experts in how their experiences feel. Their accounts should be heard not only as insights into their distress and confusion, but also as testaments to their dead children and to their own struggles to come to terms with bereavement.

Recognizing the power of stories

Accounts and stories about deceased children or siblings and their relationships with other family members provide the listener with clues about how each of them is making sense of the death or of the diagnosis of a life-threatening illness. Major differences in how they perceive these events and the ways they give meaning to them can help supporters understand major relationship problems within the family (Coles 1989; Gersie 1991; Nadeau 1998). Death threatens many bereaved people's sense of reality. Talk and the creation of stories help to construct a new reality that begins, in time, to incorporate what had previously been unimaginable. We may not know what we think or feel until we have heard ourselves saying it (Morgan 1985).

Suspending judgement

Feelings of grief and perceptions of the lost relationship are often unique to individual family members. The 'meanings' they eventually discover, and their consequent behaviour may increase marital and family relationship problems rather than reducing them. Supporters should not judge how bereaved people feel or what they want to do.

Accepting that help may only be of limited value

There may be no solution and no positive way of making sense of the death and, as Nadeau (1998) argues, attempts to impose such interpretations may only cause more distress. Time should be spent simply trying to appreciate the cultural perspectives that bereaved people are using to explain their experiences, and the assumptions on which they are basing their perceptions of how the rest of the family are reacting and coping. The degree of informal social support they are receiving from others will only gradually become apparent, as will the part played by the family as a whole in each individual's adjustment.

Reaching out to offer help

Bereaved people or those having to bear the anxiety of a life-threatening diagnosis in their child or sibling ought not to be left to take the initiative in seeking support. Many have noted the value of being contacted and of their own inability to seek out support. To know there is someone who can provide information, who really cares and who will be around for a long time if they are needed may be reassuring. Offers should not only be made in the early stages. Time is not necessarily a great healer and need will almost certainly increase rather than decrease over the next few months and years. Formal services appear to provide very little systematic follow-up in bereavement care.

Giving information as fully as possible

Supporters ought not to assume that parents and siblings will have already been given all the information they need by medical or emergency services. Systematically check on what they have been told. Do they know their rights and obligations over the coming days and weeks – the benefits they may be entitled to, opportunities to stay at the hospital with their sick child, their right to have the body of their child at home or to visit them at the mortuary or at the funeral home, the role of the coroner's court and the procedures of post-mortems, their degree of freedom to chose how, where and when their child's body is buried or cremated and so on?

Death disorients and disempowers. Bereaved parents and brothers and sisters may be highly dependent on professionals and other experts for help in knowing what to do and in knowing how to cope. Yet, more than anything, they need also to find ways of regaining their sense of lost purpose and personal capacity to act. Information provides the basis for clarifying problems, for making decisions, and for acting in ways that help self and others 'regain control of their lives' (Bright 1996).

Reassuring them they are not abnormal

Help them understand that confusion, stress, dreams, hallucinations, marital tension, isolation, physical symptoms and so on are not unusual following bereavement. Help them make some order out of their lives by listening to their stories and encouraging them to reflect on them. Help them listen to each others' stories and appreciate their different ways of coping, under-standing and adapting to bereavement.

Bereavement often brings in its wake a whole catalogue of minor disasters that appear totally unconnected with the loss. Reassure bereaved family members that awkwardness, illness, tiredness, impatience and frustration with seemingly ordinary challenges can be experienced for years rather than months after the death. Help them be more patient with themselves and with others close to them.

Helping families share reactions to the death

Supporters could check early on the degree to which hospitals or other settings in which treatment has been offered or where the bad news has been communicated have enabled and encouraged family members to be with each other and share their thoughts and feelings. This is crucial in cases of unexpected or violent deaths, deaths where the children are out of contact with parents or siblings, and deaths where parents or siblings are not living together.

Helping family members be involved

Check on the degree to which all family members are allowed or encouraged to be centrally involved with the care of sick children and the arrangements for memorial, funeral, burial or cremation ceremonies. Nadeau (1998), Lauer *et al.* (1985), Rubin (1996) and others recognize how beneficial third parties can be in helping families air and negotiate different ways of hearing the bad news and trying to make it fit their own ways of coping. There is evidence from our own experience that many family members know their partners or surviving children desperately need support yet feel totally incapable of even talking to them about it, let alone trying to help them.

Helping retain control of disoriented lives

At the centre of many bereaved people's disorientation is a feeling of lost control. Huge changes have reached in and altered their lives. Any support that can help return some aspects of personal power can enable them to take up, once again, some authorship of their own story. Part of this sense of control arises simply from finding mental maps that help them locate where they are in a bereavement process, or in finding others who have been through similar experiences.

Helping put them in touch with each other

Evidence shows that distress arises not simply from feelings of being left alone by the deceased, but also from believing their intense personal grief is not shared or understood by other family members. Help in understanding each other's perceptions, and in recognizing their different ways of dealing with loss might ease family communication and help them support each other. Children especially must not be forgotten and should be included in sharing feelings and memories.

Noticing the forgotten mourners

At the end of a year in which his brother was taken sick and died, one adolescent took home a school report that showed a string of D and E grades against each of his subjects. His form teacher had written 'very disappointing year. Martin needs to concentrate more. Could do better'.

Though thankfully rare, the chasm that exists between the perceptions and priorities of recently bereaved people and those with whom they share everyday lives cannot be overestimated.

Perceptive bereavement support should recognize family members who cannot ask for help, who appear to be giving rather than receiving support and who silence their own pain out of concern for the distress of others. Acknowledgement of the sometimes overwhelming burdens they carry, unknown to anyone else, can help them feel a little lighter.

Remembering lost relationships and permanently changed lives

One of the things parents cherish most, especially those bereaved long-term, is the recognition by others of their dead son's or daughter's birthdays and the anniversaries of their death. They also value beyond measure people who remember that they will always have a child or sibling who has died, and that this sense of loss continues to deeply affect their lives. Recognizing the never-ending impact of this event, and offering opportunities for them to share memories and sadnesses without having to explain themselves constitutes a major form of support.

Liaising with others who share lives with the bereaved

Supporters can help co-ordinate and re-educate those in organizations with key responsibility for individual family members. Insensitivity from colleagues or supervisors – the unfortunate remark and the quickly forgotten loss – fuels feelings of anger and exclusion among all family members. Some parents have felt this to be the case even in the larger hospitals where an impression is sometimes given that they have little time to take account of the needs of the family of sick or recently deceased children.

Liaising with others who shared lives with the deceased

Unfinished business and ambivalent relationships with the deceased may be eased for a parent or sibling through sharing the different perceptions that friends, teachers or colleagues had of the dead child. In any event, conversational remembering with those that knew the deceased is a central part of the process of 'writing the last chapter', making sense of the life that was lived, and coming to terms with the death and its causes.

Helping put them in touch with others in the same position

A number of schemes operate on the basis that individual support can be combined with groups sharing their own particular perspective according to age and family position (such as Winston's Wish). Back-up can be offered through telephone help-lines, liaison with hospitals, social work or community teams and drop-in centres. More than anything else, parents and siblings value flexibility, a sense that they are able to choose themselves what they feel is helpful, and time and opportunities to talk and think through their experiences with others who understand what they are talking about.

Helping find others who might help

Support groups for parents, grandparents and siblings of children with life-threatening illnesses can be of immense value, with a professional coordinator setting up initial meetings and providing facilities for adults to talk together while their children play or meet separately. Here, a skilled helper can encourage mutual support, work for parents to take over the running of the group but be on hand for individual discussion if needed. Siblings' discovery that other children and adolescents are in the same circumstances as themselves can provide a stimulus to share feelings and resentments they might otherwise keep to themselves. It also enables the helpers recognize and maybe work on growing exclusions and misunderstandings within individual families.

Appendix: Shoe-strings and bricolage: some notes on the background research project

Approach and methods

Research often appears systematic and carefully planned; the reality is more messy. Our experience of this qualitative research project confirms Newby's observation that in spite of the appearance of systematic, logical and objective procedures, research is as much dependent on luck, intuition and insight as it is on 'scientific method' (Newby 1980).

Many of the ideas for this book and most of the quotations we have used come from an ongoing project, begun in late 1993 and funded by the University of Derby. This appendix offers a brief outline of our project and a history of the coincidences and chance events that mark its hesitant and stumbling progress. In terms of our analytical approach, we agree with McLeod that the qualitative researcher resembles the amateur 'do-it yourself' enthusiast, learning by trial and error and drawing on a whole range of tools and techniques. Citing Denzin and Lincoln, he argues that qualitative research is essentially *bricolage*; it is a pieced together solution that meets a specific problem in any one given setting that might well change in another: 'The product of the bricoleur's labour is a bricolage, a complex, dense, reflexive, collage like creation that represents the researcher's images, understandings, and interpretations of the world . . .' (McLeod 1996: 72).

McLeod's description reflects the history of our project and its relationship with this book. Our theoretical assumptions, our approach and certainly our methods of data collection and analysis fully reflect the post-modern condition that we have attempted to explore. Our findings are eclectic, partial, inevitably superficial at times and draw happily from a wide range of theoretical positions, which at first glance appear unconnected. If we were alone in this approach we would be more concerned, but there exists a 'movement' of sorts that argues that research should take itself less seriously, with researcher's owning up to the fact that the 'eureka' moment is as much the result of mistakes and 'playing' with data as it is the result of systematic logical thought (Wrigley 1995). We have neither found, nor offer, any single model or foolproof approach to discovering the 'correct' explanation of the problems and differences in how family members grieve and adjust to bereavement. What we have found is a range of views – conceptual tools – that each contribute something to our understanding.

Background

Much of the project has grown from the partnership between Gordon Riches and Pam Dawson. Not only has Pam conducted a substantial part of the fieldwork, is (at the time of writing) a practitioner with a substantial case-load and ongoing first-hand experience of bereaved families, but she also began this research partnership with an invitation for Gordon to attend a bereavement conference back in 1991. Gordon has been teaching social sciences at Derby University for a number of years and, prior to this project, had been researching the effects of disabling accidents on self-identity.

Another foundational element of the project is the University of Derby, which provided two initial grants – one to fund transcription of the interviews and one to pay for a temporary research assistant to start up a literature database. Gordon's employers continue to support this work through travel, conference expenses, colleague and library support and a salary for his teaching. Nevertheless, working, as many academics do, on a 'shoe-string budget' is a significant factor both in the choice of methods and in the time we are able to devote to research.

The third important element is The Compassionate Friends (TCF). They have supported our research and contributed significantly as informants, in giving us access to bereaved parents and siblings, and as constructive critics of our ideas. Our first publication was based on an early interview with a TCF regional organizer. Other groups – Support after Murder and Manslaughter (SAMM), Survivors of Bereavement following Suicide (SOBS) and the Kathmandu air disaster network – have also provided us with generous access and much 'insider' information. Professional and voluntary groups – Action for Bereavement Care in Derby, the Laura Centre in Leicester in the form of Jan McLaren, the Eclipse Bereavement Centre in Cheshire, Cruse and The National Association of Bereavement Services, not to forget the London Borough of Bromley – have also given resources, information, access to further bereavement networks, moral support and critical feedback.

Finally, in terms of making sense of the progress we have made, the annual symposium on Social Aspects of Death, Dying and Bereavement (sponsored by the British Sociological Association) and the biennial Conference on the Social Context of Death, Dying and Disposal have supported our ideas, introduced us to new ones, provided contacts with others working in similar fields and provided invaluable advice on writing up our research for publication.

Discovering the problem

Our starting point for this research was a question posed by a friend from TCF: 'Why do so many marriages appear to break down following the death of a child?' Wider discussion confirmed this to be a familiar problem for other befrienders in The Compassionate Friends and for staff in the bereavement support agencies with whom we subsequently talked.

Our initial literature search appeared to suggest that marital tension and relationship breakdown following the death of an offspring was common (Littlewood *et al.* 1991; Schwab 1992). However, while a number of studies linked marital conflict to child bereavement, fewer researchers attempted to trace patterns of marital or wider family adjustment to bereavement over time, or to link them to earlier patterns of family interaction. More recently, Moos (1995) has applied family systems theory to bereavement and Nadeau (1998) notes the same lack of research into *family* grief, though her excellent study goes a long way towards filling this gap in our knowledge.

Helmrath and Steinitz (1978) were exceptional in describing a process model that used gender and parental roles to map out how differences in mothers' and fathers' coping strategies built into misunderstanding and marital conflict. This 'cultural' analysis of grief was helpful in confirming our aim to investigate marital relations from the 'inside' and from an interactional perspective (Burgess 1984).

The choice of ethnographic methods – primarily in-depth, unstructured interviewing and participant observation – was made for a number of reasons. First, although the question posed to us was framed as a request for explanation, we felt that we had first to identify and *describe* patterns of change in couple relationships. How did irritation with each other, increasing inability to share a common grief and family tension arise? As Nadeau (1998) notes, citing Loffland, 'If you are asking "what are the causes?" . . . you are asking a quantitative question . . . [but] if you are asking "how did this build up, how did it happen?" . . . you are asking a qualitative question' (Nadeau 1998: 16). Second, through TCF and other professional contacts we had legitimate access to a number of bereavement 'subcultures'. We also had access to voluntary organizations involved in bereavement support. Third, not only did we both have a preference for face-to-face work rather than for structured interviewing or questionnaire-based surveys, we felt uncomfortable using 'remote' tools to investigate such emotionally sensitive experiences (Brannen 1993). Also, our shoe-string budget and work patterns fitted far more easily into a research programme that was flexible and fairly open-ended. Fourth, our literature search had shown that work done so far tended to be theorized on the basis of psychological or medical models. Philosophically we both have problems with essentialist views of grief and bereavement. A qualitative approach offers the opportunity to discover sequences of events during and after the child's death that contributed to differences in the family's *perception* of its meaning and significance. At the same time, the 'story-telling' approach allowed us to take account methodologically of our own biographically driven perceptions in the construction of data (Hollway 1989; Jorgenson 1991; Cotterill and Letherby 1993). We were interested in how bereaved families themselves *felt* and made sense of their 'lived experience' of bereavement and grief (Ellis and Flaherty 1992).

Constructionism assumes that most behaviours and feelings can be accounted for – but only using frameworks of meaning from *within* the culture of those whose actions are being studied. This demands that the researcher spends a little time with his or her informants, trying to understand the world from their point of view (Abramson 1992). A certain degree of credibility, sympathetic 'gatekeepers' and numerous opportunities for fieldwork within bereavement settings that fitted in with our principle employment pattern also confirmed the appropriateness of choosing a qualitative project.

Case history interviews

During the last six years we have conducted extended taped interviews with over 50 bereaved parents and siblings. At their shortest, these have lasted one and a half hours and some have taken over three hours or more. We have remained in contact with many of our informants receiving 'updates' on their progress and being privileged to hear of developments, both positive and negative in their attempts to survive without their children.

Some of our interviewees – particularly parents bereaved for some time and parents trained as counsellors or health workers – have become 'key informants' in the sense that they have not only been willing to complete follow-up interviews, but also have shown a willingness to discuss our ideas and share their knowledge of other bereaved families.

Our original analysis of the impact of a child's death on marital relations was presented in the Summer of 1994 at a conference marking the International Year of the Family at Plymouth University (Riches and Dawson 1996a). By the Autumn of 1994 we had discovered Douglas and Calvez's cultural analysis of late modern society and presented our synthesis of marital and cultural influences at the 4th Symposium on the Social Context of Death, Dying and Disposal at Leicester University (Riches and Dawson 1997). By this point we had completed interviews with 32 bereaved parents living primarily in the midland counties of England. In many cases we had managed to interview both partners. We aimed to speak to them separately and in some cases we also interviewed them together. Comparisons between their accounts and analysis of their interactions when interviewed together, offered us direct evidence of differences, similarities and interpersonal pressures in creating meanings around the deaths of their children. Road traffic accidents, an air disaster, accidental falls from buildings, fatal illnesses, murder, suicide, miscarriage, stillbirth, cot-death and voluntary termination were among the causes of deaths of the children whose parents we spoke to. Their ages at death ranged from unborn through to 30 years.

The time between the children's deaths and our interviews varied from 11 months to 23 years (with the exception of one 85-year-old mother whose infant had died 50 years previously), though the bulk fell into a narrower period of between two and six years. Interviews were conducted primarily by the two of us and we each aimed to gain accounts with a minimum of direct questioning, following a loose agenda that sought to gain details of the child's life, death, and events in the family since then. We also encouraged them to recount their feelings, thoughts and events during and since the death, their perceptions of support given, their involvement with professionals and self-help groups if any, their perceptions of their partner's and surviving children's grief, and their perceptions of the affect of the child's death on their marriage and their family's relationships.

Since 1994, we have added considerably to our tape-recorded case-histories. Our database now includes a growing number of siblings, most of whom were bereaved during childhood or adolescence but with two or three exceptions of adult and more elderly siblings.

Participant observation

We have conducted participant observation in a range of settings where death and bereavement features significantly in the culture of their members. We found that bereavement support groups and meetings of professional and volunteer workers offered many opportunities to experience patterns of relationships that members use in attempting to make sense of their losses 'first-hand'. These fieldwork observations have also helped develop our thinking and certainly provided an additional source for checking out our findings in the case history interviews. Hence, our links with groups and organizations listed above allowed us to explore bereavement subcultures both from the point of view of those who offer bereavement support and from those who have sought it.

We stress the word 'exploration' rather than 'observation' to note the explicit collaborative nature of our methods. We have talked informally and at length – taking notes during and after conversations – with many bereaved people at support group meetings and annual gatherings. Our fieldwork has also taken us into a range of settings, including coroners' courts, post-mortem rooms, conferences for bereaved parents and siblings (both in the UK and the USA), meetings of officiants for humanistic funeral services, centres for bereavement support, training venues for bereavement support workers, and hospital-based support groups.

Practice

In addition to extensive experience of one-to-one support with bereaved people, of liaison with public sector and voluntary agencies and mounting training courses in bereavement care, Pam Dawson's practice as Bereavement Co-ordinator for the London Borough of Bromley includes the setting up of support groups for parents and siblings of children with life-threatening illnesses. Both of us have counselling or pastoral responsibility as part of our professional roles, and these experiences also have contributed to the qualitative nature of our research design, to our fieldwork approach and to our critical use of existing models in analysing our data and creating the framework developed in this book.

Through regular discussion of our experiences, we have managed to put some analytical distance between personal experience and its translation into data. On a few occasions where our experiences have been particularly relevant to the research, one of us has acted as interviewer and we have tape-recorded the other's response in the same way as we have done with our case-study interviews.

Collaboration and 'face' validity

Many of our 'key informants' continue to read and comment on our work before it is submitted for publication. Both of us regularly accept invitations to present our findings to groups of bereaved people and to professionals and volunteers who work with them. We have close and continuing contacts with many of the latter who also read and comment on our ideas. Chapter 4, for example, appears in the shape that it does largely through feedback obtained from parents and professional bereavement counsellors during a seminar set up for us by the National Association of Bereavement Services in the Autumn of 1998. Following the circulation of a draft of this chapter, we received a number of telephone calls and letters confirming aspects of our analysis but suggesting amendments to others. Chapters 2, 3 and 5 are the result of feedback from presentations to bereaved people and counsellors based on draft and published papers circulated between 1996 and 1998. Chapter 6 has been re-written three times to accommodate comments made by bereaved parents in response to its first draft. Most of the people we work with live in the UK, but, following contacts made through presentations to international conferences, we also have received data from parents and surviving children living in the USA, Canada and parts of the West Indies. By returning to our informants, and by checking out the utility of our ideas with practitioners, we can constantly modify and develop our findings, so checking out their face validity and the utility of our interpretations.

Access, bias, ethics and confidentiality

We accessed our interviewees using personal contacts with bereavement groups and through our own professional networks. As it was TCF who approached us, all our interviewees from this source were 'volunteers' in the sense that they either came forward after learning of our project, or were 'invited' to talk to us by fellow members who felt their stories would be useful to us. This led inevitably along the threads of established support networks in which some informants knew each other. Half of the parents studied were accessed in this way and so at least part of our data were biased towards particular subcultural perceptions of grief, although the different support groups we worked with had little or nothing to do with each other. While at one level this presented a problem in generalizing our findings to all bereaved parents, it also offered the opportunity of investigating how specific bereavement subcultures help make sense of children's deaths and offer support to newly bereaved parents and siblings. We presented our findings on communities of bereaved parents at the 'Ideas of Community Conference' at the University of the West of England in September, 1995. Feedback provided from academics immediately helped modify the paper for presentation to the Second International Conference of Death, Dying and Disposal at Sussex University a week later.

The other half of our sample was just as 'opportunistic' as those coming from support groups. This second set of individuals on the whole had no links with other bereaved people. Their involvement was also voluntary. They (or their sons, daughters or siblings) offered their stories following discussion of our research project through our teaching or professional work. Again, as many of these individuals were contacted through a Higher Education setting their experiences were also likely to contain some cultural bias.

From the outset, we have stressed the importance of 'collaboration' in our research (Riches and Dawson 1996c) as a way of avoiding an instrumental approach to vulnerable people. We have not approached any bereaved parent or sibling directly or from a 'cold' position. All interviewees have either been introduced to us through a third person in their support, family or friendship network, or have come forward in the course of professional discussions about our work. All interviewees have given their informed consent to the interview and to our use of their stories, and in cases where we have used specific ideas, we have checked again that they have no objection to our publishing them.

Similarly, all participant observation of bereavement subcultures has been overt. At best we were seen as 'sympathetic' outsiders, but as our work has become more generally recognized within TCF, we have come to be accepted as 'associate' or 'honorary' members of the groups with which we work. In all cases, confidentiality has been maintained by changing names, locations and identifying characteristics.

Throughout our research, presentations and within this book, we have attempted to stress the tentative nature of our findings. Collaboration involves us continually being open to the possibility that we have got it wrong and we encourage our informants to feedback their views of what we have written. On numerous occasions our conceptual framework has leaped forward or gone back to the drawing board following discussion with parents, surviving children and bereavement workers. Through these collaborative mechanisms we have sought to avoid 'appropriating' our interviewees' stories, unfairly representing them or preventing them from changing in the light of new information.

Sample limitations and the nature of our analysis

Originally our study set out to describe the range of ways in which individual parents and their primary relationships change following a child's death. Since we relied on opportunity sampling we made no claim to representative findings. We attempted, rather, in exploring a range of specific case histories, to identify 'typical' orientations that parents adopted in responding to the deaths of their children. Thereafter, using both published literature and the more general opportunities for discussion presented by our participant observations, we began to build these typical orientations into a broader social and cultural framework. This strand of our research began, again totally fortuitously, through the visit of Marcel Calvez to Derby University early in 1994 during which he presented the conceptual framework that he and Mary Douglas were using to analyse attitudes to HIV and AIDS in modern society (Douglas and Calvez 1990). At the same time, we had read with enthusiasm the seminal paper by Mellor and Shilling (1993) on the sequestration of death and its impact on identity construction. We presented a synthesis of these ideas and their use in explaining differences in grief response to the fourth annual symposium on Social Aspects of Death, Dying and Bereavement at Leicester University in November, 1994. Noting the importance of gender in this cultural model we embarked again on a literature search for concepts that might further this analysis. The work of Hart (1996) on the gendering of identity, based on a constructionist model that integrates both psychoanalytical and feminist perspectives was especially useful. We found it not through a systematic library search, but simply because it appeared next to our first paper in the *Journal of Family Therapy*. Such is the serendipitous nature of qualitative research!

Throughout our research we have transcribed, indexed and categorized interviewees' accounts, identifying recurrent themes and analysing them using a whole range of conceptual frameworks. Many of these frameworks appear in Chapter 1 of this book, but our discovery of them was far more piecemeal and accidental than this first chapter implies. From the outset we have been committed to viewing interviewees' accounts as 'storytelling' – as attempts to create meaning using narrative or metaphor to make sense of their lives – rather than as a 'true' record of what actually happened. In this we were influenced strongly both by Gidden's argument that late modernity was a period in which many individuals had to continually 're-order their reflexive self narrative' to make sense of their current circumstances (Giddens 1991) and by the work of discourse analysts (particularly Hollway 1989) in which culture is viewed as a reservoir of ideas and beliefs through which individuals, in interaction with others, actively build meaning out of their lived experiences.

We have similarly analysed expressions of isolation or support, of experiences of grief and playing out the role of 'normal' using Symbolic Interactionist and Social Constructionist theory (Mead 1934). Both related frameworks allowed us to interpret bereaved individual's negotiation of meanings within the context of supportive or non-supportive social relationships. We have analysed accounts of families and couples negotiating meaning using family systems theory (Nadeau 1998), which is where we came in 1993 (without really knowing it) by applying the work of Reiss (1981) and Roger (1991) in the creation of family paradigms. We are now able to make this connection having read Nadeau's review of Reiss's contribution to past attempts to 'capture' meaning-making within families.

Maybe the biggest 'find' of all in terms of analytical frameworks were the complementary ideas of Walter (1996) and Klass et al. (1996) as they helped us solve two key 'problems' discovered within our data. One was the extreme passion with which many parents and siblings refused to 'let go' of their deceased children, even many years after their bereavement (as with the 85-year-old mother who still felt guilt over her infant dying). This theme resurfaced time and again in open-ended interviews. The second problem was opposite in terms of its overtness. Visits to spiritualists and clairvoyants, dreams, visions and sounds of deceased children were part of a 'mystical' theme we only gained access to late on in our work when we had demonstrated we could be trusted not to criticize or reframe parents' stories. The vital role of deceased children in some parents' inner life-worlds and in some family's conversations provided yet another important framework for examining conflict and fundamental differences not only between family members, but also between bereaved people and those professionals who seek to help them.

Hence problems of personal loneliness could be linked to the failure of others to understand, especially of those partners or parents sharing the same bereavement. These frustrations were central to most interviewee's accounts. Anger or disbelief at the ordinary world of non-bereaved people, disorientation and pressure to return to normal were also regularly mentioned. Support from others in the same position, from close friends who allowed them to be upset, and from professionals who became friends, figured among things that 'helped'. The importance of these principle themes was demonstrated both in the number of times they were returned to within each open-ended interview, and in the strength of feeling that was reflected in interviewees' use of words and emphases.

Links between research project and this book

Hence the 'findings' we present in this book are the result of the coming together of many influences and voices – primarily of bereaved people themselves, but also of those who work to support them, and of the researchers and theorists through whose eyes we have interpreted their stories. Accepting the limitations of our sample and the tentativeness of our analyses, we have debated with the models and conclusions set out by others in the published literature.

In particular, at a micro level, the biographical approach of Walter (1996), Klass *et al.*'s analysis of continuing bonds (1996), Nadeau's analysis of family stories (1998) and Forte *et al.*'s approach to the social construction of grief (1996) have helped synthesize many of our own findings and thoughts about cultural resources, identity reconstruction, representations of the deceased and negotiation of them with the living. Throughout, the excellent findings from Schwab's more empirically based research (1992–1998) have provided evidence that our own thoughts may apply to a wider sample than just those we interviewed.

At a macro level these conceptual frameworks still needed locating within a larger structural (or post-structural!) perspective. It was our discovery of the continuing relevance of Durkheim's analysis of 'moral authority', as reflected in the analysis of Douglas and Calvez (1990), that helped us argue the connection between diversity of grief responses and cultural pluralism in late modernity.

So, our research project does not provide 'evidence' in terms of scientific proof. Qualitative research can never do that, nor does it aim to do much more than add depth and detail to the theoretical propositions that appear to explain the causes of things. What our research has done is to provide themes, insights and experiences with which to consider the value of the grief models that we have identified, and to provide both a stimulus for, and examples of, the explanatory frameworks we have developed. The project is ongoing.

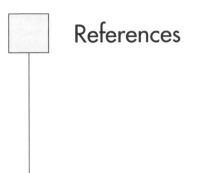

References

Aadalen, S. (1980) Coping with Sudden Infant Death Syndrome: interventions and strategies and a case study. *Family Relations*, 29(4): 584–90.

Abramson, P. (1992) *A Case for Case Studies*. London: Sage.

Altschuler, J. (1993) Gender and illness: implications for family therapy. *Journal of Family Therapy*, 15: 381–401.

Anderson, M. (1998) Speaking of death: language, conversation and narrative in the management of grief, paper presented at *The Seventh Annual Symposium on Social Aspects of Death, Dying and Bereavement*, The Open University, Milton Keynes, 27 November, 1998.

Apter, T. (1985) *Why Women Don't Have Wives: Professional Success and Motherhood*. Basingstoke: Macmillan.

Apter, T. (1997) *Secret Paths: Women in the New Midlife*. New York: W.W. Norton.

Arlidge, J. (1997) Bitter exodus of Dunblane families. *The Observer on CD-ROM*, 9 March.

Attig, T. (1991) The importance of conceiving of grief as an active process. *Death Studies*, 15: 385–93.

Balk, D. (1983) Adolescents' grief reactions and self-concept perceptions following sibling death: a study of 33 teenagers. *Journal of Youth and Adolescence*, 12(2): 137–61.

Balk, D.E. (1990) The self-concepts of bereaved adolescents: sibling death and its aftermath. *Journal of Adolescent Research*, 5(1): 112–32.

Ball, S.J., Bignold, S. and Cribb, A. (1996) Death and the disease: inside the culture of childhood cancer, in G. Howard and P.G. Jupp (eds) *Contemporary Issues in the Sociology of Death, Dying and Disposal*. Basingstoke: Macmillan.

Barbarin, O. and Chesler, M. (1986) The medical context of parental coping with childhood cancer. *American Journal of Community Psychiatry*, 14(2): 221–35.

Barrett, R.K. (1996) Adolescents, homicidal violence and death, in C.A. Corr and D.E. Bald (eds) *Handbook of Adolescent Death and Bereavement*. New York: Springer, 42–64.

Bauman, Z. (1992) *Mortality, Immortality and Other Life Strategies*. Cambridge: Polity Press.

Beeghley, L. (1997) Demystifying theory: how the theories of Georg Simmel (and others) help us to make sense of modern life, in C. Ballard, J. Gubbay and C. Middleton (eds) *The Student's Companion to Sociology*. Oxford: Blackwell.

Benfield, D., Leib, S. and Vollman, J. (1978) Grief response of parents to neonatal death and parent participation in deciding care. *Pediatrics*, 62(2): 171–7.

Berger, A.S. (1995) Quoth the raven: bereavement and the paranormal. *Omega*, 31(1): 1–10.

Berger, P. and Luckman, T. (1966) *The Social Construction of Reality*. Harmondsworth: Penguin.

Berman, A.L. (1986) Helping suicidal adolescents: needs and responses, in C.A. Corr and J.N. McNeil (eds) *Adolescence and Death*. New York: Springer.

Bernstein, B. (1970) Education cannot compensate for society. *New Society*, 26 February: 344–7.

Birenbaum, L.K., Robinson, M.A., Phillips, D.S., Stewart, B.J. and McCown, D. (1989) The response of children to the dying and death of a sibling. *Omega*, 20(3): 213–28.

Black, D. (1996) Childhood bereavement. *British Medical Journal*, 312(7045): 1496.

Blinder, B.J. (1972) Sibling death in childhood. *Child Psychiatry and Human Development*, 2: 169–75.

Bonanno, G., Keltner, D., Holen, A. and Horowitz, M.J. (1995) When avoiding unpleasant emotions might not be such a bad thing. *Journal of Personality and Social Psychology*, 69(5): 975–89.

Bor, R., Legg, C. and Scher, I. (1996) The systems paradigm, in R. Woolfe and W. Dryden (eds) *Handbook of Counselling Psychology*. London: Sage.

Boston, S. (1981) *Will, My Son: The Life and Death of a Mongol Child*. London: Pluto Press.

Bowlby, J. (1969) *Attachment and Loss: Attachment* (Vol. I). New York: Basic Books.

Bowlby, J. (1973) *Attachment and Loss: Separation, Anxiety and Anger* (Vol. II). New York: Basic Books.

Bowlby, J. (1979) Self-reliance and conditions that promote it, in J. Bowlby *The Making and Breaking of Affectional Bonds*. London: Tavistock.

Bowlby, J. (1980) *Attachment and Loss: Loss, Sadness and Depression* (Vol. III). New York: Basic Books.

Bowling, A. (1987) Mortality after bereavement: a review of the literature on survival periods and factors affecting survival. *Social Science and Medicine*, 24: 117–24.

Brabant, S. (1997–8) Death and grief in the family comics. *Omega*, 36(1): 33–44.

Brabant, S., Forsyth, C.J. and McFarlain, G. (1997) The impact of the death of a child on meaning and purpose in life. *Journal of Personal and Interpersonal Loss*, 2(3): 255–66.

Brabant, S., Forsyth, C. and McFarlain, G. (1994) Defining the family after the death of a child. *Death Studies*, 18: 197–206.

Brabant, S., Forsyth, C.J. and McFarlain, G. (1995) Life after the death of a child: initial and long term support from others. *Omega, Journal of Death and Dying*, 31(1): 67–85.

Bradach, K.M. and Jordan, J.R. (1995) Long-term effects of a family history of traumatic death on adolescent individuation. *Death Studies*, 19(4): 315–36.

Brannen, J. (1993) The effects of research on participants: findings from a study of mothers and employment. *Sociological Review*, 41(2): 328–46.

Braun, M.J. and Berg, D.H. (1994) Meaning reconstruction in the experience of parental bereavement. *Death Studies*, 18(2): 105–29.

Brice, C.W. (1987) What forever means: an empirical existential-phenomenological investigation of the maternal mourning of a child's death, *Dissertation Abstracts International, 49/01-B*, 0234. (University Microfilms No 88-05348).

Bright, R. (1996) *Grief and Powerlessness: Helping People Regain Control of Their Lives*. London: Jessica Kingsley.

Brown, G.W. (1995) Depression: a sociological view, in B. Davey, A. Gray and C. Seale (eds) *Health and Disease*. Buckingham: Open University Press.

Bryan, E.M. (1995) The death of a twin. *Palliative Medicine*, 9(3): 187–92.

Bryant, C.M. (1989) Fathers grieve, too. *Journal of Perinatology*, 9(4): 437–41.

Burgess, R.G. (1984) *In the Field: An Introduction to Field Research*. London: Allen & Unwin.

Burkitt, I. (1991) *Social Selves: Theories of the Social Formation of Personality*. London: Sage.

Byng-Hall, J. (1979) Re-editing family mythology during family therapy. *Journal of Family Therapy*, 1: 103–16.

Byng-Hall, J. (1998) Evolving ideas about narrative: re-editing the re-editing of family mythology. *Journal of Family Therapy*, 20: 133–41.

Campbell, S. and Silverman, P. (1996) *Widower: When Men are left Alone*. Amityville, NY: Baywood.

Carroll, R. and Shaefer, S. (1994) Similarities and differences in spouses coping with SIDS. *Omega*, 28(4): 273–84.

Cherney, P.M. and Verhey, M.P. (1996) Grief among gay men associated with multiple losses from AIDS. *Death Studies*, 20(2): 115–32.

Chodorow, N. (1978) *The Reproduction of Mothering*. Berkeley: University of California Press.

Clark, S.E. and Goldney, R.D. (1995) Grief reactions and recovery in a support group for people bereaved by suicide. *Crisis*, 16(1): 27–33.

Colarusso, C.A. and Nemiroff, R.A. (1981) *Adult Development: A New Dimension in Psychodynamic Theory and Practice*. New York: Plenum Press.

Coleman, J., Lyon, J. and Piper, R. (1996) Suicide and self harm: helping distressed young people. *Rapport*, 3(1): 6–9.

Coles, R. (1989) *The Call of Stories*. Boston: Houghton Mifflin.

Comer, R. (1995) *Abnormal Psychology*. New York: W.H. Freeman & Co.

Conrad, B.H. (1998) *When a Child has been Murdered: Ways You can Help the Grieving Parents*. Amityville, NY: Baywood.

Cook, J.A. (1988) Dad's double binds, rethinking fathers' bereavement from a man's studies perspective. *Journal of Contemporary Ethnography*, 17(3): 285–308.

Copley, M. and Bodensteiner, J. (1987) Chronic sorrow in families of disabled children. *Journal of Child Neurology*, 2: 67–70.

Cordell, A. and Thomas, N. (1990) Fathers and grieving: coping with infant death. *Journal of Perinatology*, 10: 75–80.

Cornwell, J., Nurcombe, M.D. and Stevens, L. (1977) Family response to loss of a child by sudden infant death syndrome. *The Medical Journal of Australia*, 1: 656–8.

Corr, C. and Corr, D. (1996) *Handbook of Childhood Death and Bereavement.* New York: Springer.

Corwin, M.D. (1995) Cultural issues in bereavement therapy: the social construction of mourning. *In Session: Psychotherapy in Practice,* 1(4): 23–41.

Cotterill, P. and Letherby, G. (1993) Weaving stories: personal auto/biographies in feminist research. *Sociology,* 27(1): 67–79.

Craib, I. (1995) Some comments on the sociology of the emotions. *Sociology,* 29(1): 151–8.

Das, V. (1993) Moral orientations to suffering, in L.C. Chen, A. Kleinman and N.C. Ware (eds) *Health and Social Change in International Perspective.* Boston: Harvard University Press.

Davies, B. (1988) Shared life space and sibling bereavement responses. *Cancer Nursing,* 11: 339–47.

DeFrain, J.D. and Ernst, L. (1978) The psychological effects of Sudden Infant Death Syndrome on surviving family members. *The Journal of Family Practice,* 6(5): 985–9.

DeFrain, J.D. (1991) Learning about grief from normal families: SIDS, stillbirth, and miscarriage. *Journal of Marital and Family Therapy,* 17(3): 215–32.

Deits, B. (1992) *Life after Loss: A Personal Guide Dealing with Death, Divorce, Job Change and Relocation.* Tuscon, AZ: Fisher Books.

DeMaso, D.R., Meyer, E.C. and Beasley, P.J. (1997) What do I say to my surviving children? *Journal of the American Academy of Child and Adolescent Psychiatry,* 36(9): 1299–302.

DeMinco, S. (1995) Young adult reactions to death in literature and life. *Adolescence,* 30(117): 179–85.

De Montiguy, F., Beaudet, L. and Dumas, L. (1996) Repercussions de la mort d'un enfant sur la famille. *The Canadian Nurse,* 92(10): 39–42.

DeM'Uzan, M. (1996) La mort n'avouse jamais (Death never confesses). *Revue Française de Psychanalyse,* 60(1): 33–47.

DeVries, B., Lana, R.D. and Falck, V.T. (1994) Parental bereavement over the life course: A theoretical intersection and empirical view. *Omega,* 29(1): 47–69.

Doka, K.J. (1989) *Disenfranchised Grief: Recognising Hidden Sorrow.* Lexington, MA: Lexington Books.

Doka, K.J. (1996) The cruel paradox: children who are living with life-threatening illness, in A. Corr and D. Corr (eds) *Handbook of Childhood Bereavement.* New York: Springer.

Donaghy, B. (1997) *Leaving Early.* Sydney: HarperCollins.

Douglas, M. and Calvez, M. (1990) The self as risk taker: a cultural theory of contagion in relation to AIDS. *The Sociological Review,* 38(3): 445–64.

Duker, A. (1966) What is culture shock?www.wooster.edu/oisa/handbook/culture.html

Duncombe, J. and Marsden, D. (1993) Love and intimacy: the gender division of emotion and 'emotion work'. *Sociology,* 27(2): 221–41.

Duncombe, J. and Marsden, D. (1995) Workaholics and whingeing women: theorising intimacy and emotion work – the last frontier of gender inequality? *Sociological Review,* 43(1): 150–70.

Dyregrov, A. (1990) Parental reactions to the loss of an infant child: A review. *Scandinavian Journal of Psychology,* 31(4): 266–80.

Dyregrov, A. (1991) *Grief in Children, A Handbook for Adults*. London: Jessica Kingsley.

Dyregrov, A. and Matthiesen, S.B. (1987) Similarities and differences in mothers' and fathers' grief following the death of an infant. *Scandinavian Journal of Psychology*, 28: 1–15.

Dyregrov, A. and Matthiesen, S.B. (1991) Parental grief following the death of an infant: a follow-up over one year. *Scandinavian Journal of Psychology*, 32(3): 193–207.

Elders, M.A. (1995) Theory and present thinking in bereavement. *Issues in Psychoanalytic Psychology*, 17(1): 67–83.

Ellis, C. and Flaherty, M.G. (1992) *Investigating Subjectivity: Research on Lived Experience*. London: Sage.

Ender, M.G. and Hermsen, J.M. (1996) Working with the bereaved: U.S. army experiences with nontraditional families. *Death Studies*, 20(6): 557–75.

Erickson, E.H. (1980) *Identity and the Life Cycle: A Reissue*. New York: Norton.

Fickling, K.F. (1993) Stillborn studies: ministering to bereaved parents. *The Journal of Pastoral Care*, 47(3): 217–27.

Fitzpatrick, T.R. (1998) Bereavement amongst elderly men: the effects of stress and health. *Journal of Applied Gerontology*, 17(2): 204–28.

Forte, J.A., Barrett, A.V. and Campbell, M.H. (1996) Patterns of social connectedness and shared grief work: a symbolic interactionist perspective. *Social Work with Groups*, 19(1): 29–51.

Fortier, L. and Wanless, R. (1984) Family crisis following the diagnosis of a handicapped child. *Family Relations*, 22: 13–24.

Freud, S. (1913) *Meaning and Melancholia* (Pelican Freud Library, Vol. II). London: Pelican.

Furnham, A. and Bochner, S. (1986) *Culture Shock: Psychological Reactions to Unfamiliar Environments*. London: Methuen.

Geertz, C. (1983) *Local Knowledge. Further Essays in Interpretive Anthropology*. New York: Basic Books.

Gentry, J. and Goodwin, C. (1995) Social support for decision making during grief due to death, *American Behavioral Scientist*, 38(4): 553–63.

Gersie, A. (1991) *Storymaking in Bereavement*. London: Jessica Kingsley.

Giddens, A. (1991) *Modernity and Self-identity*. Cambridge: Polity Press.

Gilbert, K.R. (1996) 'We've had the same loss, why don't we have the same grief?' Loss and differential grief in families. *Death Studies*, 20(3): 269–83.

Gilbert, K.R. and Smart, L. (1992) *Coping with Fetal or Infant Loss: The Couple's Healing Process*. New York: Brunner/Mazel.

Gilroy, P. (1997) Diaspora and the detours of identity, in K. Woodward (ed.) *Identity and Difference*. London: Sage.

Goffman, E. (1963) *Stigma: Notes on the Management of a Spoiled Identity*. London: Penguin.

Goffman, E. (1971) *The Presentation of Self in Everyday Life*. Harmondsworth: Pelican Books.

Gordon, R. (1978) *Dying and Creating: A Search for Meaning*. London: Society of Analytical Psychology.

Gorer, G. (1965) *Death, Grief and Mourning in Contemporary Britain*. Garden City, NJ: Doubleday.

Gottlieb, L., Lang, A. and Cohen, R. (1994) 'Coming to terms with infant death: changes that couples experience'. Poster presented at the International Nursing Research Conference, Vancouver, B.C., March 1994.

Grinwald, S. (1995) Communication-family characteristics: a comparison between stepfamilies (formed after death or divorce) and biological families. *Journal of Divorce and Remarriage*, 24(1/2): 183–96.

Gubrium, J. (1988) The family as project. *Sociological Review*, 36(2): 273–96.

Guidano, V.F. (1991) *The Self in Process: Towards a Post-Rationalist Cognitive Therapy*. New York: Guilford.

Hagemeister, A.K. and Rosenblatt, P.C. (1997) Grief and sexual relationship of couples who have experienced a child's death. *Death Studies*, 21(3): 231–52.

Hagman, G.H. (1995) Mourning: a review and reconsideration. *International Journal of Psychoanalysis*, 76(5): 909–25.

Handley, N. (1991) Death awareness and personal change, in C. Newnes (ed.) *Death, Dying and Society*. Hove and London: Lawrence Erlbaum Associates.

Hart, B. (1996) The construction of the gendered self. *Journal of Family Therapy*, 18(1): 43–60.

Hartrick, G.A. (1996) The experience of self for women who are mothers. *Journal of Holistic Nursing*, 14(4): 316–31.

Hazzard, A., Weston, J. and Gutterres, C. (1992) After a child's death: factors related to parental bereavement. *Journal of Development and Behavioural Paediatrics*, 13(1): 24–30.

Hearn, J. (1987) *The Gender of Oppression*. Hemel Hempstead: Harvester Wheatsheaf.

Heiney, S.P. (1991) Sibling grief: a case report. *Archives of Psychiatric Nursing*, 5(3): 121–7.

Helmrath, T.A. and Steinitz, E. (1978) Death of an infant: parental grieving and the failure of social support. *The Journal of Family Practice*, 6(4): 785–90.

Hindmarch, C. (1995) Secondary losses for siblings. *Child: Care, Health and Development*, 21(6): 425–31.

Hogan, N. and DeSantis, L. (1992) Adolescent sibling bereavement: an ongoing attachment. *Qualitative Health Research*, 2(2): 159–77.

Hogan, N. and DeSantis, L. (1994) Things that help and hinder adolescent sibling bereavement. *Western Journal of Nursing Research*, 16(2): 132–53.

Hogan, N. and DeSantis, L. (1996) Adolescent sibling bereavement: towards a new theory, in C. Corr and D. Bald (eds) *Handbook of Adolescent Death and Bereavement*. New York: Springer.

Hollway, W. (1989) *Subjectivity and Method in Psychology*. London: Sage.

Huber, R. and Bryant, J. (1996) The 10 mile mourning bridge and the brief symptom inventory: close relatives? *The Hospice Journal*, 11(2): 31–46.

Hunfield, J., Mourik, M., Tibboel, D. and Passchier, J. (1996) Parental grieving after infant death. *The Journal of Family Practice*, 42(6): 622–3.

Iphofen, R. (1990) Coping with a perforated life: a case study in managing the stigma of petit mal epilepsy. *Sociology*, 24(3): 447–63.

Irish, D.P., Lundquist, K.F. and Nelsen, V.J. (eds) (1993) *Ethnic Variations in Dying, Death and Grief*. Washington: Taylor & Francis.

James, I. (1995) Helping people with learning disability to cope with bereavement. *British Journal of Learning Disabilities*, 23(2): 74–8.

Johnson, S. (1984) Sexual intimacy and replacement children after the death of a child. *Omega*, 15: 109–18.

Jorgenson, J. (1991) Co-constructing the interviewer/co-constructing 'family', in F. Steiner (ed.) *Research and Reflexivity*. London: Sage.

Jurk, I.H., Ekert, H. and Jones, J. (1980) Family responses and mechanisms of adjustment following death of children with cancer. *Australian Paediatric Journal*, 17(2): 85–88.

Kalnins, I.V., Churchill, P. and Terry, G.E. (1980) Concurrent stresses in families with a leukemic child. *Journal of Pediatric Psychology*, 5(1): 81–92.

Kandt, V. (1994) Adolescent bereavement: turning a fragile time into acceptance and peace. *The School Counselor*, 41(3): 203–11.

Kaplan, D.M., Grobstein, R. and Smith, A. (1976) Predicting the impact of severe illness in families. *Health Social Work*, 1: 71.

Kaplan, L.J. (1995) *No Voice is Ever Wholly Lost*. New York: Simon and Shuster.

Kerner, J., Harvey, B. and Lewiston, N. (1979) The impact of grief: a retrospective study of family function following loss of a child with cystic fibrosis. *Journal of Chronic Disease*, 32: 221–5.

Kirchberg, T.M. (1998) Beginning counselors' death concerns and empathic responses to client situations involving death and grief. *Death Studies*, 22(2): 99–120.

Klass, D. (1991) Religious aspects in the resolution of parental grief: solace and social support. *Prevention in Human Services*, 10(1): 187–209.

Klass, D. (1996a) Grief in an eastern culture: Japanese ancestor worship, in D. Klass, R. Silverman and S. Nickman (eds) *Continuing Bonds: New Understandings of Grief*. Washington DC: Taylor & Francis.

Klass, D. (1996b) The deceased child in the psychic and social worlds of bereaved parents during the resolution of grief, in D. Klass, R. Silverman and S. Nickman (eds) *Continuing Bonds: New Understandings of Grief*. Washington, DC: Taylor & Francis.

Klass, D., Silverman, P.R. and Nickman, S.L. (1996) *Continuing Bonds: New Understandings of Grief*. Washington, DC: Taylor & Francis.

Klein, S.J. (1998) *Heavenly Hurts, Surviving AIDS-Related Deaths and Losses*. Amityville, NY: Baywood.

Lang, A., Gottlieb, L.N. and Amsel, R. (1996) Predictors of husbands' and wives' grief reactions following infant death: the role of marital intimacy. *Death Studies*, 20(1): 33–57.

Lang, A. and Gottleib, L. (1991) Marital intimacy in bereaved and nonbereaved couples: a comparative study, in D. Papadatou and C. Papadatos (eds) *Children and Death*. New York: Hemisphere Publishing Corporation.

Lang, A. and Gottlieb, L. (1993) Parental grief reactions and marital intimacy following infant death. *Death Studies*, 17(3): 233–55.

Lauer, M.E., Mulhern, R., Wallskog, J.M. and Camitta, B.M. (1983) A comparison study of parental adaptation following a child's death at home or in hospital. *Pediatrics*, 71(1): 107–12.

Lauer, M.E., Mulhern, R.K., Bohne, J.B. and Camitta, B.M. (1985) Children's perceptions of their sibling's death at home or hospital: the precursors of differential adjustment. *Cancer Nursing*, 8: 21–7.

Layne, L.L. (1996) 'Never such innocence again': irony, nature and technoscience in narratives of pregnancy loss, in R. Cecil (ed.) *The Anthropology of Pregnancy Loss*. Oxford: Berg.

Lee, C. (1994) *Good Grief: Experiencing Loss*. London: Fourth Estate.

Lehman, D., Lang, E., Wortman, C. and Sorenson, S. (1989) Long-term effects of sudden bereavement: marital and parent-child relationships and children's reactions. *Journal of Family Psychology*, 2(3): 344–67.

Lewis, M. and Schonfeld, D. (1994) Role of child and adolescent psychiatric consultation and liason in assisting children and their families in dealing with death. *Child and Adolescent Psychiatric Clinics of North America*, 3(3): 613–27.

Lindemann, E. (1944) Symptomatology and management of acute grief. *American Journal of Psychiatry*, 101: 141–8.

Lindstrom, T.C. (1995) Anxiety and adaptation in bereavement. *Anxiety, Stress and Coping*, 8: 251–61.

Littlewood, J.L., Cramer, D., Hoekstra, J. and Humphrey, G.B. (1991) Gender differences in parental coping following their child's death. *British Journal of Guidance and Counselling*, 19(2): 139–48.

Lofland, L.H. (1982) Loss and human connection: an exploration into the nature of the social bond, in W. Ickes and E.S. Knowles (eds) *Personality, Roles and Social Behaviour*. NY: Springer-Verlag.

Loo, R. and Shea, L. (1996) Structure of the Collett-Lester Fear of Death and Dying Scale. *Death Studies*, 20(6): 577–86.

Lovell, A. (1983) Some questions of identity: late miscarriage, stillbirth and perinatal loss. *Social Science and Medicine*, 17(11): 755–61.

Lupton, D. and Barclay, L. (1997) *Constructing Fatherhood: Discourses and Experiences*. London: Sage.

Mahan, C.K. and Calica, J. (1997) Perinatal loss: considerations in social work practice. *Social Work in Health Care*, 24(3/4): 141–52.

Martinson, I. (1991) Grief is an individual journey: follow-up of families postdeath of a child with cancer, in D. Papadatou and C. Papadatos (eds) *Children and Death*. New York: Hemisphere.

Martinson, I. and Campos, R.G. (1991) Adolescent bereavement: long-term responses to a sibling's death from cancer. *Journal of Adolescent Research*, 6(1): 54 69.

Martinson, I.M., McClowry, S.G., Davies, B. and Kuhlenkamp, E.J. (1994) Changes over time: a study of family bereavement following childhood cancer. *Journal of Palliative Care*, 10(1): 19–25.

Marwit, S.J. and Klass, D. (1995) Grief and the role of the inner representation of the deceased. *Omega*, 30: 283–98.

Maslow, A. (1968) *Towards a Psychology of Being* (2nd edn). New York: Van Nostrand.

McCown, D.E. and Pratt, C. (1985) Impact of sibling death on children's behaviour. *Death Studies*, 9: 323–35.

McGreal, D., Evans, B.J. and Burrows, G.D. (1997) Gender differences in coping following loss of a child through miscarriage or stillbirth: a pilot study. *Stress Medicine*, 13(3): 159–65.

McLaren, J. (1998) A new understanding of grief: a counsellor's perspective. *Mortality*, 3(2): 275–90.

McLeod, J. (1996) The humanistic paradigm, in R. Woolfe and W. Dryden (ed.) *Handbook of Counselling Psychology*. London: Sage.

McNamee, S. and Gergen, K.J. (1995) *Therapy As Social Construction*. London: Sage.

Mead, G.H. (1934) *Mind, Self and Society*. Chicago: University of Chicago Press.

Mellor, P.A. and Shilling, C. (1993) Modernity, self-identity and the sequestration of death. *Sociology*, 27(3): 411–31.

Merrin, W. (1999) Crash, bang, wallop! What a picture! The death of Diana and the Media. *Mortality*, 4(1): 41–62.

Merrington, B. (1995) *Suffering Loves: Coping with the Death of a Child*. Leamington Spa: Advantage Books.

Middleton, D. and Edwards, D. (1990) Conversational remembering: a social psychological approach, in D. Edwards and D. Middleton (eds) *Collective Remembering*. London: Sage.

Middleton, W., Raphael, B., Burnett, P. and Martinek, N. (1998) A longitudinal study comparing bereavement phenomena in recently bereaved spouses, adult children and parents. *Australian and New Zealand Journal of Psychiatry*, 32(2): 235–41.

Miller, W. I. (1998) Fixin' to die, in M. Mitchell and A.M. Gilroy (eds) *Proceedings of The Social Context of Death, Dying and Disposal*. Glasgow: Glasgow Caledonian University.

Milo, E.M. (1997) Maternal responses to the life and death of a child with a developmental disability: a story of hope. *Death Studies*, 21(5): 443–76.

Mirren, E. (1995) *Our Children: Coming to Terms with the Loss of a Child: Parents' Own Stories*. London: Hodder and Stoughton.

Moos, N.L. (1995) An integrative model of grief. *Death Studies*, 19(4): 337–64.

Morgan, D. (1985) *The Family: Politics and Social Theory*. London: Routledge & Kegan Paul.

Moriarty, H.J., Carroll, R. and Cotroneo, M. (1996) Differences in bereavement reactions within couples following death of a child. *Research in Nursing and Health*, 19(6): 461–9.

Mulkay, M. (1993) Social death in Britain, in D. Clark (ed.) *The Sociology of Death, Theory, Culture, Practice*. Oxford: Blackwell.

Murphy, F.A. and Hunt, S.C. (1997) Early pregnancy loss: men have feelings too. *British Journal of Midwifery*, 5(2): 87–90.

Murphy, S.A. (1996) Parent bereavement stress and preventive intervention following the violent deaths of adolescent or young adult children. *Death Studies*, 20(5): 441–52.

Murray, J. and Callan, V.J. (1988) Predicting adjustment to perinatal death. *British Journal of Medical Psychology*, 61(3): 237–44.

Nadeau, J.W. (1998) *Families Making Sense of Death*. London: Sage.

Najman, J., Vance, J., Boyle, F., Embleton, G., Foster, B. and Thearle, J. (1993) The impact of a child death on marital adjustment. *Social Science and Medicine*, 37(8): 1005–10.

New, C. (1996) *Agency, Health and Social Survival: The Ecopolitics of Rival Psychologies*. London: Taylor and Francis.

Newby, H. (1980) In the field: reflections on the study of Suffolk farm workers, in C. Bell and H. Newby (eds) *Doing Sociological Research*. London: Allen & Unwin.

Normand, C.L., Silverman, P.R. and Nickman, S.L. (1996) Bereaved children's changing relationship with the deceased, in D. Klass, P.R. Silverman and S.L. Nickman (eds) *Continuing Bonds: New Understandings of Grief*. Washington: Taylor and Francis.

Oakley, A. (1980) *Women Confined*. Oxford: Martin Robertson.

O'Hara, M., Taylor, R. and Simpson, K. (1994) Critical incident stress de-briefing: bereavement support in schools. *Educational Psychology in Practice*, 10(1): 27–34.

Parkes, C.M. (1993a) Psychiatric problems following bereavement by murder or manslaughter. *British Journal of Psychiatry*, 162: 49–54.

Parkes, C.M. (1993b) Bereavement as a psychosocial transition: processes of adaptation and change, in D. Dickenson and M. Johnson (eds) *Death, Dying and Bereavement*. London: Sage.

Parkes, C.M. (1996) *Counselling in Terminal Care and Bereavement*. Leicester: BPS Books.

Parkes, C.M., Laungani, P. and Young, B. (eds) (1997) *Death and Bereavement Across Cultures*. London: Routledge.

Papadatou, D. and Papadatos, C. (1991) (eds) *Children and Death*. New York: Hemisphere Publishing.

Parsons, T. and Bales, R.F. (eds) (1956) *Family, Socialisation and Interaction Process*. London: Routledge and Kegan Paul.

Pedicord, D.J. (1990) Issues in the disclosure of perinatal death, in G. Stricker and M. Fisher (eds) *Self-disclosure in the Therapeutic Relationship*. New York: Plenum Press.

Peppers, L. and Knapp, R. (1980) *Motherhood and Mourning a Perinatal Death*. New York: Praeger Publishers.

Pettle, S.A. and Britten, C.M. (1995) Talking with children about death and dying. *Child: Care, Health and Development*, 21(6): 395–404.

Pfeffer, C., Martins, P., Mann, J., et al. (1997) Child survivors of suicide: psychosocial characteristics. *Journal of the American Academy of Child Adolescent Psychiatry*, 36(1): 65–74.

Plopper, B.L. and Ness, M.E. (1993) Death as portrayed to adolescents through top 40 rock and roll music. *Adolescence*, 28(112): 793–807.

Powell, M. (1995) Sudden infant death syndrome: the subsequent child. *British Journal of Social Work*, 25: 227–40.

Prior, L. (1989) *The Social Organization of Death*. London: Macmillan.

Puddifoot, J.E. and Johnson, M.P. (1997) The legitimacy of grieving: the partner's experience at miscarriage. *Social Science and Medicine*, 45(6): 837–45.

Pynoos, R.S. and Eth, S. (1984) The child as witness to homicide. *Journal of Social Issues*, 40(2): 87–198.

Radley, A. (1990) Artifacts, memory and a sense of the past, in D. Edwards and D. Middleton (eds) *Collective Remembering*. London: Sage.

Rando, T.A. (1991) Parental adjustment to the loss of a child, in D. Papadatou and C. Papadatos (eds) *Children and Death*. New York: Hemisphere.

Raphael, B. (1994) Loss in adult life: the death of a child, in B. Raphael (ed.) *The Anatomy of Bereavement*. London: Routledge.

Reif, L.V., Patton, M.J. and Gold, P.B. (1995) Bereavement, stress, and social support in members of a self-help group. *Journal of Community Psychology*, 23(4): 292–306.

Reiss, D. (1981) *The Family's Construction of Reality*. London: Harvard University Press.

Reissman, C. (1991) When gender is not enough: women interviewing women, in J. Lorber and S. Farrell (eds) *The Social Construction of Gender*. London: Sage.

Rennie, D. (1994) Client's deference in psychotherapy. *Journal of Counselling Psychology*, 41(4): 427–37.

Riches, G. and Dawson, P. (1996a) An intimate loneliness: evaluating the impact of a child's death on parental self-identity and marital relationships. *Journal of Family Therapy*, 18(1): 1–22.

Riches, G. and Dawson, P. (1996b) Communities of feeling: the culture of bereaved parents. *Mortality*, 1(2): 143–61.

Riches, G. and Dawson, P. (1996c) Making stories and taking stories: methodological reflections on researching grief and marital tension following the death of a child. *British Journal of Guidance and Counselling*, 24(3): 357–65.

Riches, G. and Dawson, P. (1997) Shoring up the walls of heartache: parental responses to the death of a child, in D. Field, J. Hockey and N. Small (eds) *Death Gender and Ethnicity*. London: Routledge.

Riches, G. and Dawson, P. (1998a) Lost children, living memories: the role of photographs in processes of grief and adjustment among bereaved parents. *Death Studies*, 22(2): 121–40.

Riches, G. and Dawson, P. (1998b) Bereavement by murder: spoiled identity and the subordination of parental grief. *Mortality*, 3(2): 143–59.

Riddoch, V. (1998) Real lives: I'm glad it's all over. *The Big Issue*, June 15–21: 10.

Robinson, L. and Mahon, M. (1997) Sibling bereavement: a concept analysis. *Death Studies*, 21(5): 477–99.

Roger, J. (1991) Family structures and the moral politics of caring. *Sociological Review*, 39(4): 799–822.

Rogers, C. (1957) The necessary and sufficient conditions for therapeutic personality change. *Journal of Consulting Psychology*, 21: 95–103.

Rogers, R. and Man, J. (1990) *Reaching for the Children*. London: Arrow Books.

Rosen, E.J. (1996) The family as healing resource, in A. Corr and D. Corr (eds) *Handbook of Childhood Bereavement*. New York: Springer.

Rosenblatt, P.C. (1996) Grief that does not end, in D. Klass, R. Silverman and S. Nickman (eds) *Continuing Bonds: New Understandings of Grief*. Washington, DC: Taylor & Francis.

Rubin, L.B. (1983) *Intimate Strangers*. London: Fontana.

Rubin, S. (1984) Mourning distinct from melancholia: the resolution of bereavement. *British Journal of Medical Psychology*, 57: 339–45.

Rubin, S.S. (1996) The wounded family: bereaved parents and the impact of adult child loss, in D. Klass, R. Silverman and S. Nickman (eds) *Continuing Bonds: New Understandings of Grief*. Washington, DC: Taylor & Francis.

Rynearson, E.K. (1995) Bereavement after homicide, a comparison of treatment seekers and refusers. *British Journal of Psychiatry*, 166(4): 507–10.

Schwab, R. (1992) Effects of a child's death on the marital relationship: a preliminary study. *Death Studies*, 16(2): 141–54.

Schwab, R. (1996) Gender differences in parental grief. *Death Studies*, 20(2): 103–14.

Schwab, R. (1997) Parental mourning and children's behaviour. *Journal of Counselling and Development*, 75(4): 258–65.

Schwab, R. (1998) A child's death and divorce: dispelling the myth. *Death Studies*, 22(5): 445–68.

Seale, C. (1995a) Dying alone. *Sociology of Health and Illness*, 17(3): 376–92.

Seale, C. (1995b) Heroic death. *Sociology*, 29(4): 597–613.

Segal, L. (1997) Sexualities, in K. Woodward (ed.) *Identity and Difference*. London: Sage.

Segal, N.L., Wilson, S.M., Bouchard, T.J. and Gitlin, D.G. (1995) Comparative grief experiences of bereaved twins and other bereaved relatives. *Personality and Individual Differences*, 18(4): 511–24.

Seguin, M., Lesage, A. and Keily, M.C. (1995) Parental bereavement after suicide and accident: a comparative study. *Suicide and Life-Threatening Behaviour*, 25(4): 489–98.

Seidler, V.J. (1991) *Recreating Sexual Politics*. London: Routledge.

Silverman, E., Range, L. and Overholser, J. (1994/5) Bereavement from suicide as compared to other forms of bereavement. *Omega*, 30(1): 41–51.

Sims, D. (1997) 'Wallowing'. Paper presented at The Second International Gathering of The Compassionate Friends, Adam's Mark Hotel, Philadelphia.

Sinclair, I. and McCluskey, U. (1996) Invasive partners: an exploration of attachment, communication and family patterns. *The Journal of Family Therapy*, 18(1): 61–78.

Smart, L.S. (1992) The marital helping relationship following pregnancy loss and infant death. *Journal of Family Issues*, 13(2): 81–98.

Smith, S.C. and Pennells, M. (1995) *Interventions with bereaved children*. London: Jessica Kingsley.

Snyder, C.R. (1997) Unique invulnerability: a classroom demonstration in estimating personal mortality. *Teaching of Psychology*, 24(3): 197–9.

Sprang, G. and McNeil, J. (1998) Post-homicide reactions: grief, mourning and post-traumatic stress disorder following a drunk driving fatality. *Omega*, 37(1): 41–58.

Spratt, M.L. and Denny, D.R. (1991) Immune variables, depression, and plasma cortisol over time in suddenly bereaved parents. *Journal of Neuro-psychiatry*, 3(3): 299–306.

Stahlman, S.D. (1996) Children and the death of a sibling, in A. Corr and D. Corr (eds) *Handbook of Childhood Bereavement*. New York: Springer.

Stark, E. (1978) *Intimacy*. New York: Norden Publications.

Storr, A. (1997) *Solitude*. London: HarperCollins.

Strauss, A. (1962) Transformations of identity, in A. Rose (ed.) *Human Behaviour and Social Processes*. London: Routledge and Kegan Paul.

Strauss, A. (1993) Dying trajectories, the organisation of work and expectations of dying, in D. Dickenson and M. Johnson (eds) *Death, Dying and Bereavement*. London: Sage.

Stroebe, M. (1993) Coping with bereavement: review of grief work hypothesis. *Omega*, 26(1): 19–42.

Stroebe, M. (1994) The broken heart phenomenon: an examination of the mortality of bereavement. *Journal of Community and Applied Social Psychology*, 4(1): 47–61.

Stroebe, M. and Schut, H. (1995) The dual process model of coping with loss, paper presented at *The International Work Group on Death, Dying and Bereavement*, St Catherine's College, Oxford, UK, June 26–29, 1995.

Stroebe, M. and Schut, H. (1998) The social context of grief and grieving, in M. Mitchell and A.M. Gilroy (eds) *Proceedings of the Social Context of Death, Dying and Disposal*. Glasgow: Glasgow Caledonian University.

Stroebe, M., Gergen, M., Gergen, G. and Stroebe, W. (1992) Broken hearts or broken bonds? *American Psychologist*, 47(10): 1205–12.

Stroebe, M., Van den Bout, J. and Schut, H. (1994a) Myths and misconceptions about bereavement: the opening of a debate. *Omega*, 29(3): 187–203.

Stroebe, M., Stroebe, W. and Hansson, R.O. (1994b) *Handbook of Bereavement: Theory, Research and Intervention*. Cambridge: Cambridge University Press.

Stroebe, W. and Stroebe, M. (1995) *Social Psychology and Health*. Buckingham: Open University Press.

Stroebe, W., Stroebe, M., Abakoumkin, G. and Schut, H. (1996) The role of loneliness and social support in adjustment to loss: a test of attachment versus stress theory. *Journal of Personality and Social Psychology*, 70(6): 1241–9.

Swisher, L.A., Nieman, L.Z., Nilsen, G.J. and Spivey, W.H. (1993) Death notification in the emergency department: a survey of residents and attending physicians. *Annals of Emergency Medicine*, 22: 1319–23.

Talbot, K. (1997) Mothers now childless: structures of the life-world. *Omega*, 36(1): 45–62.

Taner Leff, P. (1987) Here I am, Ma: the emotional impact of pregnancy loss on parents and health-care professionals. *Family Systems Medicine*, 5(1): 105–14.

Taylor, K.M. (1988) Telling bad news: physicians and the disclosure of undesirable information. *Sociology of Health and Illness*, 10(2): 109–132.

Tedeschi, R.G. and Calhoun, L.G. (1995) *Trauma and Transformation: Growing in the Aftermath of Suffering*. London: Sage.

Tehrani, N. and Westlake, R. (1994) Debriefing individuals affected by violence. *Counselling Psychology Quarterly*, 7: 251–9.

Theut, S., Zaslow, M., Rabinovich, B., Bartko, J. and Morihisa, J. (1990) Resolution of parental bereavement after a perinatal loss. *Journal of the American Academy of Child and Adolescent Psychiatry*, 29(4): 521–5.

Thomas, J. (1995) The effects on the family of miscarriage, termination for abnormality, stillbirth and neonatal death. *Child: Care, Health and Development*, 21(6): 413–24.

Thomas, V., Striegel, P., Dudley, D., Wilkins, J. and Gibson, D. (1997) Parental grief of a perinatal loss: a comparison of individual and relationship variables. *Journal of Personal and Interpersonal Loss*, 2(2): 167–87.

Thuen, F. (1997) Social support after the loss of an infant child: a long-term perspective. *Scandinavian Journal of Psychology*, 38(2): 103–10.

Torrez, D.J. (1992) Sudden Infant Death Syndrome and the stress-buffer model of social support. *Clinical Sociology Review*, 10: 170–81.

Turner, V. (1974) *Dramas, Fields and Metaphors: Symbolic Action in Human Society*. Ithaca, NY: Cornell University Press.

Umberson, D. and Terling, T. (1997) The symbolic meaning of relationships: implications for psychological distress following relationship loss. *Journal of Social and Personal Relationships*, 14(6): 723–44.

Videka-Sherman, L. (1982) Coping with the death of a child: a study over time. *American Journal of Orthopsychiatry*, 54(4): 688–98.

Videka-Sherman, L. and Lieberman, M. (1985) The effects of self-help and psychotherapy intervention on child loss: the limits of recovery. *American Journal of Orthopsychiatry*, 55(1): 70–82.

Viney, L.L. (1993) *Life Stories: Personal Construct Therapy with the Elderly*. Chichester: John Wiley and Sons.

Von Bloch, L. (1996) Breaking the bad news when sudden death occurs. *Social Work in Health Care*, 23(4): 91–7.

Walker, C.L. (1993) Sibling bereavement and grief responses. *Journal of Pediatric Nursing*, 8(5): 325–34.

Wallerstedt, C. and Higgins, P. (1996) Facilitating perinatal grieving between the mother and the father. *Journal of Obstetrics and Gynecology and Neonatel Nursing*, 25(5): 389–94.

Walsh, F. and McGoldrick, M. (1991) Loss and the family: a systematic perspective, in F. Walsh and M. McGoldrick (eds) *Living beyond Loss: Death in the Family*. New York: Norton.

Walter, T. (1996) A new model of grief: bereavement and biography. *Mortality*, 1(1): 7–27.

Walter, T. (1991a) Modern death: taboo or not taboo? *Sociology*, 25(2): 293–310.

Walter, T. (1991b) The mourning after Hillsborough. *Sociological Review*, 39(3): 599–625.

Walter, T., Littlewood, J. and Pickering, M. (1995) Death in the news: the public invigilation of private emotion. *Sociology*, 29(4): 579–96.

Ward, B. (1996) *Good Grief, Exploring Feelings, Loss and Death with Over Elevens and Adults*. London: Jessica Kingsley.

Wass, H. (1991) Helping children cope with death, in D. Papadatou and C. Papadatos (eds) *Children and Death*. New York: Hemisphere.

Wellman, B., Carrington, P. and Hall, A. (1988) Networks as personal communities, in B. Wellman and S. Berkowitz (eds) *Social Structure: A Network Approach*. Cambridge: Cambridge University Press.

Wetherell, M. and Maybin, J. (1996) The distributed self: a social constructionist perspective, in R. Stevens (ed.) *Understanding the Self*. London: Sage.

Wheeler, I. (1994) The role of meaning and purpose in life in bereaved parents associated with a self-help group: Compassionate Friends. *Omega*, 28(4): 261–71.

Wiener, L., Aikin, A., Gibbons, M.B. and Hirschfeld, S. (1996) Visions of those who left too soon. *American Journal of Nursing*, 96(9): 57–61.

Winnicott, D.W. (1969) *The Maturational Process and the Facilitating Environment*. London: The Hogarth Press.

Worden, J.W. (1981) Coping with suicide in the family, in A. Milunsky (ed.) *Coping with Crisis and Handicap*. New York: Plenum.

Worden, J.W. (1991) *Grief Counseling and Grief Therapy: A Handbook for the Mental Health Practitioner* (2nd edn). New York: Springer.

Worth, N.J. (1997) Becoming a father to a stillborn child. *Clinical Nursing Research*, 6(1): 71–89.

Wortman, C.B. and Silver, R.C. (1989) The myths of coping with loss. *Journal of Consulting and Clinical Psychology*, 57: 349–57.

Woodward, K. (1997) Motherhood: identities, meanings and myths, in K. Woodward (ed.) *Identity and Difference.* London: Sage.

Wright, J.B., Aldridge, J., Gillance, H. and Tucker, A. (1996) Hospice-based groups for bereaved siblings. *European Journal of Palliative Care*, 3(1): 10–15.

Wrigley, K.M. (1995) Constructed selves, constructed lives: a cultural constructivist perspective of mental health nursing practice. *Journal of Psychiatric and Mental Health Nursing*, 2: 97–103.

Index

ON BEREAVEMENT
THE CULTURE OF GRIEF

Tony Walter

Insightful and refreshing.

> Professor Dennis Klass, Webster University, St Louis, USA

A tour de force.

> Dr Colin Murray Parkes, OBE, MD, FRCPsych,
> President of CRUSE

Some societies and some individuals find a place for their dead, others leave them behind. In recent years, researchers, professionals and bereaved people themselves have struggled with this. Should the bond with the dead be continued or broken? What is clear is that the grieving individual is not left in a social vacuum but has to struggle with expectations from self, family, friends, professionals and academic theorists.

This ground-breaking book looks at the social position of the bereaved. They find themselves caught between the living and the dead, sometimes searching for guidelines in a de-ritualized society that has few to offer, sometimes finding their grief inappropriately pathologized and policed. At its best, bereavement care offers reassurance, validation and freedom to talk where the client has previously encountered judgmentalism.

In this unique book, Tony Walter applies sociological insights to one of the most personal of human situations. *On bereavement* is aimed at students on medical, nursing, counselling and social work courses that include bereavement as a topic. It will also appeal to sociology students with an interest in death, dying and mortality.

Contents

256pp   0 335 20080 X (Paperback)   0 335 20081 8 (Hardback)

LOSS AND BEREAVEMENT

Sheila Payne, Sandra Horn and Marilyn Relf

- How have people sought to understand loss and bereavement?
- What are the current theoretical approaches to loss and bereavement?
- What are the implications of these approaches for interventions?

This book aims to provide students with an understanding of important theoretical perspectives and specific models of adaptation to loss. It is assumed that loss and change are normal processes that occur within a social and cultural context, and the reader is introduced to historical and cultural perspectives which illustrate the diversity of approaches to loss. Major theoretical perspectives are explored to enable students to understand their origins and influence. The authors go on to review the development of common models used to conceptualize individual reactions to loss and provide a critique of these models, highlighting the assumptions that underpin them. Finally, they discuss how these conceptual models have actually been used in clinical and community interventions. This is a comprehensive text describing the variety of approaches available to understand the process of loss and bereavement.

Contents
Introduction – Loss in society – The impact of loss: stress and coping – Theoretical perspectives on the family – Theoretical perspectives: life span development – The development of models of adaptation to loss – The application of models of loss in clinical and community settings – References – Index.

144pp   0 335 20105 9 (Paperback)   0 335 20106 7 (Hardback)

SUICIDE – THE ULTIMATE REJECTION?
A PSYCHO-SOCIAL STUDY

Colin Pritchard

... first rate: scholarly, insightful with delightful literary touches ... and always with an eye to the struggling practitioner.

Professor Stuart Rees

Suicide – The Ultimate Rejection? is an interdisciplinary text based on Colin Pritchard's first-hand experience both as a practising psychiatric social worker and social researcher. It provides an analysis of current research on suicide, exploring possible 'causes' and how best to intervene, and makes the case for a science based practice 'art'. International rates of suicide are examined as the author looks at suicide in a cross-cultural context showing how it is differently understood in different ethnic groups, reflecting various degrees of stigma. He argues for greater recognition of these key differences between cultures and ethnic groups, and shows how important they can be to our understanding and intervention.

Suicide – The Ultimate Rejection? explores the concepts of prediction and prevention and asks how the current health and community services might work to reduce the number of suicides in line with the targets set by the government's *Health of the Nation*. Different approaches to intervention and treatment are considered, with emphasis on those which research has shown to be the most promising. Special attention is given to the families of the victim, and in the final pages a wider view of suicide which includes euthanasia is explored. Using new research, Colin Pritchard examines the practical and moral issues raised by euthanasia.

This book will be of interest to students of social work, psychiatric nursing, health visiting and medicine, as well as health professionals and counsellors.

Contents
Introduction – Suicide in history and literature: social and cultural variations – Defining suicide 1: psychiatric and substance abuse factors – Defining suicide 2: other contributory psycho-social factors – Deliberate self-harm and suicidal behaviour in young adults and adolescents – The sociology of mental health and suicide – An integrated needs-led intervention and treatment model – Family 'survivors' of suicide: hidden casualties? – Euthanasia: an epilogue to chronic mental illness? – Synthesis and conclusion – Bibliography – Index.

224pp   0 335 19032 4 (Paperback)   0 335 19033 2 (Hardback)